Principles of Interpretation

PRINCIPLES
of
INTERPRETATION

Edward Goodwin Ballard

Ohio University Press
Athens, Ohio
London

Library of Congress Cataloging in Publication Data

Ballard, Edward G.
Principles of Interpretation

(Continental thought series; 5)
Includes index.
1. Ontology. 2. Experience. 3. Perception (Philosophy) I. Title. II. Series.
BD311.B32 1983 110 83-4281
ISBN 0-8214-0688-4
ISBN 0-8214-0689-2 (pbk.)

to
K. M. K.
and to
my Students

By the same author:

Art and Analysis (1957)
Socratic Ignorance (1960)
Philosophy at the Crossroads (1971)
Man and Technology (1977)

Contents

Preface

This book was devised to satisfy my curiosity and is written in the modest hope that it would be useful to others in the same way. The curiosity concerns the underpinnings of our daily lives, lives so different from—yet in important ways so like—the generations which have preceded. When I say with surprise, "There is the Saarinean Arch!", I am using a difficult, efficient, and beautiful language, made and bequeathed me by centuries of speakers. I am also using my powers of vision and discrimination, as well as knowledge of my whereabouts in space and time, my recollections of archways and their significance, and other cultural acquisitions in a way no less complex than the language which expressed my surprised recognition. Even more centuries of endurance, change, routine, and insight have gone into the production and communication of these ways of perceiving and recognition than were needed for producing modern English. How have I acquired these skills? My dog could in principle never have learned them. What kind of being must I be that I can perceive and experience as I do? Why do I do so? The satisfaction of attempting to answer such questions is the satisfaction offered by philosophy.

Although I have expressed myself in the first person singular, this book is not an intellectual autobiography. Rather, it is a general account of a certain philosophic method and content, a phenomenological ontology. Perhaps it could be called a philosophic (ontological) interpretation of the world, where world (content) factors into such essential items as space, time, objects, self, others, and interpretation (method) factors into such parts as perception, principles, categories, context, context intention, and projection (terms to be elucidated in the text).

More particularly, the purpose of this essay is in part to discern and express the principles utilized in the composition of two books previously published, *Philosophy at the Crossroads* (Baton Rouge, La.: Louisiana State University Press, 1971. Later abbreviated as PC) and *Man and Technology: Toward the Measurement of a Culture* (Pittsburg, Pa.: Duquesne University Press, 1978. Later abbreviated as MT.) Thus the present undertaking is only a portion, though a fundamental one, of a larger enterprise. The reader will understand a little better what he may be getting himself into if the relation of the present essay to these other two be sketched briefly.

For the purposes of *Philosophy at the Crossroads*, philosophy was defined as the interpretation of archaic experience, where archaic experience is the experience of radical changes or transitions — the experiences which tend to exhibit *archai* or principles — whether these transitions occur in the life of an individual, a society, a culture, or even a world. This same book proceeded to apply this definition and associated views to several of the transitions from epoch to epoch which have already occurred in the lifetime of philosophy. Then in the second book, *Man and Technology*, the same definition and related views were utilized to determine and evaluate a possible transitional development toward which our own history may be carrying us. Thus these two books considered radical changes (those revealing important principles) first as they have occurred in the past, and second as they may occur in the future. Experience of these changes was described as archaic, not in an archeological nor in a temporal sense, but in the sense that such changes tend to force one back upon an *arché* or philosophic beginning. Once this beginning is discovered, it may be considered critically, and possibly a new beginning may be essayed upon this more clearly perceived basis. Thus the dramatic encounter with an *arché* offers a kind of gateway (an arch) through which one may pass in order to discover and develop new possibilities. Both of the books just mentioned employed a set of principles and concepts in their movement to and from the *arché* or beginning in question. But neither attempted to provide a systematic exposition of the principles for the interpretation of archaic experience. The present book, however, is directed toward eliciting and expressing just these principles.

Evidently, then, this book, being related to the two books already published, looks backward toward the past. In addition, all three of these volumes are closely allied to the classic and European tradition in philosophy. Yet I do not think this backward look, this attachment to tradition, expresses anything like a crippling tie to the past. Rather, I construe this tie as an effort to discharge responsibility to the future by appropriating preceding acquisitions, under the conviction that only if our significant past is responsibly grasped can we move through present history and toward the future with reasonable confidence and fitting irony. I should, in short, like to believe this book contributes in some measure, however small, to our living authentically in our own time and history. Indeed, if this study is successful, it should add something to our grasp of the present relationship between our knowledge of and control over the environment and our apprehension of the human situation, self-knowledge, and self-determination.

In my attempt to deal with these matters, I owe far more to other writers and thinkers than the references and notes in the following text will indicate, far more indeed than could usefully be tabulated. The same remark holds true of the help I have received from friends, colleagues, and students. Perhaps they will accept this essay itself as an expression of my debt and gratitude. Several colleagues have provided special help. Professor Michael Zimmerman of Tulane University, and Professor Charles Bigger of Louisiana State University have gone carefully over considerable portions of the typescript; both have offered many keen criticisms. Professor Kathleen Haney of Lincoln University and Professor Harold Alderman of California State College at Sonoma have read the entire essay and have provided many apt criticisms and suggestions which helped materially to improve this essay. In return, I offer these friends my very special thanks. Mistakes and confusions in the essay are, of course, my own.

Likewise I am obligated to a number of editors and publishers for permission to make use of my articles or contributions. These articles, editors, and publishers are the following: "The Visual Perception of Distance," in *Phenomenology in Perspective*, ed. F. J. Smith (The Hague: Nijhoff, 1970), 187-201; "Alms for Oblivion: An Essay on Experienced Time and Objective Time," in *Phenomenological Perspectives*, ed. Philip Bossert (The Hague: Nijhoff, 1976), 168-187; "On the Nature and Use of Dialectic," *Philosophy of Science*, XXII, No. 3 (July, 1955), 205-213; "Category and Paradox," *Tulane Studies in Philosophy*, ed. J. K. Feibleman, vol. V, 1956, 5-23; "On Being and the Meaning of Being," *Southern Journal of Philosophy*, vol. IV. No. 4 (1966), 248-265; "The Nature of the Object as Experienced," *Research in Phenomenology*, VI, (1976), 105-138. "On Dialectic, Mechanical and Human," in *Communication Philosophy and the Technological Age*, ed. Michael Hyde (University of Alabama Press, 1981).

Also I owe a very special debt of gratitude to administrators and colleagues of Tulane University, the University of Missouri (Columbia), and the University of the South for providing the leisure and environment necessary for bringing this essay to completion.

Finally, my thanks for the preparation of the typescript go to Mrs. Freda Faber of New Orleans, La.

September, 1981

ἐν ἀρχῇ ἦν ὁ λόγος

St. John I.1.

I

Introduction

§1. THE APPROACH

How does one "do" philosophy? Two ways meet over this question: the direct and the indirect way.

The indirect way is to make philosophy into a scholarly study. The student of this kind reads and annotates, analyzes and compares. He produces chronologies, topical studies, word studies, historical essays, and often makes a fetish of historical and linguistic precision. The outcome is frequently an academically admirable accumulation of essays on the sacred texts of philosophy. Those who read them become vastly learned about the detail of these texts. One has the suspicion, though, that philosophy itself often gets obscured in this textual examination, for it tends to pass from word to word rather than from experience to word.

The more direct way to philosophic study carries the student to life, to experience, to "the thing itself"; such a way re-directs observation and reflection. This way to philosophy is, perhaps, more difficult, for "life," the "thing itself," "experience," are more mysterious than our most sacred texts. It is not even evident how one begins philosophic study; what is "life" that one need examine it, or the "thing itself" that one should return to it, or "experience," that one should analyze it? Perhaps we have some hint of how to acquire the physicist's insight into a physical object, now that the way has been shown by the Newtons and the Einsteins, but how does one go about acquiring philosophic insight into an object or into the self? Which philosopher offers us the exemplary model? The questions remain: What sort of thing is an object? What is the object of philosophy? One needs already to be a philosopher to respond to such questions.

The phenomenological epochē was supposed by Edmund Husserl to provide a route of ingress into philosophy. But this epochē seems effective chiefly in setting aside a naturalistic metaphysics which, being constructed upon non-philosophical assumptions, directs the student's attention upon philosophically misleading characteristics of the object. A more general epochē would, no doubt, aim at setting aside all presuppositions and, consequently, at exhibiting the object just as it presents itself before being interpreted by the perceiving mind. This would be an ambitious program, and one whose meaning is not entirely clear: can one indeed set aside all interpretation, all presuppositions, or even all the philosophically irrelevant or misleading assumptions? Does such an act really yield access to the object "as it itself is"? But how does one know when one has reached the thing itself? Is this the object of everyday experience or of some other and more recondite experience? Again, one needs already to be a philosopher in order to deal with these questions.

In any event, I conceive this essay within the phenomenological orbit although I make no mention of the epochē (cf. MT § 5). Instead of engaging in the Husserlian epochē and reductions, I shall recognize at least three modes of experience — scientific, ordinary, mythological — and I shall seek to become aware of the presuppositions of each so far as appropriate to my topic by way of a kind of dialectic (see chap. 8 and § 51 below).

As in other phenomenological philosophies, thought in this essay will move in two directions: (1) toward the phenomena, whose presuppositions are either removed or recognized and perhaps criticized, and (2) toward the ontological basis of these phenomena. Thus my method will in one important part be descriptive. The descriptions, moreover, will quite consciously be developed within explicitly differing contexts. I shall have initially to describe the object as I myself experience it, but my intention is to move from this individual experience to that which is valid for anyone; that is, I shall move from the particular experienced fact to the universal essence (when there is an essence). And then I shall reflect upon this movement — the classical movement of philosophy — and ask how and why it is accomplished. The different contexts, presenting the object in different perspectives, will operate like a thought experiment, working variations upon the experience of an object. What these several variations have in common will be, or will indicate, the essence of this object. The way will then be opened to discern the interpretative principles used in the delineation both of the object and its essence, and both of the self and its ontological basis or possibilities.[1] In fact, interpretation, its factors, its ontological conditions, and its method of proceeding will form the chief themes of this essay.

Let us begin with a brief description. Consider the contents of this room where I am sitting. I find in it piles of books and papers on the floor, books in bookcases along the walls, two desks littered with papers, a typewriter, several chairs, filing cabinets, some drawings made by students, a copy of a Van Gogh painting, and myself and a friend with whom I have been discussing the philosophical problem of intersubjectivity. A bell rings; immediately we hear the shuffle of students' feet, some leaving their classrooms, others coming to take their places. We both maneuver to bring our conversation to an appropriate end, for my friend is to lecture during the next hour on Sir Isaac Newton and the Neutral World View.

Present in this thumbnail sketch are references to all the items which ordinarily fill our experience: space, time, objects, self, others, and world. I shall call them "the essential items." We shall need to have descriptions of them, of experienced space and time, and of the things in space and time, all of which are said to be in a world. There are also ideal objects which will, however, not be our immediate concern until chapter 5. Notice should be taken that the objects to be described have been chosen in such a way as to provide a view of our place in the world and of that toward which we are moving and to which, if our existence is to be healthful and our ultimate meaning is to be at least glimpsed, we must be explicitly related.

In all that follows, I shall approach my topics by way of common everyday experience of these items, for everyday and common experience is indefeasibly familiar to everyone; thus it forms a kind of natural gateway to philosophy, and we shall do well to enter through it. In philosophy, avoiding the common and obvious is risky; there is enough which is unavoidably obscure.

But in truth we may be multiplying terms beyond necessity. There is no radical difference between description and interpretation. Both refer to a translation of some sort. Description is the first translation of experiences into language. It begins with the interpretation of objects as they spontaneously or unreflectively appear to one in everyday experience, whereas "interpretation" in the narrow sense refers to a further probing of the description and to a reflection upon it in the pursuit of its meaning, essence, or basis. Thus we approach philosophy directly through a descriptive study and interpretation of common experience and certain other experiences.

§2 THE BIAS OF THIS ESSAY

What do we expect of a phenomenological description? The preceding section has suggested that four factors characterize such a description. First there is a negative characteristic, an effort to purify experience of carry-overs from theoretical explanations and beliefs pertinent to other contexts, carry-overs which have the consequence of adulterating perception, e.g., persuading us that we directly experience factors which actually are not perceptible at all. Husserl's famous epochē is a systematic effort to discover and eliminate such adulterations. A second characteristic expected of a phenomenological description is a more acute awareness of the phenomena as presented. This achievement is often a consequence of the purification just indicated. It is a sensitiveness to just what is presented and just as it is present but may not have been explicitly experienced before. Thirdly, phenomenologists seek to carry their probing and descriptions of phenomena to the point where essences (meanings, universals, the logoi of the phenomena) become evident and communicable. Fourthly, phenomenologists strive to become critically aware of the principles and techniques employed in the preceding three steps and of their limitations. Our direct approach to philosophy in this essay will be concerned with all four of these factors but will place some emphasis upon the fourth, the principles, methods and limitations of interpretation.

In developing my account some bias, some special aim, is inevitable, for if its purpose were merely to examine the principles at work in any experience, then it might begin anywhere, for any experience is as much an informing by principle as any other. The bias of this study, however, is in a broad sense humanistic. It will deal with those interpretative principles which become evident in human experience and change and to which we turn under conditions of stress. Since its especial concern is with the principles involved in human change, the following questions will be a guide: What is the nature of human change? What may be taken as the goal of this change? What are the conditions necessary for approaching this goal?

There is, however, a catch; these questions are not simple and straightforward, for when a man genuinely changes, his whole world changes with him. The way he lives in his space, the quality of his lived time, all these are altered. The character of the objects with which he deals, his feeling for and his relation to himself and to other persons undergo a correlative change, and the texture and sense of his world become dramatically different. To understand such change thoroughly entails that all these essential items be understood, reinterpreted, and brought into harmony with the new man. Now, one way of studying these very important alterations would be to examine a notable instance of them and then to work out the detail in regard to each of the items mentioned. Let it not be supposed, though, that this book is intended to offer an illustration of the dramatic movement back to basic principles. Although something like a literary technique of description is sometimes employed, this study is philosophical and is intended to exhibit the general way principles are embodied in, and can be elicited from, objects of experience and human living and change. And these interpretative principles are the ones to which archaic experience returns us. Acquaintance with such principles and the manner by which they develop in and structure experience should provide an appropriate protreptic to the dramatic movement toward our archaic foundations.

In other words, I want to undertake a general treatment of the phenomena of human change. To this end, there will be need first to examine the several essential items as they are experienced (space, time, object, self, others, world), and then there will be need to develop a view of the categories and principles of change, of the way they operate, and of their source and orientation. These matters will be taken up at length presently. The next four chapters will describe and interpret the essential items, or at least the most relevant aspects of them. Then the last four chapters will reflect upon the preceding and will undertake to elucidate the principles of interpretation, the process of interpreting, and the ground and goal of interpreting. All this achieved, the reader should have before him, illustrated and analyzed, what may broadly be called the principles of a descriptive philosophy. He will have an exposition of the principles for the interpretation of archaic experience, and at least one view of the orientation of that experience. A difficulty: Which apprehension of the essential items is genuinely archaic?

The difficulty is perennial. Many generations of philosophers have sought assurance that their philosophies have begun appropriately and exhibit a harmony between the world and its contents and our experience of them. Kant showed that pragmatic success yields no such assurance in principle. So we must still ask: Is the world as we experience it? How in fact do we experience the essential items? Why not otherwise? At the very threshold, however, of our efforts to grasp these items they can be made to seem unstable and to elude us. For only a little investigative questioning is needed to demonstrate that these items and their interpretation are apprehended by different people in quite different ways.

After this questioning, anyone will admit that he hardly knows in any fixed or absolute sense what is meant by these items. Consider the different ways in which an American regards a bit of bone with a feather tied to it and the way the same is apprehended by a native of Haiti. Or recall the different senses in which a tin can is understood by a housewife, a chemist, a painter, or a garbage collector. A change of culture, a shift of context can be understood to operate rather like Socratic questioning. We particularly desire that our treatment of principles should be subjected to this questioning and should emerge flexible yet sharp enough to account effectively for the many possible kinds of interpretation.

§3. PRESENTATION, PERCEPTION, EXPERIENCE

Consider again the brief description offered a few paragraphs above of my somewhat disorderly office. All the things mentioned there are easily classifiable items. But why, the curious will ask, do these things appear in just the way they do? To many viewers, even to many in this country, most of these contents would have been totally unfamiliar. They would have appeared quite strange and would have been classified in categories not used by me. How do we gain access to things such that they appear in definite but different kinds of ways to different peoples? Finally, one may ask: Why do things appear at all? These three questions will point the way to the ontological basis of this essay, a basis which we are particularly concerned to reach and to understand so far as possible (cf. chap. 9) since a view of man's place and function in the world can be reached only upon this basis.

Let us begin here with the second of these questions: How do we gain access to things? Most observers will agree that the world, its contents, and those privileged elements within its contents, ourselves, become accessible to us through perception and experience. Perception and experience both, though, are already complex notions. Perception is presentation plus interpretation. Presentation is the given; it is received in part through sensation but by no means wholly so. The passively received presentation is subject to active interpretation (PC§3).[2] The outcome of the interpretative process (or processes) is particulars, specific kinds of objects. Thus perception is interpretation of presentations as particulars. The nature and limitations of this kind of perceptual encounter with objects or persons need to be carefully thought through, not with regard to the psychological processes involved, for this book is not a text on the psychology of perception, nor even with regard to the constitution of these experienced items, for neither does this book offer a doctrine of constitutive phenomenology, but rather with respect to the conditions of objects or persons being interpreted and experienced as they are. I have in mind such conditions as first, the initial receptivity of human being; second, the context, and contexts of contexts which incline to certain interpretations rather than to others; third, the categories and derivative principles of interpretation; fourth, the world which conditions and limits all the other conditions; and finally, being itself, which I take to be in some sense the origin both of presentations and of interpretation.

Now, even casual reflection upon perception reveals a most important factor: our self-awareness, the center and reference point for perceiving. This self-function is always discovered as already operative, but when we become aware of it the quality of perceiving undergoes a change. We become aware of the self as actively interpreting and so of affecting perception in ways sometimes difficult to determine. We know, for instance, that anyone can affect the perception of a tin can by shifting it from the context of say, physics to the context of art. Thus our experience of it is altered; we behave differently toward it. We shall use the term "experience" for perception which is thus self-aware.

Interpretation, whether spontaneous or reflective, is the movement toward discovering *what* the presented may be; it is a movement toward meaning, and this movement, meaning-giving and meaning-receiving, seems to be coterminal with human nature. Notice that some interpretations of the given presentations are altogether spontaneous. For example, I observe that I cannot help interpreting certain motions of my body as preliminary to a fall. Also, I can no longer avoid interpreting some visual configurations as indicating distance; long associations have brought these interpretations to the stage of the spontaneous. Still, illusions are always possible; reflection often intervenes to correct or elaborate the first automatic judgment. For instance, in an ordinary thunderstorm I spontaneously dismiss a sudden loud noise as a clap of thunder, but in wartime combat, I carefully compare the loud sudden noise with my recollection of the sound of gun-fire to be sure that the first spontaneous interpretation was correct. Still more complex and explicit principles of interpretation could be developed and applied, for example, by the physicist who measures the speed of sound, carefully determining his own speed relative to the speed of the sounding object.

Perception, then, is interpretation of presentations as particulars; experience is perception plus self-perception. Through perception and experience we react passively and actively to the things which furnish the world, to the world itself, and to our own being. I shall, therefore, ask what experience of these beings (e.g., space, time, objects, self-awareness, others, and the world) is like and what changes this experience may undergo. Similar questions will have to be addressed to the objects, the self, and other selves we seem to encounter in space and time. To reiterate, our questions reduce to three: How do we gain access to these beings? How does perception or experience of them come to be what it is? Why is it that such things appear or come to exist in our world?

This last question is supposed by a large portion of the tradition to lead the philosopher to the consideration of being.[3] In modern times, however, as Heidegger notes, being is thought to mean either too much, since it applies to everything, or too little, since it names no object of any kind, its function being merely copulative. Thus the term is either innocuous or empty. I shall, therefore, assign it a more useful meaning. Let us say, for the present, that being is directed power. The phrase "directed power" (*dynamis*) is so used in a goodly portion of the pre-modern tradition in philosophy, and refers us now to our two primary *archai*. In an earlier writing (MT §4A), I associated the notion of directed power with the myth of our first (Greek) ancestors, Ouranos and Gaea, an association useful in that it suggested the original unity and later separation of direction (sky, Ouranos, whose regular movements directed and organized all things) and power (earth, Gaea, whose superabundant, even self-destructive, fertility required limitation and direction). Here Ouranos arches over Gaea, having been forced upward by their offspring, our ancestors, so to open the way for their own crucial entry into awareness of being in time and in a world. Thus the offspring became "distanced" from earthy and natural necessities and were able to entertain alternatives to them and to make choices. The myth refers us to the moment of transcendence of organic and instinctual determinations, of entrance into human freedom where one becomes a directing power. Yet the paradox remains: This transcendence of earthy necessities is never more than partial; those offspring retain the marks of dual inheritance in their limited freedom, a freedom whose bounds are not fixed, and hence not clearly known, but sensed, rather, in hybris.

Plato's account in the *Timaeus* of the receptacle, the foster mother of all beings, and the Demiurgos, agent of form and order, brings the myth a little more up to date. The *chora*, or place where beings appear, is like the chaos or open space between Gaea and Ouranos.[4] And again these appearing beings retain their full paradoxical character: They can, but need not, mold their souls upon the most rational and orderly traits of their world; they must, in short, make their own choices.

In ourselves, offspring of the same two, and by means of our receptivity and interpretative activity, beings are brought into the "open," perceived, identified, chosen or rejected. In us, direction does indeed become separable from power, so that power can be considered separately and thence redirected. A human being is directing power. A finite freedom comes to be perceivable within our possibility,[5] and thus a man, with practice, may come to be the master of his own powers, within certain limits (limits easily concealed by hybris). When this consideration and redirection of power are concerned primarily with objects and events in the world and with eventual control over these objects in the interests of human preference, the rationale developed is, as I shall point out, of a scientific and eventually of a metaphysical nature. When this consideration emphasizes the human self—the protagonist, his power and his freedom—the rationale developed tends to be of an ontological character and raises questions about the function of man, the ends of human life, and its relation to its ground in being.

Characteristic of all human being, common to all kinds of experience, is the need to meet conditions. Certain to be among these conditions, as Kant pointed out, is location in space and time, for anything which is perceived or perceivable must be discoverable therein. Likewise, as Kant also noted, objects and self are among these conditions, for self-awareness and selfhood are achieved through experience of objects and other selves. Hence also, the principles of interpretation of objects and the self, and the dialectic whereby experience of objects is developed and the dialectic whereby experience and knowledge of the self is generated must be among the conditions to be investigated. I mean to suggest here what we shall later find to be the case, namely, that experience is modally differientated; that is, some experience utilizes interpretative principles which are not relevant to other experience. We shall observe the differentiation of experience of objects from experience of self and shall take note of the main stages in the realization of self-awareness and human freedom; then we can attack the ontological task of specifying the meaning of the self's being and possibly of being itself. Thus we shall more closely approach an answer to the question why objects, ourselves, and the world appear (and appear to us) as they (and we) commonly do appear.

This question is related to, but is prior to, that assigned to the book, *Man and Technology*. In this study, the problem was first to determine the structure of human living; this structure was found to consist of three moments: (1) a decision concerning the protagonist's identity; (2) a struggle to persist in this identity; (3) insight into the inadequacy of the initiating decision (MT §22). Secondly, the problem was to determine the character of the human being whose living was thus structured; this character was seen to be dependent, finite, and without permanent (role) identity (MT §26).[6] Now, in this present essay the question asked concerns the conditions allowing a being to enter in on this life. What, that is, must his powers be, such that he can direct himself within the life-structure just indicated? In general, the answer to this question is that the human powers must be such that they permit a person to respond both passively and actively within an interpreted space-time environment to objects, to others, to himself, and to his world, and then to direct himself either toward the control of the environment or toward the achievement of his own freedom. Hence we need to determine what powers one needs in order to enter into this passive and active, this sensitive and interpretative, process (cf. PC §3). These powers, which together constitute a man's sensitive field, can be seen to exhibit human being and to be intrinsically related to the being within which and by which a person can exist.

§4. THE SENSITIVE FIELD

The ontological concept of a sensitive field is centrally important to this essay. The term "field" possesses several relevant connotations. It suggests a field of force; likewise, in common usage it recalls a field, an open space having fertility and natural boundaries—the river, the forest—as well as legal or customary bounds. Still, its meaning here is ontological. "Field" is concerned with being. It is not a psychological concept concerned with the processes of sensation or with the responsive contact of one object with another. Rather, the concept aims to capture an insight into the foundation, condition, or basis of such a psychological or physiological concept. The ontological concept refers to that primary and peculiar function of human being through which access is gained to itself and to other beings. Being, as has been remarked, is a difficult notion; indeed its nature or meaning may be said to be the chief problem of ontology, as the etymology of the term "onto-logy" suggests. That the concept of a sensitive field can immediately be made crystal clear will, therefore, scarcely be expected. Something, nevertheless, may be said about it.

Today *soi-disant* ontological concepts are usually of two kinds: naturalistic and non-naturalistic. The naturalistic kind are produced by philosophers who seek logical simplicity above all else. Professor W.V.O. Quine is such a philosopher, and his ontology, true to form, makes do with just two notions, set and particular, an admirably simple basis on which to organize physics. But it offers no reason why the phenomena of physics should appear to physicists as they do. Also, the tendency of this physicalist ontology to recognize the basic constituents of things in smaller things of the same kind seems to me to beg the question and to leave the most interesting problems not only unsolved but unformulated, for the interesting questions concern the nature of the elementary constituents.[7] But if these constituents are assumed from the outset to be quite the same in nature as that which they constitute, only smaller and simpler, then the interesting questions are immediately "answered" by this same assumption.

A non-naturalistic ontology makes no such assumption, but instead seeks the source, the *archē*, of natural things in something which is not another one of those things. It seeks this *archē* in something called "being," which, however, is not a thing at all but is more like possibility. Heidegger has remarked that a great part of the sense of being is possibility.[8] Possibility here does not have a statistical sense, nor a modal sense, pointing to what might be. Rather, it has much the meaning given it in the Kantian tradition; it refers us to a transcendental source, the source of knowledge or of existence. According to Kant, possible knowledge is just the structure of the powers of cognition as they are developed in the Transcendental Aesthetic and the Transcendental Logic of the *Critique of Pure Reason*. Nor does "powers," in the phrase "powers of cognition," refer to any sort of psychological mechanism or faculty; it refers, rather, to that structure, habit, need, or tendency of the being which the psychological faculty subserves. Possibility, then, is a transcendental concept; it transcends and founds the natural.[9] Thus understood, possibility plays something like the active role suggested by an adaptation of a famous phrase, "the cunning of the possible." In Husserl's *Cartesian Meditations*, possibility assumes the character of an ego possessing habitualities (definite powers); this ego is a unified complex of such powers having a life and an orientation.

Possibility, thus, exhibits two distinct characteristics: it is, first, erotic; that is, it is possessed of something like psychic energy or power. Secondly, this energy, this power-to . . . , or power-not-to . . . , has a direction. This oriented possibility is experienced by us as consciousness. Consciousness is not, as some explanatory theories would have it, the passive mirror of an external world. It is experienced, rather, as a power of transformation and is directed either toward transforming the world about us or toward self-transformation. Receptive and interpretative consciousness transforms presentations into experienced objects and events, and the latter into other objects and events, so that they appear in new ways or with new values not merely in fact but to the theoretical gaze as well. Thus nature herself is persuaded to appear to us in a progressively renewed guise. Consciousness likewise transforms the self by way of a dramatic dialectic into a new self or selves, ideally in a movement toward maturity and justice. In this manner and through a mimetic influence, a change in one self may contribute to a change in others. An overall direction in these kinds of change may become evident as each contributes its quota to the slow and secular change of the world.

Essential to understanding this intrinsically telic character of consciousness is Husserl's observation that consciousness is always consciousness-of . . . . I have in mind his doctrine of intentionality; here "intentionality" refers specifically to this intrinsic orientation. The telic property of consciousness becomes most clearly perceptible in transcendental experience. Kant would not have understood the phrase "transcendental experience"; nevertheless, we can give it a meaning. Transcendental experience is awareness of this consciousness-of before it reaches completion in its object. We can actually achieve this awareness when an act which we are accomplishing is suspended or inhibited; then our readiness to perform the act floods consciousness. Recall the experience of listening to a person with a serious speech impairment. One is ready to understand, but the communication is inhibited. One's readiness to understand can then become an awareness of an oriented power (cf. MT §25). Here our directed power-to . . . could become thematic.

Possibility, in short, is the readiness of a being to engage in certain kinds of acts, in definite kinds of behavior. Characteristic of human possibility is the power to restrict this readiness, or to inhibit or to redirect its powers, the redirection being guided by knowledge, by feeling, or by a kind of intuitive apprehension of the end pursued. Thus man's being is not only directed power, it is also directing power. In short, consequent upon an interpretation we can direct or redirect our powers. A spider, say, is without such apprehensions; though it can weave a geometrically interesting web, to speak of the spider being guided by a grasp of geometry is ridiculous. The spider is neither ignorant nor learned in geometry. It can only spread out a web which *we* may recognize as geometrically regular. Nor can it make errors in geometry even when it weaves badly. Its power and direction are fused in an indissoluable unity; hence it cannot separate its power from direction and redirect its power in consequence of its interpretations. The spider has no such possibility, no such freedom.

Here "possibility" is used in an ontological sense. On the other hand, we may speak of a person as possibly (in a modal sense) being a good geometrician even though he makes geometrical errors, for his being or his (ontological) possibility includes the right or wrong doing of geometry. In this respect, his power and direction are separated. Once thus endowed, a person may educate himself (redirect his powers) and consequently increase his possibility (in the modal sense) of making correct statements in geometry. This distinction between the ontological and modal senses of "possibility" is crucial for this essay. Our interest will center upon ontological possibility.

Being, according to Plato's *Sophist* (247E), is the power to affect or to be affected. The being, then, of anything is that which it can possibly (in the ontological sense) do or suffer. An analysis of its being consists of distinguishing the various factors or strands of this possibility, its powers to do or suffer such and such and the limits on this power itself. I give the name "sensitive field" to the tissue of (ontological) possibilities constituting human being. An ontological analysis of human being will recognize the basic powers and distinguish them from the derivative powers of man. Thus a human being experiences himself as a self among others in lived space and time, opposed to objects in a manner determined or limited by his world. Space, time, objects, self-awareness, others, and world all refer not only to their corresponding objects but also to the relevant human powers, to strands of possibility, to directed and re-directable powers-to and powers-not-to, in virtue of which we can live as we live, be as we are, and give and receive meanings as we do. We can, for example, perceive objects which appear in space because our sensitive field includes that possibility. Having this possibility, we can learn to utilize our eyes to take visual bearings upon things in the environment and to make judgments of distance.

Is perceiving objects in space a primary possibility? Patently not. Perceiving is complex. So is space. We shall begin in the next chapter of this essay by describing certain experiences, e.g., experiences of the perception of space, then determine the essence or structure embodied in this kind of experience. Thereupon we may reason that a certain strand or strands in the structure of our sensitive field are precisely the power to experience space in the sense or senses instanced. The same is also true in respect to time, objects, self, others, and world. This essay may, therefore, be conceived as an analysis of the sensitive field. It is directed toward understanding our interpretations of the essential items and the relation of these interpretations to human change.

The preceding paragraphs suggest that common experience of the essential items is not the consequence of direct enactments of the basic possibilities of our sensitive field but is derivative of more basic possibilities. This suggestion is, I think, correct. The experienced variety of kinds of these essential items, a variety observable in different cultures, attests to the derivative character of these possibilities, for if all experience were directly the outcome of the same proximate possibilities, experience would be uniform; there would be no cultural or individual variety. But there is such variety. Consider the kinds of experience of space, for example, described by Oswald Spengler in his *Decline of the West.*[10] Compare, too, the experience of space and time lived by medieval inhabitants of the Aristotelian universe with that lived by modern men (cf. PC §16f). Clearly, the possibility or power of living in space is a common human endowment, a qualitative part of human being. The way in which this power is utilized, however, varies within limits. A *way* of being in space will be a function of several factors: e.g., of the world in which one lives, of the particular expression of world in one's culture, of the tradition or epoch in time in which one's sense of space is presently evolving, and it will depend also upon individual peculiarities (for example, upon whether one is blind or not).

This variety indicates the derivative and alterable character of experiences of space. We are thus led to the question: What are the basic possibilities of our sensitive field which open to us the different kinds of experiences not only of space, but of anything which we may affect or be affected by? I begin to answer this question in the next four chapters by offering descriptions of the essential items which I take to be not uncharacteristic of a modern Westerner's current experience, and I undertake to carry those descriptions to the point where a structure or essence can be rendered evident, when there is a more or less permanent structure or essence, that is.

These descriptions and the structures in which they culminate are interpretations of that which is given or presented, for by interpreting the given we come to have perception, experience. A first characterization of human possibility, our sensitive field, is similar to the being Plato mentioned, both passive and active, both receptive and productive. It is the possibility of receiving presentations and actively interpreting them. And anything of which we are aware is initially an interpretation of presentations.

We may take this initial account of human possibility, the sensitive field, one step further. According to an ancient tradition, being, including human being, is characterized by several very general properties. These properties have been said to be being, non-being, one, many, true, false, good, evil, same, other. There are, perhaps, others, but these are the terms known to the tradition as the transcendental predicates; they were held to be analytic of being and to characterrize in some sense everything that is, including themselves. Now, I see no reason to deny the accuracy of this observation. *Everything that is in some sense is not. Everything that is, in some sense is both one and many, both true and false, both good and evil, both same and other.* Further experience and ratiocination must determine just how a something is one and many, good and evil, etc.. But *that* it is such, is hardly open to doubt. That it is so is just what brings it into the realm of the experienceable.

I find this view promising, not merely because it belongs to an ancient tradition in philosophy, and, developing the present doctrine in relation to this view, insures a continuing relationship with that tradition, but also because it seems to provide a good initial description of the sensitive field and to open the way to an understanding of interpretative activity. Of course, being and non-being, one and many, etc., the primary forms of the sensitivity and activity of our sensitive field, exhibit no kind of intrinsic experiential content. They are empty and formal possibilities. As such, these terms are fitted exactly for making reference to human possibilities not yet given content by, or rendered concrete in, actual experience. The primary strands of possibility, then, composing the sensitive field are named by the transcendentals of tradition.[11] They refer us to the formal and primary ways the mind actively goes out to meet that which is passively received, in order to, by the union of active and passive elements (of direction and power), give birth to experience.

The transcendentals are usually, in this essay, mentioned in opposing pairs, being/non-being, one/many, and the like. The point to this mode of reference is partly to provide a salutary reminder of the paradoxical character of all human experience, where being and its opposite, unity and its opposite, life and its opposite, love and its opposite are so universally mingled. Also, this mode of reference is, in part, a preparation for a way of viewing principles of interpretation and the categories which will be developed later (chaps. 6 and 7.). The present point is merely to understand the sensitive field as the aglomeration, or system, of strands of possibility in virtue of which one can either do or not do some act, suffer or not suffer some effect.

§5. THE PHILOSOPHICAL PERSPECTIVE

There should be no anticipation that this essay will end by offering a neatly programmatic set of principles for organizing the whole of human life, since in my opinion human life is not a continuous achievement, not a smooth evolution to a "higher plain." Rather, it is a series of beginnings and endings, of ambitions, frustrations, and reformulations. It is often a disappointing affair, from which systematic theory is only a refuge; often a dirty business, from which a polished ethical view is only a flight; often a sorrowful thing, where acceptance is the only choice, and always it is strange and paradoxical.

Accordingly, this essay will not undertake to reach its end by unpacking a few crucial words nor by attempting to fit certain specialized experiences into a prefabricated logical schema. Nor will this essay be developed within the bounds of a realism or an idealism of any older or contemporary sort. It will, rather, be phenomenologically conceived. By this avowal, I mean that if pressed to declare what seems to be the ultimate reality to which the following descriptions and reflections point, I would maintain this reality to be neither objective in nature nor merely subjective, but rather I would hold the subjective/objective division to be derivative and to be developed within an originative unity (cf. p. 7 above). An object is always an objective something in a subject's perspective. And a subject's perspective is very complex; world, culture, context, and the person's own leanings, acquisitions, and purposes enter into its constitution. Now, the way an object appears is always a function of its place in such a perspective. Thus, an object is never experienced as merely objective or merely subjective.

From this vantage point, realisms can be seen to abstract and reify a portion of the whole, the object. Idealisms abstract and reify another part, the subject or his sensations. Both "isms" find themselves inadequately prepared to deal with that part of the concrete whole from which the metaphysical abstraction was drawn. Dualisms commonly reify both subject and object, then discover insuperable difficulties in relating the two. More recent expressions referring to perception as meaning-giving and to man as the source of meaning, encounter similar difficulties. Is man or his intentionality the sole source of meaning? (Husserl, in *Ideas* and *Cartesian Meditations*, found that difficulties followed from this idealistic bias and retreated from it.) Or is meaning given solely by the object to the mind? (Heidegger's philosophy is occasionally interpreted in this extremely objectivistic sense and is discovered, accordingly, to be laced with difficulties.) We shall be closer to a coherent and independent account if meaning-giving be seen as the outcome of a kind of marriage of the subject and the object, of intentionality and the being intended (cf. pp. 127-30). Such a phenomenological ontology seeks to retain the whole, the object-in-a-subjective-perspective, in a unity explicitly related to its world and to its origin. Heidegger develops in his doctrine of temporality an account of the underlying unity of these two. I also want to consider this underlying unity but shall not turn to it until the last chapter of this essay and then I shall envisage this unity in a manner rather different from Heidegger's.

Perhaps, as a mnemonic device and as an aid to clarity, a diagram will help. The concrete whole just suggested may be pictured as follows:

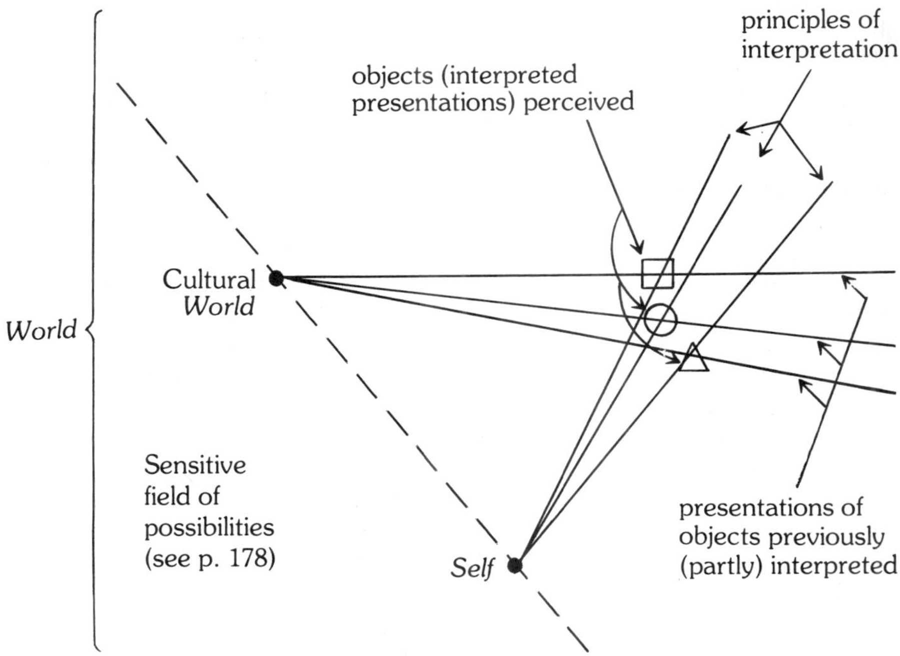

The rays issuing from the point labeled "self," the point of perspection, may be thought to begin at a central point of reference in the sensitive field. These rays, strands of the sensitive field, represent ways of taking up a perspective; that is, of passively and actively responding to object presentations. A perspective locates the experienced object in a context. The strands constituting a perspective context are possible ways of functioning; for example, they may come to expression as interpretative principles which identify and interpret the object. We noted earlier that the basic formal interpretative principles are the transcendentals of tradition, but there are other and derivative principles.

The rays which issue from the point labeled "cultural world" represent possible object sources; they are initially presentations. The points where they intersect with interpretative principles represent actual (spontaneously or reflectively) interpreted objects. Notice that "cultural world" lies on a dotted line which also moves through "self," indicating thus the unity binding self and world; this line also represents our power to make world symbols and myths about the self. These myths and symbols give concrete and communicable form to what we believe to be our nature, location, and vocation in the cosmos and are embodied in the remaining rays in the diagram; that is, they are embodied in a culture. The whole complex is the concrete reality with which we have to deal.

Although we cannot deal with this whole without breaking it up into strands, parts, traits, and aspects, the whole is prior and should not be lost to view. Parts, abstractions from this whole, are known as such only when contrasted with the whole. Abstractions from this complex—partial or specialist's views of it—are in no sense "wrong," but they are incomplete and should be recognized for what they are. An incomplete view, if unrecognized as such, becomes a distortion. Ontology is the attempt to approach an apprehension of the whole concrete reality and to correct distorted or partial apprehensions of it.

Perhaps the best way of retaining this concrete whole continually in view is to think of the philosophical task as requiring a particular sort of part-whole analysis.There are several kinds of part-whole analyses. One kind is analysis into quantitative or partitioned parts, analogous to dividing a square into two halves along the diagonal; there is no overlap, no common part, between the two. Another and opposite kind of part-whole analysis breaks the whole into qualitative parts, parts which interpenetrate each other. Analogous to this is the analysis of white light into its component colors. These components, though separable, overlap or interpenetrate each other at every point. Such, I suggest, is the character of the elements of the whole indicated on the above diagram, although the diagram, being geometrical, too easily intimates a quantitative whole. Note expecially the interpenetrating elements of the diagram labeled "self" and "world." World is not merely the whole context within which the self-function perspects objects and persons. It is the mythically invested (cf. §27) and all-inclusive structure embodied in the dominating culture and in the selves who practice the culture. A final reason why we experience things as, in fact, we do is given by reference to the world inhabited at a particular epoch.

The other primary element of the diagram, the "self," is the appropriate point of entry for an ontological essay, for the sensitive field is that collection of powers associated with the self-function through which a person can achieve access to other persons, to himself, and to objects, and by means of which he can direct himself toward ends of his own choosing and establish a relation with his source of being. In short, through his sensitive field one can make his own being manifest, more properly, making oneself manifest is precisely exhibiting one's sensitive field in acts. The self which can thus become manifest has taken (or has been given) the first step toward the dialectic of self-interpretation. By way of a repeated return to beginnings, the self can engage in dramatic change. In order to open the way for understanding such a return to *archai*, a qualitative part-whole analysis of this sensitive field is proposed. The general outlines of this task have now been delineated; the difficulty lies in the detail.

Notes

1. I find myself continually invited by the English language to use of the term "self" even though I wish to dispense with many of the meanings which now cluster about this word. "Self function" or "experience of self-awareness" often convey my meaning but become awkward upon repetition. I do not wish to suggest that the self is any sort of reification, e.g., an object, a substance, a Cartesian subject, or an ego. But what I think the self is will not be stated until the latter part of §20 and in §21 and §51. I develop a view of self in MT, see especially chapters 2 and 5, which is consistent with the standpoint of the present essay.
2. For the meaning of the abbreviations PC and MT3 see p. i.
3. I shall not adopt the convention of spelling "being" with a capital when referring to the *vis primitiva activa*, as is done by translators of Heidegger's writings, and with a small letter when referring to particular beings, for I believe that the context makes this distinction with sufficient clarity.
4. "Chaos," the name of the space between Gaea and Ouranos, is not to be associated with its modern meaning. Among the earlier meanings of this term, Liddel and Scott list in their *Greek Lexicon*: "The first state of the universe," and OED adds "the deep out of which the cosmos evolved" (and cf. PC§3).
5. To be endowed with human possibilities is already to be possessed of an ontological freedom, a freedom from the instinctual determination which defines and binds animal possibilities. For this reason, among others, I shall

say later that the self is not possessed of an essence in the sense in which an essence or an *eidos* is attributed to an animal. I shall also refer from time to time to a derivative and non-ontological kind of freedom; this is the kind of liberation which comes with self-knowledge, and is developed through the discipline and experience which enable us to learn to direct and control our own powers and to approach the ideal of autonomy. One may also achieve a freedom, in consequence of study and practice, with respect to some technique, e.g., medicine. Cf. Nicholas Berdyaev, *Dostoevsky*, trans. D. Attwater (N.Y.: New American Library, 1957), chap. 3.

6. The third task of *Man and Technology*, the use of this philosophic view to take the measure of a culture, is not relevant to the present undertaking.
7. Professor Quine is more concerned to develop a logically simple language for talking about the elementary constituents of experience than in determining what these constituents are. He remarks, "We adopt . . . the simplest conceptual scheme into which the disordered fragments of raw experience can be fitted and arranged" ("On What There Is," in *From a Logical Point of View* [N.Y.: Harper and Row, 1963], p. 15). Quine's views are further developed and applied to ontology by Professor Keith Campbell in *Metaphysics, an Introduction* (Encino and Belmont, Calif: The Dickenson Publishing Co., Inc., 1976), chaps. 9 and 12.
8. Cf. He remarks, for example, that "Possibility as an *existentiale* is the most primordial and ultimate positive way in which Dasein is characterized ontologically, "*Being and Time*, trans. by John Macquarrie and Edward Robinson (London: SCM Press, Ltd., 1962), p. 183.
9. To me it seems either arbitrary or naive to limit human cognitive possibilities to just those necessary to render the sciences possible. Also that the scientifically structured world into which physics and other sciences inquire is modally distinct from the common world of everyday living, appears too evident to require argument. That the sciences are not merely refined common sense, that they must make abstractions from common sense experience and from the value-laden environment of intersubjective living in order to initiate their measurements and to obtain their results, I take to be self-evident. Hence, to suppose that the universe constructed from these results is the only and total reality is not merely hasty generalization, it is a *reductio ad absurdum*. Generalizing the results of the sciences would not have been possible in such a reduced world. Thus, contrary to the views expressed in some naturalistic ontologies, I hold that the experienced world of ordinary day-to-day living is not reducible to the specialized experience of the scientist; it is, rather, modally distinct. I shall point to this modal distinction from time to time. Furthrmore, this distinction is demonstrated and its history outlined by Edmund Husserl in his *The Crisis of European Sciences and Transcendental Phenomenology*, trans. David Carr (Evanston, Ill.:

Northwestern Univ. Press, 1970), especially part 2. See also PC §25; MT §§33 and 36; and below §17.

10. Oswald Spengler, *Decline of the West*, trans. Charles F. Atkinson (N.Y.: Knopf, 1926), I, chaps. 5, 6.
11. The term "transcendental" is appropriate in another way. Consciousness is characterized in this essay as a power of transformation. It transforms whatever enters experience by giving it meaning, i.e., by interpreting it. This transforming and interpretative power is sometimes referred to as transcendence. The primary elements of transcendence, then, are aptly called the transcendentals. These elements are the strands of our flow of feeling, our sense of power-to or impotence-to, which receive the names of being/non-being, etc., and which initially are indeterminate but become specified upon acquiring structure from experience.

II

The Space of Experience

§6. THE TOPIC

Space is elusive though omnipresent. We cannot corner it nor escape it. We can move in it but not out of it. A man not only lives in space, he also perceives and uses it and achieves an extraordinary liberty of movement. To be able to perceive and move in space as a man does surely points to indispensable strands of his sensitive field. An understanding of the perception of space, nevertheless, is not easy to reach.

I do not perceive space in the same way I perceive this pen since space is not an object. Yet I cannot but perceive this pen as located in, and occupying, space. That is, space is indirectly perceived along with the perception of any object. And it is perceived in different ways, for its mode of appearance changes to accord with the way objects are viewed. Thus there may be said to be many spaces (e.g., physical space, life-space, play-space, ritual-space, etc.), but some of these are more basic than others. The position of this chapter will be that the life-space of common experience enjoys a methodological priority over others, a reasonable position since one gains access to the experience of other spaces through experience of common space. This chapter, therefore, will be devoted mainly to the description of the space of common experience and to discerning its essential structures, and secondarily to the determination of the other modalities of space.

Merleau-Ponty remarked that the most primitive experience of space was the infant's learning to distinguish between the inside and outside of his mouth. The remark is interesting, for it records the perception that three important spatial relations are present implicitly in that very primitive experience. These relations are contained-in, excluded-from, and overlapping (an object may be outside the mouth, inside it, or partly in and partly out). Further, the relation "contained-in" characterizes the presence of a figure on a ground and of a ground in a horizon, both surely basic structures of perceptual space. Still, there is a spatial characteristic prior to these relations. This prior function of space lies in rendering possible a basic distinction among objects, in, for instance, the separation of a figure from its ground or ground from horizon. This separative function is present and operative in every spatial experience, including the infant's. The inside of his mouth, the figure, so to speak, is "here"; the outside or ground is "there." When objects are thus distinct from each other, there is space between them. That is, some distance separates them. Also, this distance is always experienced as somehow oriented. Without a definite orientation the "there" could not be specified, for "there" is away from "here" in a specific direction. Distance and orientation are, thus, fundamental factors of experienced space. Accordingly, our initial interest in this chapter will center upon variations in the experience of objects in space with respect to orientation and distance.

The clue to change in orientation is change in appearing objects correlated with some kind of rotary bodily movement. Clues to change in distance are more numerous and complex. Some of the clues to distance are the following: if object X hides or partly hides object Y, then X is closer; if X appears to be larger than Y when one believes them to be of the same size, then X is perceived as closer; if X is seen in more detail or if it is darker in color than Y, then it is perceived as closer; if Y is vaguer or more hazy than X, then X seems closer. There are many other such clues, but practical considerations require confining our attention to only one of them, namely, variations on haziness and sharpness of the objects held in view. By this route, some grasp of the essential character of space can be reached and its modalities determined.

Initially, our sense of space is vague and unreliable. This vagueness seems to have been eliminated in modern times by an application of mathematical and mensurative techniques. Is space, in fact, clarified and simplified in this manner? Not in every sense. I want to argue later that mathematicized space is derived from a special kind of experienced space. Also, some thought will have to be given to the meaning and use of the vagueness of experienced space and to the significance of the application of mathematical techniques to it. The remarks of the next section will elaborate this aim. Thereupon, I shall work out an important way in which the clue mentioned above determines the sense of distance in ordinary experience. This topic will then be further divided into four additional sections: orientation, distance and object-properties, distance and object-identity, distance and object-context.

As these topics are developed, another kind of space will make its appearance. This I shall call dramatic or mythological space, or the space of significance. This mode of space will be seen to be prior in most respects to geometrical and physical space and also to the space of everyday life. But the space of significance is not for this reason to be ignored or disprized. Finally, to close the chapter, a section will be devoted to discerning and expressing the essence of space.

The main illustration of the experience of space utilized here will be a visit to the Saarinean Gateway Arch at St. Louis, Missouri. This Arch is so huge — 631 feet high — that it is difficult not to turn toward it if one is in its vicinity. But one may reasonably wonder whether it is ever possible to get close to it. Yet how, simply as a matter of common sense, can one avoid getting close to it if one continues to move toward it? Thus the Arch offers a propitious occasion for raising questions concerning space, distance, and orientation.

§7. THE METAPHYSICAL LINE AND THE EXPERIENCED LINE

First we should take note of the fact that one's separation from the Saarinean Arch is made possible by space, so also is one's closeness to it. Now, were the question to present itself to a person approaching the Arch, "Am I, or am I not, further separated from the north leg of the Arch than from the south leg?" how might he resolve the problem?

Any ordinary person would probably answer such a query by referring to the theory and technique of measuring. For instance, he might suggest using a device for measuring the angles of the triangle formed by imaginary lines drawn between the viewer's position and each of the two legs of the Arch. Then he might recall the Euclidean theorem about the length of the sides of a triangle being proportional to the opposite angles. But such a conventional Cartesian answer would satisfy only the average contemporary man, and neither the scientist nor the philosopher is, or ought to be, average in this sense. Perhaps the scientist would want to know why a Euclidean geometry was recommended for the measurement since he is aware that there are other geometries. Perhaps the philosopher would want to know why quantitative measurement was recommended in the first place since he recollects that terms like "direction," "close," and "far" have several senses and suspects that the art of quantitative measurement determines only one sense, and that one not necessarily the most basic or accessible to common experience.

What, after all, is there especially authoritative about quantitative measurement? Surely objects have been regarded as here or there, as close or far away, long before geometrical measurement was invented. And surely the modern geographical model for spatial perception finds its source and its referent in the perceptual world. Men lived for thousands of years either without a geographical model, or else with a simplified or distorted one. Without a perceptual world, though, there would be nothing for the geographer to talk about, and no geographer. Reflections such as these persuade the philosopher that measuring is a highly sophisticated operation, probably quite remote from its perceptual basis. In fact, the techniques of measurement not only make all sorts of assumptions which, however successful when judged by contemporary Western standards, are anything but obvious (MT §30ff.). Unfortunately, the use of such techniques also tends, when involved in a valued and successful enterprise, to conceal these assumptions within an aura of the progressive and the scientifically sacred.

The interposition of a normally unquestioned theoretical schema of measurement is most easily seen when one is asked to judge concerning certain illusions. Consider, for example, the so-called Müller-Lyer illusion. Two seemingly equal lines are given, then each is fitted at either end with arrow heads. On the first, the arrow heads point away from each other; on the second, they point toward each other. The naive viewer is apt to think the latter arrow heads are fitted on to the longer line. But his examiner can triumphantly show, by measuring the two lines, that they are "really" equal in length. So the viewer is judged to be victim of an illusion. Is he, however, victimized by his own perception or by the examiner? He can be supposed to be deluded in his perception only on the condition that the universe of Euclidean lines and measured lengths is superimposed on the perceived line, and is judged to be somehow superior to the perceived line or to be that according to which "true" or "real" lines are to be perceived and judged.

The judgment that the perception is illusory, then, is made within a context structured by geometry and its application in measurement. The operations of measurement and reasoning upon data thus gathered, it is often said, provide the means for determining what the real or objective length of the line is. The measured line length is the true, the real, the objective, length. The perceived one is illusory, false, and somehow inferior. Thus the line as phenomenally present over against the viewer is downgraded in favor of an abstract line reached only by techniques of measurement which presuppose an official quantitative universe and the validity of a certain sort of reasoning upon data gathered within it.

Suppose now that the ill-famed word "metaphysical" be accepted in its original and etymological sense as *meta ta physica* or "beyond the physical," i.e., beyond the world which actually emerges (*phyein*) into appearance, and we ask how the term is to be applied in the present instance. Consider that the measured line is an abstract line, the outcome of certain operations and inferences. It is not as such actually present and perceived; nevertheless, this abstract line is here taken as the objective, standard line and is used to "correct" our judgment of the perceived line. But such an abstract and non-perceived measured line is clearly present only in an abstract sense; it is "beyond the physical," beyond the perceptually present. This line, then, is the *meta*physical line. It is odd indeed that our period in history, which is most loud in its contempt for metaphysics, has generally accepted a view of the nature of objectivity which is metaphysical through and through, at least in the literal sense of the word.[1]

Certainly the measured line is most useful within some quite specialized contexts. Is there any justification, however, for accepting it as metaphysically, or as unqualifiedly, real? Not, I think, without narrow circularity. For perception, just supposed by our metaphysician to be subject to illusion, is employed in perceiving and using measuring instruments. And our metaphysician will have to admit that it is quite necessary to orient oneself toward any device that measures length or angles in order to be able to perceive distances on that device. Thus it seems obvious that whatever problems relating to experienced space were solved by use of a measuring device are encountered again when one inquires into the conditions for perceiving and using the device.

I mean to point out that the puzzles concerning spatial perception are not conveniently annihilated just at the moment when an experimentalist happens to be attempting to perceive the readings of a pointer or some other measuring instrument. I shall certainly not deny that there is an objective process by which perception can be clarified or corrected as judged by certain conventions and scientific standards (i.e., we do learn to perceive in modally distinct contexts and in different ways). But clearly, in order to enter in on this self-corrective process, some common and primary perceptual sense must be given to notions like the difference among points, the initial point of reference, direction, or "far" and "near," which are independent of sophisticated measurement techniques and of the particular metaphysical judgments which such techniques commonly presuppose. The common and primary perceptual sense of space is to be discovered in the sphere of common experience. An indispensible factor of this perceived space is orientation.

§8. ORIENTATION

I will now attempt to get at the senses of perceptual location and distance with as little circularity and presupposition in my procedure as possible. One orients oneself toward perceptually interesting objects almost automatically. It will be useful to begin with an illustration in which this orientation is made explicit.

A sophisticated reference to space, which is, nevertheless, quite like that which will concern us later, is illustrated by the report of a ship's lookout to the bridge. A lookout on a small naval vessel coming up the Mississippi River might typically report: "Large curved object; zero one five; three thousand yards." Whereupon the Officer of the Deck, who is chosen by a computer for possessing, like the lookout, a good Cartesian mind, could immediately turn his binoculars upon the indicated spot and pick out the object against its background. After the first general identification of the object, the report indicated the direction relative to the ship's heading, estimated in degrees, then followed a reference to distance estimated in yards. This standard report renders the position of the object sighted from the ship immediately evident to anyone appropriately trained.

Now, the Naval lookout is doing in a specialized and stylized manner just what our non-Cartesian caveman ancestors had to learn to do all but involuntarily in order to react effectively to the directions and distances of menacing or edible objects. Likewise, when a person in the common pursuits of everyday life intends to localize or situate an object, as he must if he intends, for example, to approach the Saarinean Arch, he has to be concerned with exactly these same elements: his initial position, direction, and distance.

These three elements may be understood upon several levels. In the most concrete sense, the center of reference for one's space is the self in all its temporality, subjectivity, and embodied ambiguity. That which is experienced as in space is the non-self, is an object "outside" the self or distinct from it. To determine the object's orientation and distance is to define one of its basic relations to the self. The self's orientation is like an intention. And the kind of distance which separates it from the object intended is, as we shall see later, a function of the context in which the object is perceived. Space, however, is not usually described in such concrete terms. More usually, my lived space is thought to be the field of all accessible, combined directions and distances from me here and now. Less concretely expressed, space might be described as the class of all imaginable directions and distances from anyone, anywhere. The abstract space useful in physics may be characterized as the class of all quantifiable directions and distances from any localizable point. A "localizable point" exists in some specific direction and distance from a possible observer. If the observer were reduced to a "point of origin," the description would refer to a mathematical space which might be defined as homogeneous, isotropic, and infinite.

The easiest of these spatial elements to describe is orientation, for the direction of an object is immediately given by focusing the eyes (or directing the ears) upon it. The rest of the body may then follow this lead. This easy description conceals a number of interesting questions. For instance, it may be asked: How does the body know when the plane through the shoulders and legs is rotated into the same plane as that of the eyes? Is some rapid observational and reasoning process entertained? Or are there not, rather, certain muscular or other clues spontaneously interpreted as indicating that the angle between these two planes is or is not zero?[2] Physiologists are convinced that many quite complex "calculations" are performed in the network of nerves in and around the eyes before visual messages ever reach the mind.

This is to say that we already know a good deal about the object-world and our position in it before we begin to think about it or even to orient ourselves toward any specific object in it. The matter is expressed by noting that we always already occupy a horizon whose spatial structure enables us to localize an object and move toward it. Indeed, in virtue of just such a horizon or prior interpretation we can act and think with respect to particular objects in the world. Gestalt psychologists and others have formulated the notion of the bodily schema, the already formed and operative sense of the body and its position and attitude in its familiar environments. We begin with this bodily schema; it is always the center of the space we experience; orienting ourselves toward an envisaged object is an occasion of its functioning.

We become aware of the bodily schema mainly when it does not function as desired. Maurice Merleau-Ponty has described the partial malfunctioning of the famous Schneider's sense of orientation. Schneider, who had sustained brain injury, was unable consciously to scratch a mosquito bite.[3] However, when he was not thinking about the matter, his hand automatically moved to the afflicted part and scratched. His bodily schema was not missing, it was only unavailable to conscious intention. Nevertheless, at an automatic level, his body could do what it (he) intended.

What is the structure of this bodily schema? What are its limits? To what degree do emotional and associational factors enter into it, as well as habitual movement responses and conscious intention? How does it become established? How changed or damaged? Governmental agencies may hold questions such as these to be pressing, now that the specialized spatial environment of outer space travelers needs to be understood. But our more earthy purposes confine our examination to limited aspects of these questions and to immediate and common spatial experience.

For the moment and for this section, it is sufficient to observe that I do have sufficient awareness of my body and bodily attitude in its environment to orient it in obedience to intention quite spontaneously toward points distinct from me, toward, say, the Saarinean Arch.

§9. DISTANCE AND OBJECT-PROPERTIES

The Saarinean Arch, that imposing inverted catenary and "Gateway to the West," is immensely high in comparison to other neighboring landmarks, and accordingly can be viewed in many lights and from many angles through the city of St. Louis or along the Mississippi River. Now no longer on a naval vessel, I drove toward it eastward along a winding parkway, a direction more or less normal to a plane through the legs of the Arch. As I began my approach, a primary question became the meaning of "approach." How was I to know that I was getting closer to it? The clue to the sense of distance which I selected for examination (the relative visual vagueness or clarity of the object) points to an answer to this question.

When I first turned toward the Arch, it appeared through the morning haze as a thin grey band against the sky. In effect, it first seemed to be continuous with the sky. It appeared to be paper-thin, no more solid than a darker streak in the somber color of the sky. This appearance was clearly in conflict with convictions developed through a lifetime of interpretations of perception. Nothing paper-thin could possess such magnitude. Nor could it be merely a shadow; shadows are always shadows of something else, but here there was no "something else." Such commonsense convictions lent an air of unreality to the wraith-like Arch. As I moved, it repeatedly disappeared and reappeared through the trees. It continued to offer a ghostly appearance for several miles, only it slowly grew even larger in comparison with the surrounding buildings and trees. As I watched it intently, the grey Arch seemed to stand out from the background of morning haze; then from time to time it receded into this background like a gap cut on the brighter sky. Was it a shadow against the sky? Or was the sky a light outlining the shadow?

Finally, at a moment of changing light it assumed a more permanent look; out of the grey ribbon there emerged a solid, oval or triangular column curving upward to a thinner and more indefinitely shaped transversal section, then curving back down again along the other leg to a more definitely oval or triangular form. For a considerable time during my movement, a cross section of the lower part of either leg could have been either oval or approximately triangular. When quite close to the base, I quickly decided that its cross section shape was triangular and could easily believe that it was made of separate triangular shafts of stainless steel. But even when standing quite close to it, there was a vague point where, as my eyes traveled up its great height, its shape became indeterminate, and it seemed again to be either an oval or perhaps a triangular solid.

The whole approach to the Arch from this direction seemed to be a series of ambiguities. Moreover, the language quite naturally, almost automatically, used to describe such ambiguities seems to be appropriate; this is the language of either-or. But it must be noted that the sense of ambiguity is introduced not quite in the language but rather in the conviction, illustrated in past experience and leading to present expectations, that both of the alternatives cannot hold true of the Arch "itself." The Arch cannot, for instance, be both paper-thin and yet high enough to bend over skyscrapers; it cannot be both oval and triangular. Clarity or closeness seems to be reached when one of these alternatives becomes appropriate and the other is perceptibly eliminated. Thus I knew I was getting closer to the Arch when the ambiguities in its appearance were attenuated.

There is another and quite different approach to the Saarinean Arch, by way of a boat along the Mississippi River. This approach is more or less in the south-north plane passing through both legs of the Arch. Approaching the Arch from the south, the viewer perceives one leg to be geographically closer to and the other to be further away. But, in my approach along this route, at first I found it quite impossible perceptually to determine which leg was which. As soon as one leg was identified as the south leg, the Arch would "spin around" and the appearance was reversed. Indeed, the relative position of the legs could be made to change by an act of will. Of course, having learned how shadows behave and knowing where the sun was, I could infer which leg was the northern one, but this conclusion was an inference *added* to the appearance. As for the appearances, all one could say was that the shadowed northern leg would, from time to time, become the southern leg with a change of color.

This ambiguity persisted throughout much of the approach upriver. The strange effect was most dramatically presented when one's eye was allowed to move up the near leg of the Arch and across the transversal part. Naturally, one would expect it to come down by the far leg. But it might not. It might just as well come down what suddenly turned out to be the near leg. Thus the near leg could appear to be both the near leg and the far leg, although according to my logical conviction it could not be both.

Only a few minutes before docking at the foot of the Arch did its appearance become stable and one leg became and remained near, a uniqueness which could have been verified by utilizing the category of quantity and pacing off the two distances and comparing them, or else by measuring appropriate angles; however, the category of quantity, we have observed, easily leads to an interpretation beyond the perceptual, an interpretation which we determined to omit while considering perception itself. The only conclusion to be strictly drawn from these perceptual views is that they are mainly a series of ambiguities; they seem to disappear only in a late stage of approach to the Arch. No doubt there are optimum positions for viewing the Arch, or any such object. These positions are neither too far nor too close for identifying the object. They are the positions from which perceptual ambiguity is at a minimum. Such positions are in the geographical sense, relatively "close to" the Arch.

Before turning to the literal interpretation of the meanings of distance and closeness implicit in this illustration of perceiving, it should be added that I have not dwelt upon another approach to the Saarinean Arch by way of feelings, moods, and suggestions which the Arch tends, and was intended, to evoke and which must influence the perception of it rather considerably, if obscurely. For surely the Arch is not literally a gateway, as it is called. One does not have to pass through it to get anywhere. And yet one feels drawn to approach it and to pass under it. Its magnitude, the sense of sheer rise, the strangeness of its non-utilitarian being there in the midst of a practical and busy American metropolis — such vague awarenesses as these must surely affect and even direct the experience of the object and of the distance through which one experiences it. One senses that the Arch is solidly set into the earth, yet seems to ignore gravity for all its immense weight of steel; it soars into the air like human ideals inspired by heaven. It reflects the sunlight and withstands the forces of wind and rain; it is a work of the human mind and hands unquestionably triumphing over nature.It surely represents a victory for modern technology, but a victory in what cause?

Beauty? History? Patriotism? Technology itself? It seems to invoke heroism and invites men to deeds of conquest. Though its shape is not quite the crescent of Artemis or Aphrodite, yet its partly ovoid outline brings to mind the meaning of the crescent and seems to be big with the future of America.

This Gateway to the West is part of a tradition of symbolic arches, Greek, Roman, and modern, Janus-faced structures symbolizing transitions, passages to victory or defeat, connections with other epochs, different nations and lands, North-South, East-West. How much do these background remembrances playing around the edge of perception add to or modify what is presented? Sufficient, I suggest, to lead us to something like a new arch. This is the mythological or archaic arch and the space it shapes and sets apart is dramatic space, the space of significance. I call it mythological, for its meaning is derived from myths and world symbols, and I call it significant, for in the shadow of such a symbol, or in close relation to it, decisions are made, dramatic actions initiated, old courses of action are terminated and new ones launched which are intended to embody the values projected by the Arch. Consider some of these values and their realization.

Traditionally, life is said to have begun in the East and to flow westward (so that if continued, it would end in its place of beginning). To what west is this Arch the gate? Surely it is intended to bring us closer to the history of the American West and its significance. The West once symbolized escape from the oppressions of Europe. The advice, "Go West, young man," seemed to promise freedom, land, power, a new beginning. And so awe-inspiring an archway leading from a noble past, must open onto a splendid future. The little museum at the foot of the Arch seems to offer this interpretation, as it displays accounts of the birth and growth of St. Louis and the acquisition and development of the great Western lands. It displays a series of maps depicting the conquest of the West. The first, representing the original claim of the Indian, is red-brown over the whole territory. The next map shows some inroads of white here and there, indicating the precarious holdings of a few intrepid white settlers. The following one shows many smaller red-brown sections cut apart from one another. The early settlers have been reinforced; the red man is being divided; conquest is underway and victory approaches. The white portions grow, the red ones diminish with each succeeding map. Finally, the last of the series preserves only a few red dots here and there, marking the reservations where the remaining, living Indians are permitted to eke out their existence on the least desirable land. Is the series a history of the deeds of brave settlers? Or is it a record of the violence, rapacity, and treachery of the white man? The stretch of land between this Arch and the Pacific is indeed an ambiguous stretch. Perhaps the Archway leads us close to the underside of our culture and commemorates a movement separating us from its ideals and values. Many will suspect that we are all too close to this guilty aspect of the significance of the Arch, too far removed from its ideal meaning. Is this West really the direction in which we desire to go? (West, it must be remembered, also signifies death.)

One would prefer to suppose that the Arch symbolizes a transition from the guilty side of our history to its ideal meaning. But perhaps the present reality is the ambiguity. At least this ambiguity is native to the symbolism of the Arch; hence one who wishes to approach the Saarinean Arch in all its concrete complexity will not ignore this ambiguity but will seek to interpret and to clarify the significance of this space (see also PC §§ 16-18).

Are these suspicions and recollections to which the Arch has led properly a sort of spontaneous interpretation? Do they lead us to a clearer perception of the West on which the Arch opens? Do they bring us closer to the Archway? Do they belong to perception? Where and how, exactly, does one pass from presentation to interpretation? Or is one always in a sort of passage between the two? Is the geographical approach to the Arch by way of movement along the street the literal and proper sense of approach? Or does one approach it more properly, less metaphorically, by way of these reflections and mythic recollections? Or is the closeness of approach relative to context? Do the extremes of vague-clear indicate the more primitive experience of distance, an experience which is specified as far-near for the geographical context, but in other ways for other contexts? At any rate, there is no doubt that the geographical sense of direction and approach is the closer experiential counterpart to the naval illustration concerning bearing and range and would be more unquestioningly selected today as embodying the basic sense of orientation and direction. After all, the mythological arch is generally located beyond the horizon of common experience. Let us, therefore, turn back now to complete the first mode of approach.

As a step toward understanding this more commonly experienced mode, some invariants in the appearance of the Saarinean Arch should be noted. The most obvious among these invariants is the identity of the object, the Arch itself. Throughout the variations in its appearance and during the whole approach, the identity of the Arch persisted. Indeed, the recognition of ambiguity in shape, solidity, and orientation seems to entail that the object so qualified be tacitly recognized to remain one and the same object. The object, the Arch, is the fixed meaning or invariant in the many changing visual presentations. A little later I want to point out that some changes in distance perception may be followed by loss of object-identity. But for the present it is important to note that variation in the visual distance-properties which we have observed is just that factor through which the sameness of the object is noticed. The variation of these perceptual properties is regular and is quite spontaneously interpreted by the viewer not to indicate a new object, but rather to indicate the same one "seen at a different distance." I conclude the ambiguity of these visual properties is a regularly occurring characteristic of perception and is correlated with distance.

Several phases of ambiguity in the perception of the Arch have been indicated: first, the initial conflict of its fragilc smoky appearance with convictions of what such an object must "really" and solidly be; second, the perceived ambiguous shape of the legs and transversal; and third, the indefinite north-south orientation compared with the uniqueness of shape and orientation which by conviction we presume the Arch to possess. To what invariant character of perceptual space, we may now ask, do these several ambiguities point? It is clear that they are essentially involved with the experience of distance separating me from the Arch. I suspect that the indefinite point at which we pass from what is mostly indefinite perception and hesitant interpretation to what is mostly confident interpretation and clarified perception is just that point where recognition of a conventionally identifiable object occurs. This point can be specified in one relevant detail by interpreting the perceptually ambiguous as the distance-character of the object (described already in the language of either-or) and the perceptually non-ambiguous as the near-at-handness of the object. When the Arch presents a stable and relatively unambiguous appearance, that is, when definite orientational and shape invariants perceptually dominate the flux of appearances, then it can be said to be close. Then the series of appearances clearly do converge upon one invariant object, the Arch. Thus the distance and closeness are functions of the presence or absence of certain perceptual ambiguities.

What I am suggesting reverses a traditional view. It is not because the tower was distant that Descartes and others after him were unable to determine whether it was square or round. Rather, because he could not determine whether it was square or round, he recognized it to be distant. Thus I propose perceptual ambiguity as a defining characteristic of perceptual distance.

It is worth noting that there are useful aspects of the definition just proposed, since meanings for directions of movement immediately follow from it. A movement "away" is a movement which leads into, or increases, a perceptual ambiguity. A movement "toward" is a movement which reduces and finally seems to remove this type of perceptual ambiguity. To a certain extent, this language is the language of common experience, as one might expect, since whatever the contemporary prestige of exact measurement, we always live primarily in the perceptual world. There are, nevertheless, difficulties in this ingenuous definition.

For instance, as is well-known, there are certain objects, forms, or patterns which are always ambiguous. The puzzling drawing of a stairway (Schröder's stair) will be recalled; is one above the stairway looking down, or below it looking up? Similarly, the Müller-Lyer illusion, to which we alluded earlier, is always ambiguous. Such figures, then, by our definition of distance must always be distant, even if they are only two feet away. Are we involved in a paradox? Consider the stars. On a clear night they do not seem to alter their appearance in the slightest, however the observer may move. Their appearance is unambiguous.

In the language proposed, then, we must admit that, being unambiguous, they are close at hand. Thus, although quantitatively extremely distant, they are perceptually close. Are we involved in a second and even more ridiculous paradox? The stars are "close" at hand, although their distance is measured in light years, whereas the optical illusions two feet from my eyes are not merely distant but unapproachably remote.

The source of the paradox is scarcely obscure. It arises from intermingling the context and language of perception with a language derived from practical activity, a language which, as we all know, has become official, deriving much of its persuasiveness from the emotions surrounding references to measurement and exactitude. Surely we may admit that the illusory stairs are remote perceptually, although they are close as measured and described in the technical language of measurement, but even in this respect they may be far, considering measurement from the point of view of a physicist who measures the diameter of an atom. Likewise, the stars are distant astronomically speaking — even so, they were much closer to the ancient astronomer. In any case, they may be close perceptually speaking. But again, they may appear to be perceptually remotely separated on a cloudy night or at twilight.

Clearly, there are problems connected with this first attempt to define distance by identifying it with the perceptually equivocal, and closeness by identifying it with the perceptually clear and univocal. Part of the difficulty lies in the pervasive (though remediable) confusion of the language of perception with the language of quantitative measurement. But part of it seems also to belong to perception itself and is manifested in the ease with which the perceptually clear can be made to appear perceptually ambiguous or remote by a shift of context. This illustration also points to quite another sort of perceptual ambiguity, one which brings the identity of the perceived object into uncertainty.

§10. CLOSENESS AND OBJECT-IDENTITY

Consider the area of clarity or non-ambiguity. Just what is its extent? In the illustration of the Arch, we moved from points where it appeared to be vague or ambiguous, then "toward" it and into an area where it appeared to be clear or unambiguous. Suppose, now, that we move even further in the same direction. Continuing thus, we traverse the area of clarity and eventually reach a point where the object as conventionally recognized and identified becomes ambiguous again. But in this instance it also seems to lose its identity. One might, for example, approach the Arch so closely that it would appear to be only a shaft of metal, not an arch at all. Still closer, it would seem to be a wall of indeterminate extent, and finally, from an even closer position, only a bit of stainless steel, steel which might as well belong to a steak platter as to an arch. Here a new type of ambiguity is encountered.

In the preceding example, variations of distance were associated with ambiguity in respect to various properties attributed to one and the same object, the Arch. Now the ambiguity concerns the identification of the Arch itself, to which properties are attributed. Beyond a certain point, the closer I come to the Arch the more perceptually doubtful it becomes that the standard arch-image, the interpretative principle which I bear in my imagination, corresponds to what I perceive. Indeed, the thing I see might be a steak platter held vertically. Thus, using our former terms, we might be said to be remote from the thing called the Arch. But our distance or closeness, in the present instance, has acquired a new sense.

An extremely interesting illustration of this sort of distance can be taken from the Japanese film play, "Woman in the Dunes." This play presented two persons struggling to preserve a home from being completely buried under the sands blowing in from the ocean shore. The camera was from time to time brought so close to one of the persons in the play that only a bit of sand-covered flesh was visible. Here the identity of the individual personage became ambiguous, remote, and finally was lost. But at the same time something else was brought near and made clear; perhaps this something else was a comment upon the close relation of the persons in the play to basic elements in the human struggle for preservation and life. The drama displayed the rapidity with which the accouterments of civilization which separate persons from each other may be shed and a level of common humanity reached.

The evident point is that the area of the unambiguous, of the close, is a limited but variable area. Ambiguity and nonambiguity, I suggest, are functions of context; they vary within limits which are determined by their relation to different contexts of experience and thought. One of the limits occurs when the object to be perceived begins to lose its identity and becomes too remotely separated or too close. Here "too close" has much the same perceptual meaning as "too far." Both refer to the ambiguity of the identity of the object to be perceived. One can be "too close to see," i.e., too close for perception. What, though, can the phrase "too close for perception" mean? For surely we do continue to perceive, whatever may be the distance to the Arch. The phrase acquires meaning, I want to argue, according to the context into which it is placed.

§11. DISTANCE AND OBJECT-CONTEXT

If attention be directed to the context within which perception of objects occurs, a way can be discovered for amending the earlier definition of perceptual distance while taking account of the fact that the perceived identity of the object is itself a function of distance-perceiving. The useful suggestion stems from the fact that the observations and counterinstances mentioned indicate the role of the context to which — or from which — the definition refers. The suggestion is that "ambiguous" and "unambiguous" have sense only within a specified universe of conviction, language, and behavior. The Arch, so close it is either arch or steak platter, becomes unambiguous when it is in the context of metal. It is clearly stainless steel; here the question whether it is shaped into an arch or something else does not matter. Also, the flesh which is so close it might be the flesh of anyone, might be something even more impersonal, becomes unambiguous in the aesthetic context set up by the play.

Of course, upon further questioning, ambiguity may easily be made to return. The composition of the metal alloy might be shown to be uncertain. Also, the aesthetic meaning of the flesh and sand might be brought into doubt. For example, the camera might be brought close and focused so that the flesh itself would lose its ambiguous identity and would become visible only microscopically. In such an instance, the flesh would have been brought too close to retain aesthetic relevance. It might have become biologically close perhaps, although aesthetically remote.

What, then, is the character of clarity and closeness if the ambiguity of distance is always so near at hand and can so easily be recalled? A portion of the Arch is only ambiguously steel to a perceiver who remembers that stainless steel just might be polished pewter (they look very much alike) or even a carefully painted imitation. But not in every context are these distinctions relevant. Often, where they are relevant, further tests can be devised to clarify the vagueness. But it is hardly to be supposed that all ambiguities can be forever removed in any context. The context in which a metal is determined unambiguously to be stainless steel is not often immediately related to the context in which something is perceived as an arch. Ambiguities, in other words, disappear only with respect to a given context. Evidently, the character of closeness and clarity is intimately related to the context or perspective within which these properties are identified. My second descriptive definition of closeness and distance may now be expressed: closeness is contextually removed ambiguity; conversely, distance is ambiguity elicited by a context. Thus, ambiguity and clarity, distance and closeness, separation and union, are dependent upon the context in which they are perceived, whether that context be tacit or explicit.

Although ambiguities can always be summoned up by adroit questioning or more precise investigation, still they can be ignored within certain contexts. Perhaps ambiguities are ignored because they have become familiar, or perhaps because they are recognized to be irrelevant to the task at hand. Often, closeness is ambiguity so familiar that it is passed over. Distance is ambiguity which is noticeable within the context of interpretation. The Arch was a distant object because I knew ahead of time that I was to perceive the famous structure and was striving to make out its expected features or to match up what I vaguely perceived with my standard image or principle for interpreting what was presented me. In general, perceptions occur within a context, and clarity or ambiguity are relative to the context.

A further step toward clarifying the notion of perceptual distance will be taken if the sense of the term "context" be specified more exactly. Context includes text, as ground includes figure, as perspective included object perspected. The context, ground, perspective is prior and includes within its structure elements which serve to interpret the text, the figure. I must, for example, be already acquainted with the whole context of writing before being able to draw from it the principles which interpret this object as a pen; or I must be already reasonably familiar with plastics and their utilitarian applications before being able to interpret this object (my pen) as a plastic instrument. Thus "context" is understood to refer to purposefully selected forms of language, interpretation, action, and relations among these which enable some kind of behavior (e.g., some perceiving or inquiring) to proceed. Further, these forms of language, interpretation, and action are selected in accord with some dominating intention (cf. § 25 below). Possibly, the sense of "perceptual distance" would most reliably be specified in the instance of a well-developed science since the scientist is traditionally expected to have clarified the principles and operation with which he works. Still, his environment is, after all, a limited and specialized one and depends upon the larger life-world and its more familiar contexts in which his work is given value and meaning. It will be interesting, although more difficult, to attempt to indicate in a preliminary manner something of the character of this more inclusive context.

In common and everyday usage, one is scarcely aware of living, perceiving, and speaking within a specific milieu; nevertheless, all human life does move within a scarcely definable group of beliefs, attitudes, expectations, feelings, moods, and even myths. This life-world may include, among other factors, the apperceptive mass supposed by an older psychology to mold and direct present experience. We may think of it as, in part, a sort of generalized space, organized around the central perceiver or his bodily schema, and within which he feels, perceives, acts, thinks. Such a context of contexts sets up a framework wherein certain interpretations of experience are possible, even inevitable, and tends to exclude others. Within it, we have already discerned certain general and recurrent features — the spatial features — of any context; these are the center or point of origin, orientation, and distance. Within such a space one becomes aware of oneself and whatever else appears to be present yet separated from oneself. This context varies; aspects of it change, for instance, as mood shifts, as feelings alter, as the task at hand varies. It might seem to be an almost amorphously shifting mass and quite indescribable, except that it is given form by intentionality.[4]

Intentionality is the counterpart in consciousness of bodily orientation in space. In holding it to be a basic structural element in any context where clarity and ambiguity are significant, I refer to that which some phenomenologists ordinarily mean when they define consciousness as essentially intentional. Any consciousness always intends an object, just as from the point of origin of a lived space one is always oriented upon some object (which is, therefore, separated from one or is at a distance). Consciousness, that is, is not a passively reflecting mirror of an external world, *à la* Locke. Rather, it is animated by an intrinsic teleology and resembles a biological organ having a function within the body, operating with a material, and producing a product, separable from or distinguishable from that body.

I am using the term, however, in an even broader sense; all human behavior of whatever kind is intentional, although the intention may often be obscure or pervasive. In particular, there is a context-forming intentionality (cf. §25f. below). It may be imagined to be something like the initial orientation or primary direction of movement which a person journeying through a countryside gives himself. This direction determines what comes into view, how it appears, and what is concealed. It is the initial determination of the kind of object to which one will respond and the way one will respond to it. Such a primary intention may be taken from a special study. Thus a physicist may tend to see everything, himself included, as primarily an object of physics. The primary context-forming intention may also be taken from common experience or from myth.

In our former illustration the specific intention was quite obvious. My intention was to view the thing to which my gaze was directed as the Saarinean Arch. This intention polarized all my experience at the time in a quite definite manner. It defined the context within which I interpreted visual presentations; it rendered me non-receptive to elements of the ground, to traffic, buildings, advertisements and the like, but rendered me implicitly receptive to the Arch, although up to that time I had never seen it. Still, I was ready to perceive the Arch. Would I have perceived the Arch at all without some such preparation, some determining intention polarizing my power to perceive, organizing my sensitive field, and animating my bodily schema? In this instance, my rather explicit preparation led me to seek out a series of points of perspection from which I could view what I identified as the Saarinean Arch in a multiplicity of appearings ranging through several kinds of ambiguity to relative persistence and clarity. Without the primary intention which in fact I did have, I might not have noticed the Arch at all, or I might have regarded it as a perfectly clear and obvious structure worth no further attention, or I might have taken it as an unfamiliar and vague object requiring to be identified *ab ovo*, etc.. That is, the context of my experience would have been polarized differently, or, otherwise expressed, the object itself would have been in a context which would have elicited different aspects for perceiving. It might then have appeared as far or near, vague or clear, depending upon the context as structured by my intention.

Also, my intention defined limits of perceiving as the points beyond which an expectation of seeing an arch would always be disappointed. Any movement beyond such limits could invite a transfer into a new object-context. Such a transfer might suggest, even demand, a different object identification. One such transformation of context was suggested earlier in this chapter when the mythic and symbolic sense of the Arch, the Gateway to the West, and the nearness or distance of meanings of the Western lands were adumbrated. In this mythic mode a quite different context-intention determined a quite different perception. The Arch was not perceived then as an architectural *tour de force*, nor as a tourist attraction whose physical appearances were underlined; it became a symbolic arch whose historical, ethical, and mythical qualities came to the fore. A certain mythic force or mana seemed to pervade it.

The ambiguity or clarity, distance or closeness, of a perceived object, I want to say, is its way of appearing, and its way of appearing is a function of the object within a context determined or ordered by one's intention. An object is always an object in a context and within a perspective. Distance and closeness are not functions of the object, presentations, context, intention, perceiving, or perceiver taken separately. It is safe to say that there are always unfamiliar and hence ambiguous aspects of any object in any context, and these can always be made to appear, if we know how to question the object. The questioning of an object may also consist in a shift of context and intention in such a manner as to direct attention upon new aspects of the object or upon the object as newly identified.

For example, during the Renaissance, objects were transferred to a mechanical context in which the perceiver had been generalized or made ubiquitous; from each such reference point an infinity of quantified directions and distances were available. Space, thus generalized, was held to be homogeneous, isotropic, and infinite (PC §17). This space simplified and generalized the public situating of objects and the measurements of certain of their properties. The context thus generated was and is an important one, indispensible for modern scientific and technological purposes. This is the space within which the naval lookout can take the range and bearing of a possible target. In it, however, nonmechanical properties became ambiguous, both there and yet not really there, irrelevantly present. In it, too, many human characteristics and experiences became remote. In comparison with the space of physics, experienced space seemed to be "subjective" and was so evaluated by many philosophers who failed to see the relation of perception to context.

In general, anything clearly perceived can be made to appear ambiguous if placed by our questioning intention in the appropriate context. We are brought again to the view that closeness or clarity may be termed familiar, or perhaps irrelevant, ambiguity. To term closeness or clarity a familiar, unnoticed, or irrelevant ambiguity is, then, a way of calling attention to the very important relativity of perceptual distance or apprehension generally to the context of apprehension itself. This relativity of perception to the context and its primary intention is extremely interesting for it suggests that context is instrumental in uniting pure presentation with habitual ways of perceiving and interpreting.

In summary, it should now be sufficiently evident that once one is freed from theories which tend to define *a priori* what one ought to perceive, and once one is allowed to examine just what is given in perception, the farness and nearness of an object can initially be defined by presence and absence of perceptual ambiguity. The experience of space, is, then, in an important respect, the experience of separateness among objects; it is perceiving in definite directions over distances which render an envisaged object more or less vague and ambiguous or the reverse. It is not difficult to show that any apparently unambiguously perceived object is in some respect ambiguous. Its apparent clarity or closeness can then be defined as unnoticed or perhaps irrelevant ambiguity. But the relevance or irrelevance of an ambiguity is a function of the intentionally structured context within which the object is recognized and located. And contexts can vary from an impersonal numerical or geometrical space all the way to a concrete environment weighted with symbol, paradox, and myth.

We have up to this point recognized several different contexts, each presided over by its own intention and containing its own interpretative principles. These contexts, running from the abstract to the concrete, give rise to the following modalities of space: mathematical; physical or applied mathematical; common or everyday; mythical or significant. No doubt there are other such spaces, but these are the modes most in use. Nor are they mutually exclusive. One and the same person may develop motives in significant or mythic space which send him through the space of common experience to the laboratory, where he studies the interrelations among mathematical and physical spaces.

§12. ON THE ESSENCE OR STRUCTURE OF SPACE

Although the space of common experience, "lived space," is multifold in that it is formed on the basis of many different kinds of clues — several of these clues were mentioned near the beginning of this chapter — still, perhaps, a sufficient grasp of it has been attained by the development of only one of these clues, viz., the observation of distance variations correlated with variations ranging from visual distinctness to visual vagueness or ambiguity. We took some account, also, of the two modal derivatives of this common space: namely, the abstract space of mathematics and the sciences, and the dramatic space of ritual or myth. By removing properties from the common experience of space we end up with an abstract space (e.g., that of physics). By adding properties to common space, especially human-like properties, a concrete dramatic or archaic space results. Thus the common experience of space offers an appropriate gateway to the consideration of other modes of spatial experience. With these developments in mind, let us attempt to extract the essence or structure of space.

I suggest, to begin with, that experienced space is the realm of distinctions. More ontologically expressed, space offers the possibility of making distinctions, e.g., "here" as distinct from "there," the figure "here" as distinct from the ground "there." Hence, we may say that ontological space is the field wherein distinctions among beings *can* be made. Space is the condition for discreteness among beings. As such, ontological space is surely one of the primary strands of our sensitive field.

I use words altogether literally, I believe, when I speak of myself as here and the Saarinean Arch as there. Quite frequently, "here" means within touching range from me; "there" means at a relatively greater distance, although the minimal sense of here and there refers only to distinction. That is, if I am here and the Arch is there, then at the minimum, the Arch and I are distinct and separate beings. Such a spatial distinction is not only one of the earliest in kind which a human being learns to make, but also X here, Y there, is a minimal difference or otherness between X and Y. Other perceptible distinctions between X and Y are commonly thought as analogous to this one. If X is red and Y is blue, these colors can be, normally are, thought of as lying on a scale separated from each other by yellow. Thus colors are translated into a color-space, and the distinction between "here" and "there" is given color-space meanings.

Sounds, economic values, positions in an administrative hierarchy, time, and other such entities or qualities which involve mutual separation are commonly envisaged in analogous spaces. Work space is organized to allow for somewhat different distinctions. "Here" is usually where the workman is located and the work process is actually going forward. Out from this center are located different "theres" having different values by reason of their differing relations to this center, the work process itself. Reserve wood stored "over there in the corner" is different from the hammer and chisel "there" within operative reach of the joiner's hand.

Now, I believe the here and there of space, the realm of distinctions, can be characterized in a still more fundamental way by reference to a pair of transcendental notions: same and other. Of course, taken alone, the notions "same" and "other" are so general as to be indefinite. They acquire definite meaning only when limited by some specifiable content. One such content is the spatial here and there and analogies to them. Recall that the "here" in the space of common experience is primarily just the place where I, the speaker, am located. And if I move, my "here" moves along with me. It moves along with me because my identity with my body remains the same, and "here," separate from others, is a function of this sameness or identity. That my body, or any object, should be separate entails that it should be the same as itself and other than others. What is "there" is just what is other than I, that by contrast with which my identity, my sameness, is further and negatively specified. So "here" receives a distinct sense by reason of the sameness in space occupancy; "there" is other than this continuing sameness. As same is to the other, so is my position here on this chair to my possible positions on other chairs in this room, in this house. . .

A difficulty may seem to be invoked by asking whether my hand is here or there in lived space. For my hand is a part of my body, hence a part of me; therefore, it should be "here" at the center of my space. And yet I quite intelligibly think of it in abstraction from my self and speak of it as "there," lying on the table, for example. Hence the hand is both here and there. But this is scarcely a paradox, since the self (and its "here") can be associated with a part of the body (say, the head), so that the remainder of the body is other than here, i.e., is there. The point is that the spatial distinctions of common experience are concrete specifications of the very general and formal notions of same and other; herein the most basic character of the structure of common space is indicated.

The structure of two other kinds of space — the abstract space of mathematics and the sciences and the dramatic space of myth — can easily be seen to be derived from this common space. Abstract space is a field of interrelated homogeneous points. These points are obtained from experienced space, as Section 8 indicated, by divesting common space of its personal and conscious center (its unique "here"). Each point of abstract space, then, is equally a center, equally a "here" or a "there." When each such point is such a center, each identifiable point of space is the same as itself and other than others. If such a space is marked in some manner or given a conventional identity so that its sameness can be recognized (say, by identifying it with some recurrent content), then it can be numbered, drawing as appropriate the meaning of the number from one of the languages of number (MT §31). Space, in this sense, is the possibility of making numerical or other mathematical distinctions; its formal structure is a determination of one/many and its content consists in homogeneous, abstract points.

Lastly, dramatic space ("significant space"), while still a realm of significant distinctions, may better be taken to be the possibility of becoming distinct in some mythically important sense. Recall the mythic meaning of the Arch. Passage through it signified dramatic, even radical, change. This passage was a movement from one kind of space to another, indicating a more or less profound change in being and in value. Often such passage is thought of within the province of good and evil, as a shift from a lesser good to, in some sense, a greater good. Also it is understood, and perhaps more appropriately, within the province of being and non-being. For this kind of shift is a maturing process which renders the self more distinct, more sharply defined, more cleanly separated from that which it is not. One who passes through such an arch is more distinctly the same as himself and other than others. He is more distinctly his own being and has disassociated himself more explicitly from that which he is not.

We may, then, consider that the self has at least three related modes of space at its disposal: the space of common experience where objects are discrete and are distinguished from the self and, by analogy, from each other in the ordinary ways necessary for executing the business of daily life; the abstract space of mathematics and the (hard) sciences, most usually imagined as a homogeneous field of denumerable units and often isomorphic with certain definable characteristics of its physical contents; and the dramatic space of human growth associated with the more radical changes in human being. In each of these three spaces, the formal principle yielding the spatial interpretation in question can be stated in terms of same and other, although abstract space calls upon meanings derived from one/many and dramatic space calls upon meanings derived from being/non-being and perhaps from good and evil as well. The assumption made at the outset of this chapter, that space is an essential strand of our sensitive field, is more credible now that the essence of space has been discerned.[5]

Notes

1. I shall not infrequently use "metaphysics," in the sense indicated here, to refer to the fundamental concepts of some more or less specialized study. Such fundamental concepts may or may not be understood as fundamental without restriction.
2. "Sameness of direction," for usual modes of locomotion, is maintained so long as this angle is zero, that is, so long as the two planes are Euclidean parallels. But Euclidean parallels are defined as equidistant and thus presuppose prior possession of definite notions of distance and direction. In practice, the circle is in fact broken, and the determination of sameness of direction becomes a function of the bodily schema, attesting again to the primacy of experienced space over mathematicized space.
3. Maurice Merleau-Ponty, *Phenomenology of Perception*, trans. Colin Smith (London and New York: Routledge and Kegan Paul, 1962), p. 103.
4. I shall often use the term "intentionality" as it is used by E. Husserl, cf. his *Ideas: General Introduction to Pure Phenomenology*, trans. W. R. Boyce-Gibson (London: Allen & Unwin, 1931), especially sections 36ff., 84ff., 88. Also see this essay below §20.
5. The description of the Arch used in this chapter was developed from an exer-

cise devised for the second Workshop in Phenomenology (1966) organized and directed by Professor Herbert Spiegelberg at the University of Washington, St. Louis, Missouri.

I should add that my account of the museum connected with the Arch dates from 1966. The present museum, located underground beneath the Arch, is a quite different affair. It has been beautifully and effectively organized and appointed by architects, historians, and anthropologists.

III

Time as Experienced

§13. THE TOPIC

Each of us possesses a sense of the flow of time, a sense of being in time. Awareness of this flow is awareness of a primary element of human possibility. For surely, time as such a possibility is a primary strand, if not the most basic strand, of the web of possibilities constituting one's sensitive field. So, at least, we begin by assuming, and reasonably, since each of us senses a peculiar identity with his life time and its flow. (Other reasons for this assumption will be discovered as we proceed.) The main topic for this chapter concerns this sense of flow and the basic structures which it exhibits.

When we approach an object, say, the Saarinean Arch in St. Louis, we sense that we endure through the approach, that a certain amount of time is flowing away. Notice that I speak without hesitation of an "*amount* of time." It is so clear that time always comes in definite, measured, or measurable amounts? In the preceding chapter we found it difficult, considering our particular epoch in history, to separate experienced from quantitative or metaphysical space; here we shall find it no less difficult to disentangle time as actually experienced from objective and public time whose character is formed to some considerable but undetermined extent by the instruments of its measure. So ubiquituous have these instruments become that time seems all but inconceivable to us apart from them. And the conception thus formed has determined the context in which we believe time is normally experienced. When Shakespeare remarks

> Time, mylord, hath
> A wallet at his back, wherein he puts
> Alms for oblivion,

the average modern person is apt to recall that a wallet is designed to contain discrete units of the coin of the realm, and so he may wonder what the unit of these alms is and how much oblivion each may purchase. As he moves toward the Saarinean Arch he may reflect, "Just how much of the day am I investing in this jaunt?"

The time one invests in such a reflection is clearly not objective time; it is, rather, time of actually wondering, thinking, living. How is this time to be described? What is its structure? What are the principles of its interpretation? Also, the question must be raised whether there is more than one kind of lived time. Surely there exists a lived time, in the sense ordinarily experienced by almost everyone. Is objective time also experienced in some diminished sense? Is there likewise a time characteristic of radical human change?

The task of this chapter will be to describe time as it is commonly experienced, to discern its structure (eidos), then to relate this experienced time, on the one hand, to the abstract and objective time of the sciences, and, on the other, to that time wherein dramatic human changes occur.

§14. VIEWS AND METAPHORS OF TIME

If one were asked to describe the passage of time taken, for instance, to drive to the Saarinean Arch, the reply might be that it took just seventeen minutes. If this answer were criticized as being rather too general since it failed altogether to describe the *passage* of that time and referred instead only to its conventionally measured quantity, then one might counter by pointing out that absolutely every existent thing is involved in the passage of time. Thus time is ubiquitous, like being. One is almost inclined to say time *is* being. Everything is in time and modifies time by its presence; hence an adequate characterization of the passage of time would have to take cognizance of its infinitely varied contents, a task no less impossible than providing a full description of being.

When again asked at least to make an effort to describe the passage of time, one might allude to St. Augustine's intriguing but evasive remarks about the familiarity but the inexpressibility of time. Or one might take refuge in Kant's observation that time itself is not experienced. The request to describe it is, therefore, quite unreasonable, since one must in some sense experience a definite thing in order to have something to describe. Time for Kant was the Newtonian succession of "nows" which, since they abstract from all content, scarcely provide an object for experience. What is experienced is just events in succession. There is no experience of time apart from this eventful succession. To suppose that there is, is only to allow oneself to be tricked by language; the fact that we do make use of a word like "time" does not entail that there must be either some empty substantial thing or some event-less and impalpable flux to which this word corresponds.

Just the character of this succession called time, however, is in question. There are many kinds of succession. Why is one type of succession called temporal, another geological, another dramatic, another mathematical, another spatial? The question is particularly pressing when one contemplates a noted characterization of time: that it "flows mathematically, without regard to circumstance." Such was Newton's description, and such is the belief often held by the average man, by the metaphysician, and, until recently, by physicists.[1] But such an empty succession, imagined to occur without regard to circumstances or experience, is most difficult to comprehend. By what means could one moment of this uncircumstantial flow be distinguished from another?

In any event, time is experienced as a passage of phenomena. This passage will have to be approached through phenomena and their order. It will not, then, do to identify time at the outset with the full particularity of its contents, nor with one if its abstract properties, nor with some imagined empty and contentless duration.

If one does resolve not to accept such a familiar identification of time as that associated with Newtonian physics, then the so-called temporal illusions acquire a particularly puzzling aspect. Consider something rather like a temporal version of the Müller-Lyer illusion. If one were to drive from New Orleans to St. Louis and then back again at the same speed and by the same route, the time back would doubtless appear to be much shorter than the time there. It is suggested that experienced time is affected by the content of time. But this appearance is usually judged to be illusory, since the clock-time taken up by the two halves of the journey are approximately equal. But this equality is judged by one who is persuaded he already knows what equal time intervals are. Now, who, we must ask, is suffering from a temporal illusion? The one who trusts the clock? Or the one who trusts his sense of the passage of time? The devotee of the clock is persuaded *a priori* that the clock and not the traveler's sense of time is the proper judge. He has tacitly agreed that real time is time viewed through Newtonian analogies, that any other kind of judgment of time yields only illusion.

Still, there are and have been other ways of understanding time. If we are willing to take the traveler's time-sense seriously, that is, if we are really concerned about the experience of time, such favorite ways of judging it as the Newtonian way must be put aside in favor of the view that not all ways of measuring or judging time may be commensurable; hence an independent attempt to determine the nature of phenomenal time, or time as experienced, is demanded.

Let us attempt to turn directly to the phenomena of time. Unfortunately, the decision not to be guided by sophisticated and quantitative views of time does not indicate in a positive fashion how the phenomena appropriate for study are to be selected. The initial step requires choosing events or phenomena from which the essential character of time (or the essentially temporal character of experience) can be "read off." How, though, will a temporal phenomenon be recognized prior to our knowing what time is? Will the poet, the historian, the metaphysician, or the average Western man be best able to designate such a complete temporal succession? It is persistently difficult to see at this turn why the generally credited definitions of the physicist should not be accepted as authoritative. Surely we do have experiences of time pieces. Still, clocks have not always been among us. The millenia before the invention of clocks were not timeless. The fact is that time has a history, and this history may in some way determine time as now experienced.

The history of time has been preserved in an important way by the images, figures, and analogies through which attempts have been made to describe time. Time has, for example, been likened to a spun thread, to a woven web, to a flowing river, to a thin thread of water which could be started or stopped at will, to the flow of blood marked by the pulse, to a full or empty container. The measuring of time by a wheel moving with a presumably constant angular velocity is only one among the latest of these analogies.

The analogy of the web belonged to the ancient Greeks and is expressed by Homer in terms drawn from the art of weaving. The full image to which Homer recurs suggests that the effective embodiment of fate is a web or net woven by the Morai at the instance of fate itself, or by command of Zeus and bound upon men.[2] In this web, the warp[3] threads are time or length of life. For the Greeks, this time is the duration (*chronos*) allowed for living; it is the continuing succession of events. The woof threads which work the pattern are pictured as the fated events experienced, the things, ordained. *Kairos*, meaning the opportune, the fitting moment, refers to these events, in particular to an eventful moment which in some sense differentiates itself from others as being timely or appropriate with reference to some purpose or to some act. Together, duration and event, warp and woof form the tapestry woven from day to day and bound upon men according to the design of fate or of Zeus.

Now, if this ancient analogy were taken seriously, it might be supposed to render time as duration or succession (quantity of days) separately accessible by the simple expedient of suppressing the woof threads (time as event). Thus by eliminating or ignoring human events or experiences in all their variety, the warp threads marking the orderly succession of events would be laid bare. Already an eventless time or mere duration seems to be abstracted from the concrete flow. For the Greeks, this abstraction served to emphasize certain orderly aspects of temporal succession, aspects which conserve some factors involved in the notion of an unchanging and impersonal fate. For instance, time may take from the ancient sense of fate the irreversibility of the order of events. Another fateful aspect of time is the sameness of the pace of its shuttle for all things, the necessity that each of us, indeed all things in the universe, should reach October fourth on the same calculable instant. It seems to be but a step from the observation of these two properties of temporal succession, its irreversibility and its constant flow, to the measurement of time. The Greeks, however, did not forget that the woof of the web was an essential part, the part without which the warp would fall into so many unrelated threads.

Other metaphors of time had to add their quota to the interpretation of time before the warp threads could be thought to hang together without the woof. One such metaphor holds that time is like a river, flowing irresistibly and constantly past the observer on its banks. A water clock is a small representation of this river which has the advantage that its flow can be stopped at the end of an event and the volume of water which flowed during it identified as the measure of its duration. The quantity of time and the weight of water correspond to each other in a presumably constant manner. Here also, the water retains a constant and undiversified identity independent of events. It does not fall to pieces, so to speak, upon the withdrawal of the threads of events. Thus this analogy offers a model for thinking about empty and abstract temporal duration.

Galileo, who used the water clock, seemed to sense time in this manner; it was not difficult for him to think of time as moving through other sorts of machines which would divide and measure duration by means of some handy regularity. According to legend, he sat bored by a sermon in church one day and observed a chandelier swinging to and fro in the changing wind. He idly timed its period by his pulse beat: then the essential fact concerning the pendulum broke in upon him: the relation of its period to its length. From the moment of that insight, the invention of the pendulum clock was not far distant. The metaphoric shift is not great which sees time as something flowing like a small river through a water clock, or moving through one's veins, marked by the pulse beat, or flowing, as it were, through a mechanical clock, marked by the swing of a pendulum. A more modern analogy might picture time as a magnetic tape with seconds marked on it, running through a tape recorder; the whole universe might be taken as the tape recorder. Thus time became objective, independent of men's experiences, an empty, universally measurable quantity, the independent variable of physics.

Such time runs on just as well without man as with him. It is independent of its content, "absolute"; man, events, history, are merely the contingent filling of its vacancy. Once the warp of time — its quantifiable duration — is separated from the woof — its contents — the two soon come to appear intrinsically separate and independent of each other. Time appears to be one and the same empty and characterless duration, receptive of infinitely varying contents. Of its structure we may observe a unity, arbitrarily divisible into a many. Here, we might speak quite seriously of prehistoric time, or of the eons which the nebulae spun out before the hardening of the earth and will again spin out after its destruction. Thus time, by metaphoric extension, came to refer to the mere persistence in being (the duration) of any object, however unrelated to experience or to any being which lives time. The unity of this time is the unity of a characterless duration, undivided and unmeasured, unless by man's own measures.

Objective duration, however, is abstract, independent of content; it is an irreversible, constant, divisible, and hence measurable flow or succession. For our purpose, it may be viewed as a sophistication of the warp threads of the fateful web imagined by Homeric Greeks to determine or to limit human action, or it may be like the flow of a river carrying events steadily and irreversibly upon its course. But if it be thought of in this manner, the question arises how it may be related again to the events, human and other, which happen in history.

In what way, then, are events and the empty duration they occupy related to each other? The observer of events must admit that he himself is in time; that is, he himself is a kind of object, one of those things borne along by the river of time. He does not stand non-temporally aside on the bank watching the absolute flow. All are in temporal motion relative to him; even the banks may be flowing. Now, one of those things or contents observed along the banks of time are the warp threads in our previous analogy. The constant flow of water in the clepsydra, the flow of blood punctuated by the pulse, the abstract flow in the clock, or the empty succession which the physicist measures — all are objects the observer has found or has made and has left or will leave along the banks of time as his history bears him along.

Strangest of such possibilities is the suggestion that convictions about the independence of time or its non-relation to its contents may be among the events in time which eventually are to be borne away upon its flow. Observations of this kind suggest the artificial nature of objective time and are disturbing to those who hold the objective aspect of nature to be certain, basic, and given. We may move even further in the direction of the subjective. May not the flow of feeling, so intimately associated with the self and its subjectivity, be the river which bears objectivity along? For in fact, not only was the separation of the warp from the woof of time a human act, an interpretation, but in the first place the intimation that time bore a significant resemblance to a woven web or to a river was an achievement in history.

These latter reflections loom like a comic reversal in the drama of time. It is as if the quantity of water which passed through a clepsydra were to be measured by the duration of an event rather than vice versa. The same might also be true of the more sophisticated mechanisms for measuring the constant flow of time. As soon as one considers the matter, it appears that the tape passing through the recorder of the universe must have the seconds marked upon it by someone who already knows the measure of time. The same point is made by the Newtonian philosophers who attempted to argue for the constancy, the mathematical flow, of time. This regularity simply could not be established, as Newton had hoped, without regard to circumstance. The circumstance selected by Newton was the movement of the stars as recorded on earth. But he himself was quite aware that this regularity was itself an event in time and needed to be compared to some other orderly serial event by which its regularity might be measured and judged. Some philosophers today seek in nuclear disintegration the instance of perfect regularity, but one may still ask by what measure of time this regularity is measured and authenticated. In any case, the measure of constancy would be an event or a temporal series of events, and such temporal circumstances are just that which is to be measured. Our conclusion must be that the woof and circumstance of time cannot be altogether and cleanly separated from the warp. In short, the warp is imaginable only as one of the factors in the web of time; taken by itself, it is not an independent nor even a typical temporal phenomenon.

The metaphor of the moving thread, or flow, yielding time as an independent measurable quantity, breaks down if followed out in this manner; consequently we must confess that the supposition of an empty and irreversible but real and constant flow is clearly a reified analogy, or rather it is a portion of an analogy taken apart from its total context, as if that portion possessed an independent truth. It thus becomes a metaphysical assumption.

Still, to many people, some philosophers included, this objective time appears to provide the only real temporal context; time in any other sense is "merely subjective," just a fantasy probably bred by linguistic confusion. I want to suggest that, on the contrary, this objective time is derivative; it is a human product, made for the purpose of guiding one in a certain way in selecting, ordering, and interpreting events. It is the product of a technique of measurement and is valid in some contexts but not in all. Convictions about the irreversibility, divisibility, constancy and measurability of time, which guided us to the metaphysical interpretation of it just outlined, are, as we have seen, themselves events in time, whatever else they may also be. If, therefore, we are interested in acquiring a less narrowly circular view of time, we had best return to that concrete order of events we are now living, whose sequential character we wish to understand, and begin again.

§15. THE STRUCTURE OF LIVED TIME

Time is commonly given four quite different senses; it may refer to: (1) mere duration or persistence in beings; (2) common or lived time, experienced in several ways; (3) objective, abstract, and measurable succession; (4) the dramatic time of profound human change. Now, time in the second sense is fundamental for us; it mediates, in different ways, between time in the first and in the third and fourth senses. In order to understand this function of lived time, interest must be transferred from the objective warp of time to the subjective woof. We shall seek to determine the meanings which time, understood spontaneously and then reflectively, acquires. By this route we shall reach (in §17) an understanding of the derivative, objective sense of time.

Time understood as the passage of events is subjective; it is simply unconceived and inconceivable apart from man who lives events. It is always man who imagines the woof, the warp, and the weaving of fate or history. Even the highly contrived and sophisticated Newtonian flow, providing the independent variable for physical equations, is a meaning which men conceive and give to certain events and which in this sense has its being in their subjectivity. Acquaintance with it and power to use it are acquired only through a very specific discipline open to and accepted by some but not by all. Time as eventful flow, however, is experienced by all men, even if often in a defective manner. Moreover, time as eventful flow is obviously non-existent apart from the beings, men, who live events. In order, now, to understand time-as-experienced, we need first to determine the most basic sense of time and then to proceed to examine the interpretations and meanings which this basic sense acquires or loses (MT pp. 161f.).

Time in one sense is best expressed in Spinoza's phrase as "persistence in being." It is an object's being itself, its enduring as itself and as something different from other things. That an object's mere continuation in being is ever directly sensed or experienced as such is scarcely possible. But one's own persistence in being is sensed. And no doubt it is sensed as an indistinct intention to persist which pervades all one's feeling and is illustrated in any experience whatsoever. The possibility of this intention is surely basic and is implicit always in the history and habits one carries along as potentials for further experience. Common opinion is in general agreement concerning the basic structure exemplified by any such experience. One's lived time is always a structured persistence, although at times this structure may become quite indistinct (cf. §17).

One aspect of its complex structure is always already enacted. This aspect is exemplified in previously learned muscular habits — habits, for instance, enabling me to complete the writing of this sentence. Another aspect is not yet enacted, but is tending to emerge; it is exemplified in the intended meaning which leads me to choose to write exactly this word. Indeed one might say this aspect *is* the intention. These two, the already actualized (the past) and the not yet actual (the future), intersect in the process of coming to be, the movement which is present and which depends upon and unifies the two aspects just noted (cf. § 51). Thus, I utilize my own past in order to realize my future in this present now. This intrinsic triadic structure of any instance of human persistence in being provides a clue for the selection of analogies which further interpret the sense of time. But the difficulty in selecting a complete instance of lived time is not so easily resolved, for any one of the three elements of this temporal structure might be emphasized at the expense of the other two.

The living of time might be viewed primarily from the perspective of the present, of the future, or of the past. For instance, one who emphasizes the present is aware chiefly of the peaceful waiting, the continuous and persistent, or perhaps the boring, character of his temporal movement. He lives primarily in the present boring or peaceful moment. One who perspects time mainly from the future senses it as anticipation of novelty, as anxiety, or as revolutionary excitement. He lives in an imaginative "now" which reaches toward the unactualized. Similarly, one who lives principally in the past would sense time as a determined order, a tradition which must be conserved, else life itself be lost. His experience of time is the "now" of recollection.

Though each of these emphases are experienced and might quite validly be described, each one tends to ignore the other two. It is possible, however, to acquire a sense of the wholeness of time and to discover events in which the unity of its several dimensions becomes evident.[4] But we shall, in the search after such events, also have to be careful that the concrete temporal character not be allowed to disappear either in the abstract unity of a mathematical eternity or in the ineffable unity of a mystical *totum simul*. We are interested in the whole of time as commonly experienced.

Physical or objective time having been put aside, we are returned to our earlier question: What would be a fair illustration of a complete temporal interval? And how shall we know when an adequate example has been selected? Would a concerto one hears to the end offer a fair illustration? But in this instance, one is relying upon composer and musicians to determine what a complete interval of musical time is. What of the composer's (or anyone's) life? But here one must rely upon the biographer to decide whether this lifetime was complete or not. An epoch or period in history? Here one must accept the historian's judgment, when, for instance, the epoch properly began and ended. We would be well-advised to avoid dependence upon such specialized, perhaps prejudiced or official viewpoints as these. Their authority is necessarily limited and one-sided.

More useful for indicating the nature of time would be the discernment of a temporal interval belonging to the common experience of all men. There are many such items of common experience from which to choose. There are the larger rhythms of birth, life, and death, the yearly recurrences of seasonal change, or the diurnal-nocturnal experiences of waking and sleep. But these experiences appear to be needlessly complex for the present purposes. Instead, we need an instance of the awareness of the passage of time which is both simple and experienced by all men. Let us, then, put aside not only those events which require specialized training to be experienced properly, but also these more common events involving excessive complexities; likewise we may lay to one side those temporal intervals which one may either experience or not experience, which, in other words, time may do without. There remain, after placing to one side all such complex, specialized, and optional experiences, the smaller, felt, organic intervals marked off in the course of life, intervals such as the winking of the eye, breathing, or the beating of the pulse. Of these, common agreement holds that the heartbeat is a regular and essential experienced recurrence; there is no lifetime without it. Also, it has been thus used in history; we have recalled that Galileo so used it upon a crucial occasion. I choose it, therefore, as an instance of a simple, common, and essential temporal interval.

But whose pulse shall be chosen? Surely not that of Edgar Allan Poe's melodramatic story, "The Telltale Heart," for this heart throb was the voice of fear; the persistent presence of guilt, not the passage of time, was its burden. Conversely, the heartbeat of the healthy worker is too unobtrusive, too much an unnoticed part of the background of his eventful activity. But though any person can attend to his pulse, we desire our observer to attend to nothing but his pulse, and to attend to it with sufficient penetration to perceive its structure. Perhaps such an observer will do well to recall the attitude of a heart disease patient who, as he delicately feels his pulse, wonders "will there be another?" for he, surely, is aware of the living phases of his heartbeat and of the recurrence of his pulse as the *sine qua non* of experienced time. Observe what he is experiencing: the return of the cardiac rhythm *is* the continuation of time itself; it is that upon which his persistence in being depends.

Whether our patient or observer merely feels his pulse or whether he watches the complex wave form of his cardiac rhythm shaped upon an oscilloscope, he will remember that each recurrence of this rhythm is formed by three partial phases. These phases are initiated when the auricles of the heart fill with blood from the veins. Then the auricles contract, forcing blood through stop valves into the ventricles. Next, the expanded and filled ventricles contract, forcing the blood through other valves and into the arteries. This cardiological detail is, however, not actually experienced and therefore not especially relevant to one who is concerned primarily with the experience of this rhythm. But it is important to observe that the attentive patient can experience this systolic-diastolic action as three moments within one rhythmic period: first a slight pause, then the characteristic "lub-dub,"[5] then the same period repeated throughout the remainder of lived time.

Thus the observer is aware, upon reflection, of a beginning moment, which is followed by a mid-moment, which then comes to its conclusion in an end-moment. Then, to his relief, the pattern begins over again. A sensed identity of action is exhibited in these three phases as they are continually repeated. For as they are experienced, it becomes clear that they are not three separate elements. Rather, the beginning pause is distinctive in that it is related forward to the expected systole. Similarly, the end moment, the diastole, is related backward to the systole. The systole, the mid-moment, is related in both directions. The first and the last moments might be described as monadic or unidirectional, although they are directed in opposite ways, one "forward" and one "backward." They might be symbolized thus → and ← respectively. The mid-moment, however, is related in both ways, "backward" toward the beginning of the period, and "forward" to the end. It might be symbolized thus: ↔. This symbolization suggests that the beginning and ending moments may be regarded as separated elements of the dyadic or di-directional middle moment. This latter, the middle moment, has the abstract character of a "now," or present moment, as described by Aristotle. It is always between a past and a future. However, a "now," characterized merely as between past and future moments, is remote from a present united organically to its beginning and ending phases.

Aristotle of the *Physics* was interested in time as the measure of motion; however, we are in pursuit of a time which is more like the measure of the human action phenomenally accessible to us. Its "now" is always a moment in tension, drawn both toward its immediate future and toward its immediate past. (Note that I do not mention any immediate relation between future and past in a single cardiac period, for I cannot see that in this simple organic period any such relation is sensed. The matter may fall out differently, though, in more complex illustrations; cf. §16.) A natural interval of this time is remotely reminiscent of the beginning, middle, and end of a drama as described by Aristotle in the *Poetics*. To this point we shall return later.

Our observer would further notice that the three moments of a cardiac life-interval are mutually inclusive or hierarchically ordered in a characteristic way. That is, the middle includes the beginning as leading it forward, and the end includes the middle as, so to speak, having been led forward. Hence the end moment includes the middle, which in turn includes the beginning.

At the same time, the man with his finger on his pulse projects himself beyond the end of a given pulse-beat, in anticipation or hope, to a new beginning. That is to say, the end, which includes the middle and the beginning and so completes the period, also looks forward as a whole to a following renewal of this rhythmic interval or period. Such a period includes the preceding period, which in its turn includes in memory the period immediately preceding it. Ideally, any period includes all the preceding and looks forward indefinitely to others. In fact, though, these retentions and anticipations break down into groups which coincide with — or are — recollected or anticipated events. The unity of life time is first a hierarchical order within the life interval or period; and, secondly, each period is hierarchically related to the others preceding and following. Our lived time is this kind of ordered passage; we are, organically speaking, in this cardio-temporal periodic becoming. This is the time of average continuation in being.[6]

Our patient experiences his persistence in being, his duration, as this rhythmic recurrence. It is important to emphasize that the time of which we are now speaking is not an empty flow independent of its content. At this point, container and contents are hardly separable; without this pulse there is no life, neither sensed duration or events in experienced time. The time in which the weaver lives as he weaves is a time no longer conceivable according to the analogy of a warp separate from the woof. If the analogy is to be retained, then the web must be imagined to come into existence as a unity. The living of the weaver's lifetime is precisely the continual uniting of warp and woof. Only in retrospect may the warp be considered separately from the woof. Such is the burden of the expression, "Time is life."

Three observations must now be added to amplify and modify this view. The first is to admit that this characterization of lived time differs from that offered by many philosophers, for instance by Bergson. Bergson's famous descriptions of time as duration *vécue* emphasizes its continuity. This emphasis follows, it seems to me, from his perspecting time primarily from the present. My attempt was, however, to reach a grasp of time as a whole. Time observed thus appeared partly discontinuous, its basic unit being an organic periodic interval analyzable into three components. But these periods are not altogether discontinuous. I expressed the continuity of these unit intervals in terms of the hierarchical relation among them, a relation which is available at any time to observation. This present, for example, was the future of a moment ago and contains its immediate past, which in turn contains *its* immediate past, and so on back to the beginning.

The path of time is best imagined, therefore, not as a line or a continuous, uni-directional class of temporal points. Rather, its triadic perodic structure is best seen, as I want to point out more elaborately later (§47), as something more like a circle or a spiral. Time comes toward us out of the future, through the past, and into the present. That is, our primary temporal tension is toward the future. In fact, to observe that all our intentions related to action are directed toward the future is obvious. But time coming out of the future comes through the past and is laden with all the sensation, imagery, memories, habits, opinions, and ideals which have already been accumulated. Thus directed, burdened, and empowered, it enters our experience in the present. In its structure, lived time is a hierarchical unity of many periods and classes of periods of the kind we have described, though no doubt still more complex.

My second remark must add that the significance of this cardio-time is shared by other kinds of organic rhythms.[7] We might also have chosen the rhythm of breathing to localize the sense of the passage of life-time. Indeed, we might choose any such bodily rhythm commonly identified with the continuance of life and presence as the temporal condition of one's continuation in being. Such organic rhythms constitute the time one shares with the animals and other living things. The cardiac rhythm, however, marks the shortest of these periods and the most constant. It may also be the oldest in anyone's memory. If there is such a thing as prenatal experience, this experience must be the sound of the mother's heart beating. Perhaps the security long associated with the sound accounts for the pleasantness of its rhythm, seventy-two beats per minute, so similar to the tranquil motion of lullabies and barcaroles. The cardiac rhythm is also the last which one may be thought to experience.

Thus, the cardiac rhythm is a basic instance of experienced time. Perhaps it is true for the artist, the weaver for example, that the usual temporal rhythm may become the set of habitual movements which constitute the activity of his art and its necessary divisions. His sense of time may become identified with these movements, a partly organic, partly mechanical time. But this time is quite specialized, understandable only to fellow artists, and does not prevent his sharing in the common temporal sense. Upon the basis of this common temporal sense, complex analogies and variations are constructed not only among organic rhythms but also in more contrived productions such as the sonata or certain dramatic forms (see §16).

These considerations point to an important corollary: however complex the time through which a man lives may become, it remains periodic and comes at last to its end. Human time is finite. This generalization has been denied. It has been asserted that death is a recent development in evolutionary history. Single-celled animals or single cells do not die necessarily. They divide continuously and would continue indefinitely to do so if conditions were ideal, i.e., if food were supplied and waste products completely removed. Some biologists believe that such ideal conditions may eventually be provided even for the cells constituting the human body. Then man, or his body, would be everlasting![8] But even if the survival of the organism were identical with the survival of the person, the end of the person is assured. The lifetime of the person is finite, if for no other reason than the life of the species is finite, for the species will not outlive the earth, the solar system, the galaxy. And all of these, we are assured, are moving to their "heat death" quite inexorably. In any event, though, human time is fundamentally finite. Any organic interval has an end, and any rhythmic or temporal structure of an interval, say a dramatic structure, comes similarly to an end.

In the third place, it will be useful to observe briefly at least one further characteristic of the relations which unite both the parts of an interval of time and the intervals of time themselves into a rhythmic flow. I now have in mind intervals of time more complex than such felt, organic intervals as the pulse or breathing.

An important property of these relations is indicated, I will suggest, by the concern I have already expressed for beginning with an appropriate illustration of temporality, an illustration from which the whole essential nature of time might be read. This concern points to a certain freedom for choosing one's context and one's guiding analogy. It also suggests an obscure conviction that one already somehow "knows" what time is, and needs, therefore, only take care to use this knowledge in selecting a fair example for analysis. Or, as the point may alternatively be expressed, it is as if time were already in a familiar context and were already known, though perhaps vaguely. And in fact, the anxiety and obscure prior knowledge to which I refer already constitute a reference respectively to the future and to the past. These two references are sensed now; they are unified in this present which is constituted by this inquiry into the structure of lived time. The event of this present, in other words, like an actor in a drama, defines its own interval of time by its intrinsic references to its relevant past (its beginning) and to its future. Thus the present inquiry functions like a confirming instance of the structure which has been disengaged.

This structure, furthermore, as thus exemplified, clearly contains noetic components; it is now referred anxiously to the future, and with conviction to the past. Indeed, the references of a lived present to its future and to its past are like meaning references. Lived events are significant events and are so constituted by a reflective interpretation of their meaning references. These references may be the links of mood or feeling, the relation of symbol to reference, implication, suggestion, analogy, and the like. They provide the clues to reflective self-interpretation.

The supposition that time can be used and viewed as a language is nothing new. It has been observed that time is constantly so used; for instance, in the business world the interval a person is kept waiting for an appointment with an associate tells quite unmistakeably whether the associate will be receptive, indifferent, or hostile.[9] This lapse of time indicates, therefore, the way in which their appointment will begin. In general, the relations among the elements of an interval of lived time to each other are or are like meaning relations (c.f. §§ 18, 52). For example, the beginning of a significant life-interval refers (like a symbol, or perhaps like an *implicans*) to the middle, which in turn refers to the end. If this view is true, then the ancient observation — that only man, the language-using animal, lives fully through time — becomes tautological. Other animals live only through forms of organic time, but cannot superpose upon these forms the variety of temporal meaning-relations which are available to man. Their time is, therefore, less concrete than man's.

§16. TOWARD AUTHENTIC TIME

Assuming now that the heartbeat does constitute a fairly typical and basic example of an organic life-interval, and also assuming that we have succeeded in reading off from this instance the essential structure — the hierarchically related beginning, middle and end — of a complete interval of lived time, then it should be possible to find the same structure in other more complex temporal involvements. And in fact, the discovery of a somewhat similar structure in listening to a concerto, for instance, is inevitable. It can be found, too, in an artist's acceptance of a task, his actual work, and the relatively complete embodiment of the composition in materials. Again, this structure is present in a drama, but this last is of particular significance. For changes in the particular kind of meaning-relations which structure human life are properly called dramatic only under certain circumstances. Doubtless, only some men have succeeded in living in dramatic (authentic) time.

"Drama," from *dran*, an act, a thing done, refers, as Aristotle noted, to a complete human action, one having a beginning, a middle, and an end. The beginning I identify as the protagonist's decision concerning the person he is and intends to be. Clearly, such a decision looks essentially to the future. And inevitably, the decision is made in the shadow of self-ignorance and in an atmosphere of hybris. The middle is his struggle to live out the consequences of his faulty decision. The end brings his struggle to a shocked recognition of self-ignorance and the failure to be the person he had resolved to be. The end, that is, looks essentially to the past. Thus beginning and end, decision and insight, link future to past. When, consequent upon the insight, the protagonist sees that he is not the person he had initially resolved to be, then he may begin the cycle again, chastened somewhat by his apprehension of his non-identity, his dependence, and his other limitations. Authentic time, I will suggest, is time lived in willing cooperation with this tragic movement.

Elsewhere I call this movement the non-objective dialectic (below §44). The essential element of its structure is the explicit cyclical development I have described, leading to radical human change and to the discovery of some new or renewed value. Thus the time of such dramatic change is not merely periodic as was the common time which preoccupied us in the preceding section, for authentic time introduces a relation — to the future (in the decision) and back to the past (in the ending) — which is missing in ordinary time when the identity and fate of the protagonist are not at issue. Indeed, where there is a willing cooperation with this dramatic pattern, there is, in addition, a direct relation of future to past. The protagonist's decision is made only after mature consideration of possible endings, so that the end may be said to be more or less explicitly present in the beginning. A good beginning anticipates a tragic ending. This movement has been envisaged as a repeated passage through archways, and the transition is to a qualitatively different and perhaps better life or self, (MT §25). Inauthentic time, on the other hand, is time spent evading this cyclical movement; it is time lived in nourishing an appearance of success as measured by popular standards or in preserving a mask concealing the immature egoist behind it.

A word needs to be said concerning the inevitability of the cyclical movement of tragedy. The movement originates in hybris and is inherent in the human condition. Elsewhere I have sought to show that hybris is the consequence of an "ontological flaw" (PC §53; MT §§15, 22). The character of this flaw may be expressed in terms of the cosmogonic myth to which we have already appealed (§3). The myth would say a defect follows inevitably from the infinity of Gaea's power or fertility and the limited nature of Ouranos' purpose or direction. Any definite direction he gives to power must ignore other possible directions, and thus it must forego their values. More literally, any decision made by the protagonist is a rejection of other possible decisions and a relegation of their values to the unreality of what-might-have-been. And again, the protagonist makes his decision in the light of his self-knowledge and reason. But reason must proceed by way of conceptualization which distorts the whole unless corrected by some adequate vision of the whole. But visions of the whole — e.g., the whole of man's life and fate — are theoretical and abstract. By what further vision will they be corrected and complemented? The tragic hero who is disposing of his whole life upon the basis of a reasoned decision, inevitably an abstraction, can scarcely escape error. And since he possesses no theoretical account of the whole with which to measure his abstraction, he cannot escape the overconfidence which is hybris and pride. In other words, tragic error follows from human finitude. To be a man is to have hybris — to be exorbitant and to make decisions embodying this excess. Thus, tragedy and the peculiar temporal periodicity of tragedy belong to the human lot.

Aristotle already recognized the link between elements of the tragic drama and time (*Poetics* 13). The insight or discovery, as he viewed it, can produce a catharsis of excessive pity and fear. Here pity refers to the necessities of the past, and fear to the likely happenings in the future. When the protagonist, through his own ill-advised decision, brought great misfortune upon himself or upon those whom he loved, he placed himself in a piteous position, one which, if not changed, would in the future be likely to bring even more fearful events to pass. Thus we pity him for his past errors and fear for his future. The tragic action, however, through reversals and recognitions, may lead the protagonist to understand his errors and to become more clearly aware of his self-ignorance and his pride.

The Greek tragic hero was commonly a man of noble and forthright soul, who could acknowledge his mistakes and accept their consequences. By accepting his fate, the piteousness of his past misfortunes could be changed in quality; the fearfulness of his future could likewise be altered. The catastrophic consequences of his ontological flaw, resulting from a faulty decision, could thus be taken as a means to maturity and an occasion for living in a more authentic time. Thus redirected, his past more realistically interpreted, the protagonist's life is re-evaluated, rendered more determinate, and may even become heroic. Thus past and future are bound together in a renewed and purified present by discovering the meanings of self-ignorance and pride. This binding together of future and past, exhibited in the authentic present, belongs to the uniqueness and essence of the time of radical human change.

The structure of this most concrete time is dramatic. Its unity is the unity of a human being in the process of becoming himself. Clearly, more of the human sensitive field may become involved in dramatic than in non-dramatic action. The parts of this qualitative temporal unity are the functionally different parts of a drama — its decision, struggle, and insight. This structure is analogous to a single period of ordinary time as it was exhibited in the perhaps melodramatic instance of the cardiac patient feeling his pulse, except that future and past are united in a unique manner in dramatic time. In addition, the temporality of other acts, as well as their dramatic involvements, imitate these rhythms.

"Time," may be used collectively to name the whole family of organic and lived temporal intervals and series of the same. Some of these kinds of temporal experience may include others, as a long breath may include several cardiac intervals. No doubt the expression "lived time," when not otherwise modified, is used in this complex, collective sense. But the specific difference distinguishing dramatic or authentic time should not be forgotten, whereby the three parts of a temporal interval acquire peculiar significance with regard to human change.

Here I pause to summarize. Each mode of time is a one many structure. Objective time is an abstract, unified duration arbitrarily divisible into a multiplicity of like durations or intervals which may be counted by a clock. Lived time in its most general sense is one's own given persistence in being. At the intuitive level of one's awareness of this persistence, lived time is quite involuntarily interpreted as a unity of felt, organic intervals which are further reflectively interpreted as possessing a triadic organization. Upon or within this organic time are built the structures of our daily involvement in the common businesses of life. The continuity of time results from its hierarchic structure, from the inclusion within a present phase of its immediately past and future elements and from the inclusion of other intervals in any given interval by way of memory and anticipation. Overlapping series of intervals of this sort form a family of kinds of lived time. Upon the basis of this rhythmic structure, other and various rhythms may be developed and interrelated by more complex meanings to constitute commonly experienced human time, the average continuation in existence.

In addition, the most concrete and most characteristically human time, authentic time, is exhibited in a dramatic linkage of events. This linkage constitutes the movement whereby meaning and change of meaning are given to oneself and to the events of one's life. The unity of this time is the being of the self (cf. §§51 & 54); its manyness is the multiplicity of functionally different parts — decisions, struggle, insight — whereby the self comes to be itself through confusion, suffering, and the painful passage to self-knowledge. I have heard the phrase: "The awful experiment of time"; here I refer it to man's perilous involvement in dramatic time.

One may imagine the complexity of temporal periods as analogous to ocean waves, where very small waves are superimposed upon larger, and these upon larger and larger ones still, and the latter rise and fall with the tides, and the tides ebb and flow with the moon and are affected by still larger rhythms of nature and the cosmos. But the point I am suggesting is that man's life time is no less complex when one recalls the interinvolved rhythms of time which together weave and change his life.

Let us move now from the complexity of time to its simpler forms and ask whether the latter are derived from the former.

§17. THE DERIVATION OF OBJECTIVE TIME

That common lived time can be derived from concrete, dramatic time by the omission of certain characteristics of the latter is easy to see. For instance, one may suppress the requirement that a period of time begin with a far-reaching decision concerning the protagonist's identity. The decision instead, may be quite ordinary, e.g., whether to paint one's house white or green. And the insight may be commensurately unimportant, say the discovery that the chosen color goes poorly with the color of a neighboring house. Of such a kind are the decisions, struggles, and discoveries of average everyday life. In general, one moves upon the basis of organic time from dramatic time to average continuation in being by way of omitting or attenuating important properties of the former, so that the rhythmic structure of time is retained but its significance is comparatively trivialized. Perhaps a further movement of this same kind will lead us to an experience of objective time.

I suggest that the kind of freedom from contents which objective time exhibits may best be seen by observing the kind of lived time which is most like an empty objective flow. In effect, I want to suggest that objective time may most easily be developed out of — or abstracted from — a certain sort of experience. This experience is that in which the natural articulations of an interval of time, its beginnings and endings, fade into insignificance. An empty duration, one without circumstance, may be imagined as the limit of this fading (MT pp. 160f.).

Objective time, in other words, can scarcely be supposed to be abstracted from the temporality of just any experience. Rather, it takes its orgin (or is extrapolated) from that experienced time which is already not unlike an empty flow, a time wherein the beginnings and endings of organic intervals fade away and finally become indiscernible. But even when not discerned, we must suppose that the structural elements of a temporal interval remain as aspects of the infra-structure of lived time, so to speak, only they are not used and so can be ignored. For instance, in ordinary healthful work the rhythm of time comes from one's activity; then the pulse beat or breathing or other organic intervals are not noticed. Still, these latter remain and might be elicited by an act of attention.

In fact, there is something like experience of this rhythmical flow which is familiar to all. Let us suppose that the minimal event of lived time, the cardiac and breathing rhythms, have faded into oblivion. What remains? Nothing? A nothing, perhaps, which is the possibility of sentient life, and a vague awareness of the flow we call time. This nothing is scarcely experienced, but it may be imagined as a contentless, eventless, empty flow. During periods of complete or almost complete inactivity, when attention is diffuse and expectation and memory are at a minimum, then one may experience something approaching this contentless, eventless flow. Here nothing begins, nothing ends. Time then is experienced as a kind of waiting, a gap between matters of greater moment, an indefinite readiness for a more fully lived time. This is the time which Shakespeare adumbrated when he wrote,

> Thou hast not youth nor age,
> But as it were, an after-dinner sleep,
> Dreaming on both.

The objective character of such an almost contentless somnolence is not yet evident; it is still felt duration and is sensed as a temporary oblivion. Such a time is an indefinite "now" or series of nows or mid-moments whose tensions forward and backward (toward beginnings or endings) have lost their distinctiveness. This series of "nows," with its intrinsic divisions faded, is a continuous series of like moments and may be imagined to be divisible *ad libitum*. But just this vaguely sensed duration, divisible yet undivided by anything felt or experienced, provides the experiential basis for a concept of the kind of continuous and regular flow within which physics may be carried forward. This duration without end and without beginning contains no intrinsic divisions. And because one part of it cannot be distinguished from another, it can be divided anywhere. Hence it can be divided so as to become isomorphic with the equal divisions of, say, a Euclidean line. Any point may be taken as the beginning, the zero point; then intervals may be marked by any convenient, regularly operating mechanical or organic means, and counted. Here, the living events and rhythms of time having faded away, the sense of time's passages and uni-directionality disappear also; only the fact of the geometrical or numerical isomorphism counts.

Furthermore, the experience of an impersonal flow, a mere passage, is objectively relevant in another way. Without much exercise of the imagination and without much effort of projection, this time may be attributed to unconscious objects. Inanimate objects begin nothing of themselves; they end nothing. Their time may be imagined as an endless somnolent waiting. Then, equal intervals of this impersonal time-like duration may be selected, and the objective time of physical objects may be defined into being. The important operation the imagination must perform in achieving a grasp of objective time lies in removing from experienced time every suggestion of event, every hint of human tension. This operation is performed by reversing the isomorphism just indicated and ascribing to the temporal extension just and only the properties of the line which measures it. Then, the constancy of the flow of time is interpreted as the seriality of points or intervals along a line, both in respect to the time of the (somnolent) self and the time through which an object endures and moves. Physical objects endure or persist in their being, and where we can match their endurance with the even flow of empty somnolent time and then with the ideally regular flow of abstract time, we are confident we can measure their object-time.

We are returned, it seems, to the web from which the woof threads have been removed. Only warp threads remain. Also, they are isomorphic with numbers, and so they may be counted. But now the structure of the number series holds the discrete instants, the woof threads, together, so to speak. An interpretation of time is thus reached which is innocent of beginnings and endings and of the sense of passage as well. There remains only an isomorphism between a set of numbers and of numbered objects (e.g., days); such an isomorphism is established in the eternal present of abstract relations. This homogeneous object-time lies at the opposite end of the scale from concrete, dramatic time.

Much may be gained by making this abstraction. Precise measurements of quantified and abstract time are absolutely essential to the development of the technology on which the modern Westernized world depends; without that technology, we go hungry. Surely it is unrealistic now to regret this development in our history. We do regret, though, the devotion to technology and to the sense of power and control it produces when that devotion and power are cultivated to the exclusion of living in authentic human time. Absorption in the directing of powerful machines can easily blind one to the maturing changes which direct or redirect human life. Hence the error is serious which systematically confuses abstract duration or the duration of inanimate things with human time. In the sonorous phrase of Sir Thomas Brown, "To subsist in bones, to be put pyramidally extant, is a fallacy in duration."

For humans, time is possible or actual meaning; it is the realm of possible beginnings and endings. Only by not distinguishing among such structural elements do we attain the abstract oblivion which is objective time. Objective time is still something devised by man; it has a beginning in history and may be used for an end. It will mark the end of history only when this beginning is forgotten.

§18. THE MEANING OF TIME

In this last section I wish to recapitulate enough of the preceding discussion to juxtapose the several meanings or essences of time in an order which will indicate their relationship and exhibit a common element of their structure. Time, as we have observed, runs a gamut from the series of abstract points or numbers ("nows"), to the still abstract, infinitely divisible, and regular flow of the time of physics, through the relatively trivial periodicity of ordinary lived and experienced time, to the dramatic time of human change. This gamut presents a continuous movement from the abstract to the concrete (cf. §54). That is, beginning with the concrete time of drama, and by omitting characteristic essential properties step by step, one can generate other kinds of time, and end, finally, with the most abstract form of time. These varieties of time are different kinds of being, all having different powers, and are subject to different kinds of order. Still, they manifest a certain sameness in structure. Can we now discern in this series of kinds of time some common essence or function which characterizes the being of all? I believe such a common element comes to be evident when one examines a relationship between time and space.

Let us begin with the time of personal relationships. Such relations are a function of oneself and of one's self-understanding. And this self-understanding is a state reached, whatever its degree, by a process of dramatic change. One's authentic grasp upon oneself is the consequence of having lived in dramatic time. Dramatic change lifts the actor out of the routine processes of daily work and renews him. Dramatic time, then, is a realization of the possibility of making distinctions between oneself and oneself (e.g., between one's immature and one's more mature self), or between oneself and other selves upon whom one may depend excessively, or between oneself and one's role. Thus one's being and its continuity is a function of dramatic time. Time is sameness of being throughout change.

Obviously, this kind of time is closely related to that form of space termed in the preceding chapter significant or archaic space. It is exemplified in symbolic arches which represent human transitions visually. Here a parallel with dramatic time is indicated. Just as archaic space offers the possibility of making significant distinctions, so dramatic time is the possibility of being in that space, the possibility, for example, of passing (in the dramatic sense) through an archway into a new land, a new life. Further, since other modes of space and time are more or less abstract derivatives from this concrete space and time, we may conclude generally that time is being the same in space (in the appropriate and correlative senses of time and space). Finally, since possible space is a basic constituent of that sensitive field wherein all our experience originates and is differentiated, so time, as we have found and described it, offers the possibility of being in space. Thus it offers the possibility of a differentiated being which endures, changes, begins, and ends.

Time, then, is the same being in space; it is presence in the realm where distinctions can be made. Correlatively, non-being has two opposite senses. First, non-being is that which is altogether non-temporal; any abstraction, whether reified or not, is an illustration. Time, as being in space, is the non-being of the extra-spatial. Secondly, non-being is that which is non-present, having not yet come to presence (the future) or having already fallen from presence (the past). One might conclude from these forms of non-being that the present is somehow privileged by contrast to the other two dimensions of time. Such is not the case, except in something like abstract mathematical time, which is often imagined as a continuous present. (I return to this topic in § 51.)

We turn now to review the manner in which time, as the same being in space, appears in the several temporal-spatial modes and accordingly exhibits several essential types. We utilized mere life time, the time of somnolence or the time of a senile person, to approach the notion of abstract time, for here, as in an after-dinner sleep, the differences among the elements of a temporal period are leveled out, so that each is something like a mid-moment, and the series of such moments constitutes plain sameness, undifferentiated being, or endurance. We end with the notion of a flow, equably moving without regard to circumstances. Here we have time as essentially mere continuous persistence or sameness in being, characteristic of the time of physics, or of physical bodies, or of physical space.

At the opposite end of the spectrum lies dramatic time, the fully differentiated time of maturing human being. This being it will be recalled, is characterized by a periodic movement passing through a process of decision and struggle, to an insight into the initiating decision. This is the movement into human being in the proper and concrete sense of the term, a movement in which the non-being of self-ignorance and hybris undergoes catharsis, thus bringing the self into a more realistic and harmonious relation to that which is called its fate. Characteristic of this time is a unique relation of future to past. This is the time of radical change in being. Here, too, then, the essence or structure of time is an interpretation specifying being/non-being in dramatic space. Of such is the movement from *chronos* to *kairos*.

The time of ordinary common experience is a kind of mean between abstract and dramatic time. It is periodic, unlike abstract time; yet these differentiations do not mark off anything so significant, even catastrophic, as the parts of dramatic time. They mark, rather, the rhythm of daily affairs, the dealings with objects and people in the conduct of normal business. This kind of time may be described as average continuation in being. In these dealings, beings figure, of course. Indeed, much of the business of the world consists in maintaining the being of oneself and others and in separating it from the non-being which could destroy it. Ordinary time, then, is likewise conceived within a realm where the primary principle of interpretation is drawn from the being/non-being which figures in the space of daily affairs, the space, for example, through which I moved when approaching the Saarinean Arch.

These three ways of being in time (abstract, common, dramatic) diversify time into three main modes; other forms of time-consciousness will no doubt be found nested within and among these three. We have also seen that the formal principle yielding these three kinds of time is drawn from being/non-being. This formal principle is exhibited in three temporal modes which are described as follows: (1) continuous persistence in being, (2) average continuation in being, (3) radical change in being. To this extent the essences or structures of time are uncovered. All are modes of the sameness of being in space.

The three kinds of space are paralleled by three kinds of time. Together they form three modes or strands constituting a basic part of our sensitive field. Thus our earlier assumption that existence in time refers us to a primary aspect of the sensitive field was a good assumption, for our selection and analyses of kinds of temporal experience has led to a grasp of the essence of time which is expressible in terms of being/non-being (and same/other), terms referring to the most general powers of our sensitive field (cf. §4, toward the end). Our analyses, that is, tend to support the assumption. Hence we say that the self has at its disposal three possible types of spatio-temporal fields (and their intermediate forms) which render legitimate the use of three different kinds of temporal interpretative principles, all specifications of being/non-being. The significance of this specification of being/non-being will be developed in chapter 6 (§ 35). In the meantime, other of the essential items claim our attention.

Notes

1. The Einsteinian view of the time interval's functional dependence upon the velocity of the reference frame is not relevant to the present discussion.
2. E. g., Homer *Illiad* xx. 127; cf. also Plato, *Republic* 616.
3. O. E. "*warpen*" refers to the twisting or spinning of thread.
4. Eugene Minkowski presents cases of a disintegrated sense of time which, by way of contrast, are instructive in this regard, cf. his *Lived Time, Phenomenological and Psychopathological Studies*, trans. by Nancy Metzel (Evanston, Ill.: Northwestern University Press, 1970); cf. pp. 332-337 for illustration.
5. The "lub" is the sound made by the closing of the valves from the auricles; the "dub" is the sound produced by the closing of the ventricle valves.
6. What is the nature of the unity of time? Does this unity originate in the hope or anticipation of a future? Or do we hope or anticipate because time already is, or is sensed as, a unity projecting beyond the present? I believe time already to be a unity, a constant presence, which we must assume. This assumption, however, finds a partial rationale in the structure of the concrete time of the most complex experience of change (cf. §§ 16, 47 and 51). Beyond this observation, however, I believe we can say only that time, persistence in the being of that which is, is a primary given. The unity of this primary given legitimizes the hierarchical structure mentioned above. I do not dwell upon this matter, though, for our topic is the experience of time.
7. An argument, however, for the quite fundamental character of cardiac time might be developed from the sense of close identity between the person and his heart; cf. H. Plügge, *Wohlbefinden u. Missbefinden* (Tubingen: Max Niemeyer Verlag, 1962), Chap. 4, "*Über Herzschmerzen.*"
8. Cf. Gerald Feinberg, *The Prometheus Project* (New York: Doubleday and Co., 1969), Chap. 4, "An End to Aging and Death."
9. Cf. E. T. Hall, *The Silent Language* (New York: Doubleday and Co., 1959), Chap. 1.

IV

Object and Self

§19. A FIRST DEFINITION OF THE EXPERIENCED OBJECT

What is a particular object, an individual event, within experience? Etymology suggests it is something "thrown toward or against" the percipient (cf. ob-ject; recall the German *Gegen-stand*). An object is always an object within a perspective (a self's perspective), and the awareness to which we attribute the perspective must somehow affect the objects and events falling within it. How are objects thus affected? An additional problem is entailed by the fact that the self is (or may become) an object within its own perspective. Our task in this chapter will be to reach an understanding of the experiencing self in relation to experienced objects, to some of the conditions for objects, and to itself.

It seems clear at the outset that whatever else an object may be, either it is or it has a meaning. This object in my hand, for instance, has the meaning "pen." Anything which falls within my experience has some such meaning, however vague or unfamiliar it may be. There is, moreover, no unique correlation between object and meaning. Someone native to a different culture might well have found this pen to have a quite different meaning, e.g., "magic wand."

Meanings do not occur within non-human nature. Objects acquire meanings only within a perspective, and a perspective belongs to a self. We may say that the self gives meanings to objects which fall within its perspective. But no idealism is intended by this expression; meanings may be wrongly seen or interpreted, as subsequent experience may show. Also, the notion of interpretation must be broadly construed to include all sorts of chance, customary, and unreflective couplings of objects and meanings. The point is that some beings (objects) are given meanings, and certain other beings (selves) make these interpretations. We shall in this chapter be concerned to describe these two kinds of beings.

To begin with, we need a few samples of objects. This pen and this paper would surely be considered objects by anyone. A circle, too, would be an object. But what about circularity? How about a cloud, a flash of light? Are space and time objects? Am I an object in any sense? Is Hamlet one? Is man an object? No doubt almost anything could be construed as an object on certain occasions and in the appropriate context. In this chapter, however, we cannot give equal consideration to all kinds of objects. We shall, for example, be able to give only little thought to mental or ideal objects. The kinds of objects which, for the most part will occupy the focus of attention here are objects which appear, or could appear, be used, or be contemplated by anyone.

Such objects of common experience are generally instruments in a wide sense of the term. The pavement is an instrument to facilitate walking; the tree shields one from the sun. The Saarinean Arch is meant to attract tourists. I do not intend to neglect objects other than those commonly experienced. Common objects, however, enjoy a certain priority over other object modalities, for surely scientific objects develop out of common experience by a process of abstraction, definition, specialization, and measurement. Similarly, but at the other end of the spectrum, mythologically significant objects develop in their own way out of common experience. By centering attention upon the object of common and ordinary experience, we shall secure a privileged position from which we should be prepared to understand other types of objects.

Common and average experience is, however, a variable notion. It is not specifically the same for a modern American as it was for the fourth century Greek. For the modern American, the common good is understood on the average in terms of utilitarianism (a hedonism for the masses), justice is fair play, truth is correspondence as measured by conventionally accepted standards (which are believed to be modeled upon scientific standards), reality is anything which can be squeezed with the hands (except in the remote paradise of the scientifically privileged), and common objects and persons are things useful or useless to modern technology and industry. I do not want to be so parochial as to confine the discussion to this narrow version of common experience. I shall try, therefore, to develop a more general view, one which would perhaps be as acceptable to the fourth century Greek as to a modern American.

I have in the second chapter provided a description of a large and imposing object accessible to anyone, the Saarinean Arch. We ask here what its specific object characteristics are. Surely a necessary characteristic is its presenting to perception a similar shape for a definite time interval, in this instance a salient and unusual shape easily discernable against its background. This persistence of sameness through a time interval, this continued recurrence of presentations manifesting unity and discreteness of being, is a major cue to a generalized object-status (cf. §9). Following this cue is the object's identifiability. Upon my recognition that it was an (inverted) catenary, a shape familiar to me from studies in analytic geometry, I recognized it probably to be the Saarinean Arch. "Archway," then, became the invariant meaning in the series of varying appearances as I approached it (§9). Of course, the Arch would have remained an object (only another object) even had I interpreted it incorrectly (§10). As it was, the Arch was specifically expected by me since my curiosity about it had been aroused, and since I had already been placed by preceding suggestions in a context appropriate to perceiving a historical marker, an architectural *tour de force*, a stainless steel tourist attraction. Moreover, since infancy I — like many of my kind — have been drawn and sometimes stirred by large and imposing objects and especially by archways, and cannot now refrain from remembering other archways and their manifold meanings together with this one. All lend their quota to that which now stands within my present perspective. The Arch's specific object status is derived from this context.

Had my previous experience provided me with no such context and its multitude of interpretative principles, I would have had to fall back upon some other, though partly similar, context. I might have wondered, "What a huge hairpin!", being forced into metaphor by the poverty of perspectives at my disposal. As it was, "Saarinean Arch" became the particular *logos* which I finally coupled with the catenary-like presentation. The priority of context (finally of world) in the identification of objects is clearly indicated.

Objects, then, offer to perception some persistent characteristics in their spatio-temporal location. Also, they are identifiable within a context. Unfortunate choices of context are easy to make (cf. §§10, 11). Consider a persuasive but limiting choice. The recollection that the Arch is made of stainless steel brings to mind physical and chemical contexts and suggests beliefs about the nature of objects derived from these sophisticated studies. These beliefs hold that objects are, basically, the consequence of the unequal distribution of matter in physical space-time. The true history of objects, then, would be the history of matter. Experienced properties not discoverable in this standard physical context are concluded not really to belong to the object (MT pp. 157, 214f.). They are "secondary," "merely subjective." As generalized from the second law of thermodynamics, the history of matter manifests a trend toward the equalization of the distribution of matter and energy, an equalization sometimes known as the "heat death." At the time of this death, as it might be said, there would exist only one object, the universe itself. (Yet since, at this final point there would exist no responsive subject to oppose to this object, it seems correct to doubt that the universe would be an object in any humanly intelligible sense.)

At the present epoch, matter and energy are unequally distributed. Objects, aglomerations of matter, are different from the observer and can be examined without being detectibly changed by the process of observation, except in the realm of small-particle study — or so a physical view maintains. And as everyone knows, other sciences aspire to the condition of physics; thus this view is not confined to physics. Still, I put this physical view aside since my problem concerns not what the object is as understood within the confines defined by the purposes and assumptions of physics and kindred studies. The physicist should be consulted about abstract objects of this kind. But the physicist is not an expert on the nature of contexts in general, or on the context of common experience, or on the relation of this context to the person who experiences, or to his world. Our interest, however, is directed toward objects as persons *commonly experience* them and to essential elements of this experience. Now, such notions as matter, energy, and the space-time of physics are not experienced: they are, like the second law of thermodynamics, elements which enter into a theory that provides a physical explanation of what the physicist experiences through the medium of his instruments and specialist's concepts. We legitimately turn away from a specialty like physics, therefore, when we inquire concerning the character and basis of any object as commonly experienced.

Objects of ordinary experience offer difficulties enough. We have decided to think of any experienced object as an interpreted presentation, where interpretation is not confined within some currently fashionable metaphysical context. We shall have to admit that presentation as such appears to be inaccessible. Consider the Arch merely as "something there"; already it is interpreted as a thing, vague enough no doubt, but still a something. Also, it is localized "there." Surely this classification and positioning go beyond the Arch "in itself" (as abstracted from the common perspective upon it), and are products of my interpretation, even if as yet very general products. Later we shall point out still other senses in which the pure presentation is inaccessible, even though it seems reasonable and convenient to think of the object as an interpreted presentation. Perhaps we can get no closer to a pure presentation than the minimal object, a bare something-there interpretable within, and by the help of, a more specific context. We can, though, at least consider interpretation at length (and shall do so in the next several chapters). For the present, we shall approach the object indirectly by considering what it is not, although this "is not" is ambiguous.

The questions posed at the beginning of this section took it for granted that objects are different from the person who experiences them. This distinction is not quite so easy to draw as might initially appear. I shall now try to elaborate it sufficiently for our use, for since the object is essentially set in contrast to the self, both self and object will have to be understood if either is to be made perspicuous. Also, both self (in one sense of self) and object are located in space and time. Accordingly, the next section will be devoted to describing and clarifying some of the relations among self, space, time and object in several of their senses.

In its most general meaning, an object is a discrete and enduring being experienced as a repeated unity of presentations, a something there; also, it is perceived as essentially other than the person who experiences it. The object is "outside" the person; it presents a contrast in being to the self who experiences it. An object is a being presented to, and interpretable by, the self as having a steady or recurrent structure. In this sense, all the samples mentioned at the beginning of this section, with the possible exception of "I myself," can be taken as objects. They are instances of that upon which one's attention and intention can be directed.

This otherness of the object from the self entails properties both on the part of the object and the self. One element of the otherness of objects, touched upon in the recapitulation of our description of the Arch, is perceived (or perceptual) presence in one's space and time; other elements include persisting structural properties, identifiable presence in a context or contexts and in a world, and finally, dependence upon certain factors which I shall term "mythical." All of these properties characterize objects as they are encountered in daily activity, used in technology, or given special status in the directing of human life. These important points about the general nature of experienced objects can be summarized in a statement which may be taken as a first definition: an object is a discrete being, enduringly other than the consciousness of it; it is a recurrent presentation interpreted in definite ways, a "particular" having specific feeling tones; it is in certain respects, but not in all, dependent upon the perceiver's interpretation and upon his culture. I proceed now to explicate and substantiate this definition.

§20. SELF AND OTHER-THAN-SELF

Let this section be a first effort toward untangling the relations among self, objects, and the space and time in which both self and objects are discovered, for the self is strangely involved with things in space and time. Indeed, it itself seems to be an object among objects, and no more profound paradox exists than the embodied self, the self which is both at one with its body and yet strangely distinct from, even alienated from, that same body. The self is and is not its body.

To begin, consider the several self-functions and objects as both are involved in my awareness while I drive toward the Saarinean Arch in St. Louis. The object, here the Arch, must be distinguished from my awareness of it. Drawing this distinction is not facilitated by the fact that the self, in one of its guises, is rather like an object; this similarity is underscored by the usual way of separating the two. The otherness of self and object is often expressed as a difference in their respective spatial locations. Just this way of separating the two brings forward the difficult question of the relation of self-awareness to space. Surely they are intimately related, for the body is in space just as the Arch is, only the Arch does not locate itself, and the self does. The Arch does not have the problem of distinguishing between itself and me, or between itself and its body. I, however, perceive myself and the Arch and perceive the distance which separates the Arch from my body. Were this distance imperceptible, I would have to believe the Arch to be a part of me, or at least a part of my body. For most purposes, that is, I judge the distance between me and the Arch to be the distance between my body and the Arch.

Space, we have said, is the possibility of making distinctions. But there are several kinds of distinctions. I am not distinguished from my body as the Archway is from the car I am driving. Indeed, it is more or less conventional to observe that "I" occupy the space my body occupies, for when my body neared the Saarinean Arch it seemed evident that I approached it. Still, my occupancy of that space was not exclusively physical occupancy. I am not exclusively where my hand is nor even where all the parts of my body are (MT pp. 33ff). It makes perfectly good common sense — though not good geographical sense — to say that I am closer to my friend a thousand miles away than I am to the telephone receiver at my ear, or for that matter, to my hand holding the receiver. The receiver extends my hand and my ear; still I, rather than my hand or my ear, am close to the friend.

There is, nevertheless, a danger in allowing the possible separation of self from body to develop without limit (as Descartes did), for it is only through my body "here" that I locate myself and achieve contact with the other "there." The telephone-at-my-ear is the necessary medium of contact with this other. I can intend objects, other persons, the world, only through the medium of my body (and its instruments) "here." I am related to space through my body in an essential, though systematically ambiguous manner: I may be intentionally close to my friend even when geographically distant. The instrument extending this personal closeness over the intervening miles is no less ambiguous in its status than the meaningful puffs of air I exude when I speak, or than my body itself, that organized collection of atoms and cells impregnated by personal awareness and intentional life. Thus the paradox of the embodied self begets derivative paradoxes: embodied meanings, objects which are not yet "have," sense. Again the Platonic problem of participation: how to understand that two beings or two different kinds of beings are nevertheless one.

I can intend two objects as different when they are located in non-identical spaces, even if one of these objects be my hand and the other my ear. Geometry or biology show that the two are unified in a larger spatial or organic whole. How, though, can I understand my unity with the place which I occupy? This question seems, from the point of view of modern reflective common sense, to evoke the need for a resolution to a Cartesian-like dichotomy. Such a resolution is indicated below (see p. 75). Meanwhile, consider the fact that I am able to intend my self, the one who intends, as located in a definite place, a place usually, though not always, the location of my body. It is helpful to note that I can distinguish my self (who intends) from my self (who is intended), not in a geographical-spatial sense but in an analogous sense, a sense where space is taken in its basic or generic meaning as that which renders distinctions possible (cf. §12). The self as intending, giving meaning, may be thought to be related to the self as given an object-meaning when both are located within an embracing context of originating and originated. And this non-geometrical not-yet-objective space has in common with objective space at least the generic property of enabling us to speak without confusion of discreteness and otherness, so that the noetic, meaning-giving self is differentiated from the self given a noematic (object) meaning. Still, their unity is unique and strange. Let us examine this relation as it is experienced.

How can this meaning-giving self-as-intending be rendered accessible? Since whenever a person is conscious of something, he is aware that he is conscious of it, a temptation may be felt to identify the intending self with this self-awareness. This self-awareness, moreover, always appears as part of the ground of any consciousness-of whatsoever; still, it is never directly intended, but, as it were, is only co-intended. Unfortunately, as soon as attention is shifted directly upon this co-intended background self-awareness, it becomes an intended object, something objectively definite, like a role, for example, and loses its character of spontaneous self-awareness. Self-awareness, thus, does not possess the property of persisting separateness or independence which would permit its being identified as a Cartesian or a Kantian substance. We must approach the self without such theoretical preconceptions.

A more primitive experience of self will have to be sought elsewhere. Many years ago I attempted to show that an important element in any work of art or in any experience of aesthetic value was the discovery of the self in the work (cf. *Art and Analysis*, Nilhoff, 1957, especially pp. 115ff, 192f, and chapter 13). My suggestion is that this observation holds generally. In any productive work, in any activity, for example in any perceiving, the self is discoverable, like the style of a painter in his canvas. The self is projected into whatever it makes or does. Even the workman at the conveyor belt tightens a bolt in his own paticular way, though the inspector looks only to the tightness of the bolt. In our choices, acts, friends acquired, life led, it is palpably we who are engaged, we who leave our thumb prints, our personality signatures, behind us indellibly in each living encounter. This mark of the intending self in all its activity opens a way to apprehend the self. An aspect significant for us in this translation of the self into its work is its priority to any particular experience.

Certainly the self is prior to its works and often outlives them. I have in mind, however, another kind of priority. Before any particular act has been performed, logically before any engagement or reflection, there must be the self ready to be projected into its characteristic products, ready to perceive in its own unique way (MT pp. 132ff., 142). This readiness is the self's "world." This is world in the sense of the totality of operative (noetic) powers, or it is world in the sense of the sensitive field which is prior to the environment and its furniture. (And since selves reflectively grasped as objects are articles of furniture in the environment, selves so grasped are posterior to this more primitive apprehension of self-world.) This self ready to be projected into its works is that which renders possible particular experiences of objects or of the perceptible world. We come to be aware of it in many ways, perhaps especially in the sense of "power-to," for instance in the first pervasive sense of power to live in time. Is self reflected in its time?

To utilize this suggestion, we must draw a distinction between the experience of self and experienced time. We have decided already (chap. 3) that time, or being in space, offers the real possibility of making distinctions. An object, given our analysis, is a distinguishable, unitary, persisting being. Thus if one is in the appropriate kind of space, one can proceed to utilize the power of making distinctions to separate objects from each other and from the self, and to separate the self (ambiguously) from the self. Can self and time be so separated?

The close relation of time, space, and self is entailed on the one hand by the necessity of enduring in time in order to make use of space, and on the other by the need to use space and spatial metaphors in order to think about time, perhaps even in order to become aware of time. This awareness of time, "my" time, seems to be intimately related to, even identical with, the self. This identity, I suggest, is not an embarrassment; it is just the point. The time to which I refer is lived time, time (common or dramatic) in which there is human experiencing. If there is a distinction between the self and lived time, this is the distinction between the self and its life, a distinction "merely in thought" if ever there was one. Recall the heart disease patient with his hand on his pulse; the precariousness of his time is the precariousness of his self. Time conceived apart from this perspective is reached only by a feat of imaginative abstraction which replaces the lived being by an objective, empty and regular flow. The time of experience *is* life time, the life span of possible self-awareness, and in its basic form is a *sine que non* in the structure of my sensitive field whereby objects appear and are experienced. Man *is* a being in time, a temporal being.

Any intending self, always its own life time, can intend itself as an object sharing a time in common with other objects. Still, the self which intends objects is that which experiences objects as always other than itself, at least as differently located and as enduring through a time not identical with its own lived time. Even if the self intends, or refers to itself as an object, it must do so with the reservation that the self which performs this intending or referring function is not an object. And the self as intended, the objective self, can be sensed upon reflection as other than the intending self. Rather, the intending self is unique in being that to which objects appear and by whom they are located and given sense. A primary sense thus given is that of a unified and enduring being which is my self as observed, tested, judged. This is the objective sense of self.

I experience myself as something like an object when I experience myself in the role of, say, a tourist or a teacher of philosophy, for such roles have permanent objective characteristics which are largely independent of me. But playing such roles does not exhaust my being, and I do not — or should not — *identify* myself with them (but cf. MT § 37). We hold, then, that the self experiencing and the self experienced (e.g., as playing a role) are distinguishable aspects of one person. The experiencing self *is* its own life time: it is partial and temporal awareness of its being, whereas the self as experienced is, as we say, *in* time. Despite these different relations to time, we observe that the experiencing self, and the self as experienced object share the same time.

By sharing the same time (whether perceptually present, present in memory, or existing by inference or in imagination), I mean that the object sharing time with me is present during the same span of time in which I am existing or living my own lifetime while perceiving, imagining, conceiving. Thus I can be contemporaneous with perceived, imagined, or remembered objects. The characteristic unity of this contemporaneousness is marked by participation in some essential structural element by both me and the object. This participation-effecting structure, I suggest, is intentionality (cf. § 11). The act of intending an object and being that object intended form a unitary structure embraced in the one time which is the life of the intending self and which also "contains" the object intended. That this structure is a unity is shown by the thorough-going experienced correlation of intending and intended; every consciousness is "consciousness-of"; every consciousness-of is intrinsically directed toward an object of consciousness.[1] In addition, the time which the intending self lives is the same time in which the object intended exists. Thus the unity of the time in which I live with the time containing objects of my experience is expressed in the unity of intention. Later (in §51), I shall show in detail that the unity of intentionality is the same as the unity of lived time. The self thus bears a double relation to time and to temporal objects. On the one hand, the intending self lives time; on the other hand, the self is intended as an object contained in that time. The one self is structured by these two relations.

The effective and communicative unity of self and object is closer than this temporal relation suggests, even though the division between them has appeared to be unbridgeable in the Cartesian tradition. In its original Cartesian formulation and in many others, the problem constituted by this division is rendered insoluble by definition. Descartes needed to define matter as excluding the mental, the intentional. We, however, are confronted with the experienced fact of mind-body communication, accept it, and need to describe and to discover its essence. Theories which fail to accept and to describe it are *ab ovo* inadequate. The present view provides such a description while recognizing the paradoxical unity of the embodied self.

The self, functioning as center and organizer of its sensitive field, can utilize its possibilities to form contexts of various kinds, extents, and functions. The context of writing, for instance, is animated by a quite well-understood context intention and includes among its contents the experiences of writing materials, books, desks, printing presses, and other dismembered items of that sort which have been acquired through past experience. These items are re-memorable or are recoverable in memory, and offer numerous principles useful for interpreting present presentations and objects. Such a context is prior (in experience) to any particular item within it.

Suppose I offer you this object, a pen, for your inspection and identification. Its shape, weight, color, texture — all abstractable traits — are objective properties of which the pen-presentations are and continue to be patient. Being familiar with the writing context, you immediately draw from it a standard image or concept of a pen, developed in your past, and resembling the present pen-presentation. A Cartesian might believe that he observes its isomorphism with the pen-presentation and the physical pen, so can correctly interpret the presentation as a pen-object. Here, though, we hold that interpreting the object-presentation by use of the intention (principle) "pen" *is* the experience of the pen. Here object and image (principle) coalesce; their union is the experience. We come to experience of the pen-object through that particular image just because there is a prior relation between the interpreting image and the pen-object. This prior relation is the writing context. This context guides and particularizes one's interpretative intention or image of the pen-presentation. It is the self's readiness to perceive the pen, or to discover an aspect of itself reflected in or completing the pen-as-writing-instrument.

This context, evolved in past experience and evolving now, goes back to one's sensitive field structured in its earliest phase by the primitive apprehensions, being/non-being, one/many, same/other, etc.. No longer, though, need one ordinarily go back to so primitive a stage. The pen, or any object, is taken as the thing identified in the present context. Of course, it might have been interpreted in a chemical or other context. The point is that the context bridges the "gap" between the object and the interpreting self, between noema and reality phenomenon, between what the modern tradition calls the mind and the body. The final context, bridging all such gaps which are bridgeable, is the world itself. The Cartesian gap between mind and body is itself understandable and accessible to one only because it is located like an object within the world and is united to the present thinker by a (prior) philosophic context within which it makes a certain historical sense.

Within that historical context Descartes conceived his task not so much to understand experience as to construct or discover a metaphysics which would be favorable to the nascent science of physics. To that end, Descartes had to stipulate that physical matter be purged of all human and soul-like qualities, expecially of value properties. The outcome of a meditation which banished all non-measurable qualities and characteristics to the realm of the psychic, was a universe admirably fitted for the advancement of the new physics. However, when mind and body are conceived as metaphysically ultimate, no context remains which might unite the two, and mind becomes a stranger in the physical realm having no intelligible point of contact with any object in space (including its own body!). But from the vantage point of a philosophy which seeks first to return to experience itself purged of explanatory additions and subtractions which the special interests and purposes of physics might require, Descartes' two concepts of mind (self) and matter (object) appear as abstractions. Both are abstracted from the concrete unity of self-experiencing-an-object-intended-within-a-context (cf. §39).

Further consequences of Descartes' mistaking an abstraction for the concrete are exhibited in contemporary pan-psychism and materialism or physicalism. Some philosophers still seriously ask: is the mind identical with the brain or distinguishable from it? The question is a pseudo question. It can only be asked after the questioner's prior and unwitting reification of the abstraction, brain-object. The reification, however, is recognizable as such only after a return to the concrete experience of self-intending-an-object and a comparison of this concrete experience with the abstraction. Why does this fallacy of misplaced concreteness continue to attract speculators? Perhaps a motive for persisting in this confusion lies in the desire of many philosophers to be mistaken for scientists and thus to share in the prestige of science. For if the mind (self) is the brain and the brain is an object accessible to scientific study, then the philosopher who holds this physicalist view can participate in the glory of founding or maintaining a truly scientific psychology.

Still other difficulties lie in the way of understanding the interrelations among self, time, space, and objects. They may be elicited by asking whether space and time are objects. In one sense, space is indeed an object. It is a being different from myself and may be examined very much as this pen may be examined. The problem, for example, whether physical space has Euclidean characteristics may be expressed in a manner which can be decided by experiment. Similarly, the question concerning the physical meaning of temporal simultaneity can be expressed within an appropriate context and experimentally considered.

In another and more general sense, as Kant argued, space and time are not so much objects as conditions under which something can be an object to me. That something can be distinct from me and be at a distance from me, the perceiver, and enduringly so, are conditions which must obtain if I am to encounter or perceive anything, including space or time in the physical sense just mentioned. Space allows me to make these and other distinctions. Space in this second sense is that which is "between" me, the perceiver, and that which I experience. The enduring, unified otherness of an object is the persistence of this "betweenness" which separates and also links. This usage of space is not geometrical; rather, it is that context of concrete places and possible places around me which is reflectively interpreted by application of geometrical and physical concepts. It is the condition of objects being distinct from each other and hence of their being related. Space is, in essence, I recall again, the possibility of making distinctions (§12).

Observe that the artist, as he draws, feels his pencil to be an extension of his hand.[2] He feels the pencil-hand moving over the surface of his model as he produces the drawing on his sketch pad. The hand, the pencil, the sketch pad, the model, are all different and occupy different spaces. A possible spatial "betweenness" here becomes a condition; it is intended to separate hand from pencil, otherwise the artist would not have had to pick up a pencil. And yet the pencil extends the artist's hand in one sense to the model and in another sense to the paper. In this structure, space is both the condition rendering possible the distinctness of the several items and that which renders possible their unity in a functionally complex organization. The space of the pencil is both that which separates the artist's hand from the sketch pad and that which enables hand and pad to be joined.

In a somewhat similar fashion, the unreflective self identifies itself with the space occupied by its body (or with a part of it), and is spatially separated from objects at a distance from its body; to these same objects it is also joined by the same space since it can come into immediate proximity with other objects through that same separative-unitive space.

Analogously, let us recall, the self is one with its life time yet distinct from the time in which it exists as an object. It *is* its life time but also presents itself as an object *in* time. Such is the subtle structure separating the self from the self and rendering possible one's acceptance of an aspect of oneself as an object. An illustration is offered by the "I" who is playing through some object-like role defined within a social structure. This latter self is different from, at a perceptible "distance" from, the self who is so aware and through whose sensitive field both itself and other things appear. Space in this separative and unitive sense we are describing is evidently an essential element of this sensitive field.

In the more familiar physical-geometrical sense, an object is spatially or geographically removed from me, the perceiver. It is set over against me and occupies its own space; likewise, it is in its own time. That is, it inherits its own past and is projected into its own future. This independence and stability of an object were once expressed in the conviction that an object has an essence from which it does not depart. This essence is like a law limiting possible changes. The requirement that essential structural properties persist may be expressed by saying that different appearances of the object are always transformable into the object itself. Chapter 2 took it as obvious that an object like the Saarinean Arch remained the same even though its appearance changed as the angle and distance from which it was viewed shifted. By a return to a given point and under given conditions, essentially the same appearance to me could always be recovered or its differences could be accounted for by reference to other normal changes (e.g., change of lighting) which takes place in a regular manner. Thus the object is experienced as enduringly other than the self who perceives objects.

The same kind of regularity does not determine the changes of self-experience, for the self who intends and experiences can engage in radical change (cf. above §16 and MT, §21ff.). When it does undergo radical change, it (generally) retains some elements of its previous identity, yet it is no longer so fully transformable into itself as an object commonly is. The self in this dramatic sense exists in time in a manner quite different from the way an object is perceived as occupying time. We express this difference by saying the self can transcend itself; indeed, its self-consciousness is the power of self-transformation. In other words, the self can exist in dramatic time (cf. §16); an object never does unless it be given the meanings which so place it by a self who is there by nature.

The contrast between the kind of change objects undergo and the more radical change to which self-experience may be subject is often expressed by noting that human self-change consists in acts which are self-determined or free, whereas the changes undergone by objects are determined by something other than themselves. Correspondingly, the persistence of the self is the result of habit and also of commitment and loyalty, whereas the typical persistence of an object is the consequence of endurance, or of mere repetition or routine. This distinction between two forms of change and persistence may not be the clearest. For instance, it may appear that certain objects are intrinsically determined. The protagonist of a well-written drama, for example, may seem to exhibit changes that are autonomous or intrinsically determined. Thus, he or she appears to be like a self, but still is not an independent self in a literal sense, because the entire play depends upon a skilled artist for its production and upon others for its presentation and interpretation.

On the other hand, it might be pointed out, persons in daily life are often engaged in occupations which prevent their exercising self-determination. And there is no question but that persons playing roles are not always intrinsically determined. Consider the industrial chemist; he may operate as an intrinsically determined self when he decides to become a chemist. Having made this decision, however, he submits himself to determination by the structure of the role he has assumed, unless he discovers that the role is inappropriate and must be radically changed or terminated.. More obviously requiring a quasi-object-like behavior of a self is the function of an automobile driver; the more a driver acts like a machine with an efficient feed-back, the better driver he is. No pause, however, will be made at this point in order to decide which are the acts or events most aptly exhibiting self-experience and its radical changes. I want only to notice that the persistence and change of objects are different in kind from the persistence and change of persons (however rare dramatic self-change may be).

We have now amassed a number of characteristics belonging to objects but denied to the self, so that experience of objects and experience of self appear to be radically different. Objects (ideal and mental objects to one side) occupy space and time. If the self is in time or space, it is so in a quite different sense. An object has various physical properties such as weight; the experienced self has no such properties. Objects change in determined and routine ways; self-change follows the quite different dramatic pattern. Objects appear to the self largely through interpreted (outer) sense presentations; the self may be said to appear to the self but mainly as reflected by perception of objects or else through interpretation of other kinds of (inner) presentations. Objects are intended; the self is experienced as intending objects (and itself). Objects are given meanings; the self gives meanings to objects and to itself. Thus the self is not an object as this book is, nor even as a dog is, who does not have language and is therefore, a stranger to the dramatic dialectic.

But even if the experiencing self cannot be sensed and described as if it were an object, it is felt; its effects can be observed. We note, for instance, that as the conscious center of human life, it thinks of and refers to itself in the first person singular. It owns a sensitive field by reason of which it itself and other beings can appear or be perceived, distinguished, and interpreted. It is aware of itself as in passage, a concrete passage which it identifies as its own life time, yet a time which contains objects. It is concerned about these other beings and also about itself, its changes, its fate, and its well-being. And finally, it is aware of itself as living under myths and with world-symbols which impart a final ordering to its life and unite it in some sense to its origin and to its end. Man is a being in time, who perceives in accord with his culture, and who discovers his own non-being.

No doubt the self is distinguished from objects in yet other ways. To suggest these quite profound differences, we note that self and objects are altogether different sorts of beings. They differ ontologically. Yet they are united at least by the meaning-giving and context forming powers of the self. The self in its most proper sense gives meanings; in its derivative and object-like sense the self is given meaning, or its meaning is discovered.

In order to conclude this section, there follows a brief review of our observations on the self and objects. First, the self is appropriately taken as an object by the sciences, unquestionably to be studied and measured just as any other kind of object would be. Second, for common experience and for other persons, a self is both an object and not an object. A self is experienced as an object in that it plays a role in society and serves in many ways as an instrument (a human instrument or human resource, to be sure) for other persons to employ. At the same time the self is experienced and (ideally) recognized to be non-objective, a person, an "I," and in the Western world has been held, in consequence, never to be merely a means to an end but as an "end in himself." In any event, the self can engage in the dialectic of self-interpretation and self-care (MT §8). Finally and ontologically, the intending self can be recognized as that paradoxical being, a non-object, a no-thing.[3] Yet he lives in the world, has effects and undergoes changes there. We also assign him an ontological function: he is that unique non-being, a sensitive field, to which other beings (e.g., objects) appear and by whom objects are perceived. He is that which takes up the perspective within which beings become objects in space and time. He is that which gives meanings. Objects, on the other hand, are intended; they are perceived in space and time and undergo changes in the fairly well-known and regular ways consistent with one's world and culture.

§21. ON THE ESSENCES OF OBJECT AND SELF

Can there be any common element of structure in objects as different as cubic and spherical objects, present objects and objects of the paleolithic age, physical masses, cellular objects, useful objects, human beings? With reservations relative to the last mentioned (reservations which should now be understandable), I think we can certainly answer in the affirmative. For all objects are perceived in space and time and, hence, have spatio-temporal characteristics. All are beings, yet not just beings as such. Each is not another being, or each has non-being with respect to any other; each, that is, is a persisting, discrete, unified being. And all stand in contrast to the self who gives these and other object-meanings. Such is the minimal characterization of object.

We have already observed, additionally, that in common experience, objects for the most part are instruments. As such, they fall in a particular grouping. This pen is an instrument for writing; more generally, it is a tool. Tools are efficient or inefficient; they are good or non-good for their tasks. Essential to retaining tool-status is some positive degree of excellence or virtue for the task assigned.

Notice further that a collection of objects is not always a type of, say, instrument. Objects can also be observed to fall into natural groupings of definite particulars having common properties, a common unity. One such group of phenomena (a species) is different from another in ways which can be specified. Thus, a live oak and the moss growing on its boughs belong to different groups. Two live oaks, though, are essentially the same, though individually different, for one is here and the other is there. Of course, observing and accepting different sameness and differences as standard would issue in a different classification. For instance, in a different context a certain sameness and difference in size might be accepted as an adequate principle for the classification of trees. The point is that principles for the initial interpretation of objects in space-time are obtained, on the one hand, from the formal principle same/other, associated in section 12 with the essential function of space, and on the other hand, from the formal principle being/non-being associated in section 18 with the essential function of time. Let us add here that an object is a certain type of unity shared among the many belonging to its group. This unity is to be understood in several senses and is to be contrasted with its correlative many. For instance, the unity of this pen is a whole of its many material parts. This whole is unlike the unity or wholeness of an organic body whose functioning parts (organs) are the conditions of its existence. Thus an object is a discrete being in time, the same kind of unit as others in its group, and other than the others. These matters will be considered further in chapter 6 (MT pp. 156f.).

Individual objects and groups of objects are encountered in different modalities. Modes are certain, very general kinds of being, such as physical objects, instrumental objects, organisms, human being, mythical being. These modes are further divided into genera, subordinate genera, and species as indicated by the observed samenesses and othernesses to which common experience has taught us to be sensitive. We also have in mind the distinction among the various modes of the interpretation of objects: e.g., abstract, common, existential, and mythological (cf. §27 and §52). A species of tree, e.g., an oak, is interpretable in all four modes. The scientist makes an abstract study of a tree when he analyzes its cellular structure. For common experience, an oak may be a handy shelter during a spring shower. For self-understanding, the tree may become the source of analogies concerning personal growth and transformation. For a more primitively thinking person, an oak may be an object of reverence (Zeus once spoke through the Oak of Dodona).

Much of the energies of our civilization have gone into the observation and description of the kinds or groups of beings, mainly those in the first two of the above four modes of interpretation. Such observation can become complex. It is not enough merely to note that the same identical tree reappears whenever I direct my glance in a certain direction, and that a tree is the same as (or similar to) many other individual trees and is other than others; in addition, this sameness and otherness need to be described in detail. When the relevant sameness (species) is adequately described, and when that type of tree is related to others, then we may say we have at least the beginning of a scientific apprehension of that kind of being. We apprehend its structure in the chosen mode, a structure repeated approximately and endlessly in other trees of that kind experienced in the same mode.

This sort of description of a being or of a mode of being is a function of context and context intention. Obviously, a botanist's description of a tree, a farmer's, and a poet's will differ, although each may be accurate and true in its own mode. This observation bears on the fact that a tree is a tree, and even is a tree of this or that kind, only in a context. Other factors determining perspective are disposition, projection, and finally world. These matters will be elaborated in the next chapter. Such a perspective is constituted by and is dependent on a self, a being of the human kind, who elaborates interpretations in more than one mode. But what he can see in any mode is that as one and the same being is to many other similar beings, so one identifiable object is to many other analogous ones.

We are now prepared to note briefly the essence of an object. An object, a particular in time, is a unitary being located in lived space, one to be specified by contrast with the being it is not; it is the same as (or similar to) certain other beings, a sameness which is observable and describable, and different in characteristic ways from others. And it is interpretable in the several modes with which we are acquainted. An alternative formulation: An object Z is, at minimum, the class of all presentations interpretable as Z, where Z is other than self, localized, enduring, a unitary particular, perceived or perceptible in several modes. In short, an object is a separate, enduring, unitary being.

We turn now to consider the essence of self, if it has an essence. The peculiar function of the human kind of being (one having or being a sensitive field) is to open up the perspective where object-beings (and events), their samenesses, differences, and their modalities, can appear and be experienced appropriately. To the question, then, whether human beings are objects sharing in common traits with other (real) objects, the answer can only be a qualified yes, as the preceding section indicated. Surely human beings are in one sense in experienced space and time; they are present here or there; they have traits which can be perceived and studied, even scientifically studied, in appropriate contexts, and the like. But in addition, the self (in the most proper sense) has the peculiar non-objective function of mediating (or being) the sensitive field whereby itself, others, and objects appear. As an illustration of a self experiencing an object I refer again to the account in § 9 of my approaching the Saarinean Arch in St. Louis. Obviously, this account also included a reflective awareness of the self who was experiencing. This complex activity was rendered possible by my sensitive field. Now, we have observed that this sensitive field or perspective is not an object. Rather, it is possibility, a presupposition of the appearing of objects in whatever region or mode; it is not a logical or an empirical but an ontological presupposition. We may be aware of this sensitive field, but not as we are aware of a tree or other object. This awareness is a self-consciousness and includes an awareness of one's "power-to . . ." or "impotence-to. . . ." This sense of power or readiness for something is a very important (and neglected) bit of evidence pointing to one's own being and non-being, notwithstanding the fact that persons commonly misinterpret it in the direction of hybris. It is a feeling of indefinite ability to be or to become oneself by directing one's power in a certain way and actually engaging oneself in this way. Clearly, true/false and good/evil are related to this directing power (MT pp. 132-4).

This sense of one's possibility of experiencing is initially a vague anticipation of experience and perception yet to be had; only in the course of experience does it come to be felt as a definite pre-apprehension of the possible. The lines of experience come naturally to be sketched out in advance in the definite and seemingly given manner one has learned from one's culture and past experience. I cannot doubt, for instance, that this paper on which I am writing will retain its own unitary being separate from other objects for a noticeable time. Such expectation, a feeling for what is within one's power, a pre-recognition of the possible and impossible, give one's sensitive field a definite orientation and a clearly defined character prior to particular experiences. (It should be added that these pre-formed expectations, the particular sense of the possible in experience in which each of us in a given culture is trained from infancy, include shared possessions and form the basis for sociality and communication among people. Thus much of that which is termed "self" is a social construct and is relative to a culture.)

This feeling or sense of power to experience is awareness of one's basic opening upon the world. The work of this opening is the bringing of beings to self-manifestness; it has appropriately been called discovery, the *aletheia*, or truth process.[4] Since this uncovering of the existence of an object of experience (a *that*) is the initial contact with the object and the condition of any other, I speak of it as initial truth or primary interpretation.

There is also a secondary interpretative process, a process of acting toward definitely envisaged objects, once uncovered, or of making confirmable or deniable statements about them. We shall be concerned with this secondary truth in greater detail in the next chapter. These two powers of the self in relation to truth, uncovering and secondary interpretation (stating truely or falsely *what* the object is), correspond to the directing, or intellectual, powers traditionally ascribed to man. They fall clearly among his basic endowments.

Having a sense of the concretely possible in experience, a man can intelligently direct his activity toward ends, toward values, and judge the outcome to be good or evil. Thus the awareness of "power-to . . ." extends to work and to relations among persons. The trained worker, the artisan or artist, is aware of his power to operate on materials and to embody his imagination and his conceptions in external and socially available objects. Work is power expended for an end or for an audience; it is subservient always to a greater value and finally to man. The sense of "power-to . . ." likewise includes work relations with others. For example, one works with others in the performance of some role necessary in the production of a complex product. Here the worker is associated with other artisans in a structure determined by the final product and by the techniques for producing it. His work, his activity, thus embodies various senses of good or evil, understood as use-value.

Also, some among the others may be accepted in friendship, a relation where the other is valued for himself as a human being and not merely as a use-value or as a convenient role player. Here one is concerned with the welfare and happiness of the other, with something approaching his whole being, not merely with his efficiency as a worker. Finally, perhaps in rare instances, the other may be apprehended as a person in full concreteness, the object of love, love which issues in a strange sort of cherished unity in difference which the poets and religions celebrate. In this unique relationship, two autonomous individuals can achieve something like a shared identity through a remarkable mutual empathy and acceptance. In this respect, the self is again involved with good and evil, but in a different sense, for in this relationship each takes the other as an intrinsic good, as an end-in-himself. And each discovers in the other his own being in himself, progressively and authentically revealed.

Man as feeling, thinking, and acting (as being intellectual and conative, as directing power, and as receptive), clearly has effects, in the world and upon others, which are related to true/false, to good/evil, and are describable in other ways as well. In his relation to good/evil, a man has powers of expressing his feeling for himself (his inchoate sense of being) in decisions which interpret himself to himself, and of struggling against opposition in order to verify and retain his decisions. In relation to truth/falsity, a man has powers of discovery or insight which enable him to recognize the inappropriateness of his decisions and the inadequacy of his grasp upon his own identity. Thus a person's powers of feeling, acting, and understanding are just those required for his living in authentic time (cf. §16), or for engaging in the dramatic movement of self-discovery.

The unique quality of these transforming powers of the human being is perhaps best conveyed by observing that they are linguistic. And traditionally, man is recognized to be the living being possessing language. His linguistic consciousness, with its characteristic bonds to past and future time, mirrors both itself and other things and is aptly said to be that which brings the world to appearance. It is the spatio-temporalizing unifying being which is the locus of discovery or of the truth process. Man, that is, is the being which interprets; he is a unique opening upon the world and can engage in the dramatic dialectic.

Let us now ask whether these powers of interpretation provide ground sufficient for assigning the self an essence. The answer must be in the negative. For one thing, the sense of "power-to . . ." and "impotence-to . . ." is initially amorphous and becomes definite only after experience, following upon the subjective dialectic, has endowed it with a character and a style. And the character of matured selves, moreover, varies enormously from epoch to epoch and from culture to culture. In addition, the self's possibility of radical change stands always ready to refute any given definition of self.

Decisive, though, is the fact that the self, not being an object, possesses no fixed object-like essence. Thus although each self is or possesses a sensitive field, which is the possibility of experiencing, it is altogether non-objective and lacks an object-like essence. But if self has no object-like essence, it does have certain boundary characteristics (MT §26) and can engage in the non-objective dialectic in pursuit of knowledge of these boundaries and of self-understanding and action within them. Thus the self is possessed of a non-objective character and function necessary to the experience of objects and of itself, but is itself never an object of experience and is not, therefore, definable in the usual sense. We may at least say here that a man's being must be sufficient to unite his bodily presence with the dimensions of time necessary to his functions of feeling, intellecting, and acting. But *what* this unifying being is varies over so wide a range as to forbid easy definition; it is as various as the events and contents of time itself. (Discussion of this topic will be continued in § 51.)

To deny a fixed essence to the self is to affirm its great malleability and adaptability. Men seem to get along and even to become quite human under almost any conditions, which they could hardly do were their essence as eternally fixed as the classic and rationalistic traditions often appear to affirm. Also, to deny the self an essence is to affirm its strangeness. One to whom things and essences appear has itself no predetermined being, no fixed essence. It is a no-thing among things, a non-being among beings; it is the stage of the world whereon objects appear and acts are played out, yet is more mysterious than any play it has ever composed or witnessed.

In earlier times man was defined as the living being having language (*logos*). But this "definition" does no more than call attention to the power of giving meaning, of reflecting upon appearances, of recognizing recurrent elements in experience, of naming, grouping, and discoursing upon them. It does not say *what* this power is; nor does it indicate anything like limits upon this remarkable and unique power. In more recent times, apprehension of this power seems to have become dimmed. For now experience of the object and of the self as object have been developed under the modern mythical investiture of the objective and technological world and the non-objective dialectic has been neglected. The consequence of this neglect is that Western man's opening upon the world (the structure of his sensitive field) is undergoing more or less unobserved and uncriticized change, the result of which is that he now tends to appear to himself primarily as a means to maintaining or improving his technological machine[5] or else as a commodity for exchange in the economic system associated with technology.[6]

This self as means or as commodity tends to abstractness as compared with the object of some other investitures (e.g., classical Greek or medieval). In a similar way, we have already observed in chapters 2 and 3 the comparative abstractness of the space and time of modern common experience, so deeply affected by the space and time defined for the sciences and technology. Perhaps this development was necessary for purposes of elaborating a scientific and technological culture. The limitation of human being to its scientifically accessible traits is, however, equivalent to assigning it an essence and thus tends to slight or even directly to deny the crucial non-objective dimension of the human being.

Can humanity survive this denial? Is the modern technological culture destructive of man and of itself? Questions of this kind have not infrequently been raised with respect to twentieth century Western cultures. The possibility of their pertinence imparts an urgency to investigations into the spectrum of human powers and their uses. This book will not attempt to deal with such questions (but see MT). It does observe, though, that the effort to answer these questions with completeness must wait upon a secure grasp of the processes and principles of interpreting the given and especially upon the principles and their uses as they are implicated in human being.

Our efforts have so far discerned in man his basic flow of feeling and presentations and two other interpretative powers: intelligence and conation (intellect and will).[7] We have turned these powers back upon his experiences of space, time, objects, and self, and have been able to express the *sine qua non* of these powers. Time, we concluded, is being in space. Space is otherness, the condition of being separate. An object or thing (event) is a unified spatio-temporal being. A self is a unified spatio-temporal being which is the place of appearances, the locus of the primary truth process. Now we need to examine the use of human powers in interpretation and to discover the principles and operations of the interpretative process, their conditions, structure, use, origin, and end.

Notes

1. Cf. E. Husserl, *Ideas*, trans. by W. R. Boyce-Gibson, 1931, §§34ff. The doctrine of intentionality offers no solution to the problem of participation. On the contrary, it is an illustration of this problem and a testimony to its ubiquity in human experience. Cf. Charles P. Bigger, *Participation, A Platonic Inquiry* (Baton Rouge, La.: Louisiana State Univ. Press, 1968), passim, esp. pp. 89ff. and chap. 4.
2. Cf. Don Idhe, *Techniques and Praxis, Boston Studies in the Philosophy of Science*, vol. 24 (Boston, Mass.: D. Reidel Publ. Co, 1979), chaps. 1-4.
3. On the nothingness of the self, see Michael E. Zimmerman, *The Eclipse of the Self: The Development of Heidegger's Concept of Authenticity* (Athens, Ohio: Ohio University Press, 1981), passim, but see especially chapters 3, 4, and 8. Also see § 51 below.
4. Heidegger, *Being and Time*, trans. by John Macquarrie and Edward Robinson, 1962, §§44.
5. See MT §§35F.
6. See Erich Fromm, *Sane Society* (N. Y.: Holt, Rinehart, & Winston, 1955), pp. 111-31, on the marketing personality. See also Joe Girard, *How to Sell Yourself* (N. Y.: Warner Books, 1981); the author's pitch: sell yourself (your "package") first; make people like you, have confidence in you. Then they will buy your services or your product, and you will be on your way to becoming number one.
7. In *Man and Technology* intellect or the power of seeing is further described and discussed in chapter 4, will in chapter 3, and action and self in chapter 5.

V

Interpretation of Objects and World

§22. INTERPRETATION AND ITS FUNCTION

Objects are to us always objects in a perspective. We have, then, to consider not only the object but also the perspective in which it appears. We shall now concern ourselves principally with the latter, remembering that a perspective contains interpretative principles by reason of whose operation presentations appear as they do.

Interpretation is the act of discovering the *logoi* (i.e., meanings) referred to some given presentation or object. Thereupon the object or presentation is perceived as embodying, indeed as being, that meaning. Meanings are developed by the use of principles in the act of interpretation; but meanings so given may or may not truly interpret the presentations or objects to which they are referred or upon which they are projected. The discovery of their interpretative excellence or deficiency may take a long time — as witness the career of the phlogiston hypothesis — but the truth eventually will win out, or so we commonly suppose. Furthermore, these interpretative *logoi* function as mediators between power and direction, for the directive function refers to such meanings or intelligibles as are available in order to determine action, the use of power. Human activity in its pursuit of wholeness could not proceed otherwise. Knowing and behaving, thus, are consequent upon interpretation. The understanding of interpretative excellence is a primary theme and obligation of philosophy.

Let us consider an act of interpretation or meaning-giving and note its factors. We begin with our former illustration. The Saarinean Arch breaks upon my sight suddenly and for the first time. Still, there is no doubt but that I recognize it. How? In the first place, I am in St. Louis, where the Arch is located, and I am now on the street which, as I know, leads toward it. Also, I have a clear memory image of archways and even of an inverted catenary. It is easy to relate what is presented me here with past acquisitions, even though the thing presented is much higher and more impressive than I had been led to expect. The location, the time, and the present complex image coalesce into a principle which, grasped together with the presentation, enables me to make a correct interpretation, to perceive the present presentation *as* the Arch, a typical — if, in this instance, a rather simple — interpretative act.

Clearly, my primary and necessary means of access to the experience of the Arch itself is through visual perception; my perspective upon it is a visual perspective.[1] One element of the perspective, the context in which I perceive the Archway, provided me with more than one clue to recognizing it. The known locus in time and space are part of this context, and so is my purpose in being there as a sightseer. I gained access to this context in part through a complex route which we may call "world." World and context were important in determining the kind of memories I retained and the ones I recalled on this occasion for use in interpreting what struck my sight when I looked toward the Arch. This chapter will be devoted to elucidating experiences of this kind. We shall deal with these general questions: How does the interpreter gain access to objects? What are the factors of interpretation? What are the dimensions of meaning attributed to objects?

These questions are closely related. Very generally put, we gain access to objects by placing them in an object-perspective, that is, by giving object meanings to the appropriate presentations. I have called the act of giving meanings "interpretation," bearing in mind that one does not give meanings without restriction, as one might be imagined to give them to some sort of utterly formless matter. One seeks to give them appropriately (i.e., truly). I am not free, for instance, to give the Arch-presentation the meaning of square, for its shape presents nothing angular, hence, the term "interpretation," which suggests the intimate relation between the presentation of an object (to be interpreted) and its outcome in experience. Meanings, then, are regularly given and acquired in acts of perceiving and experiencing. To be noted also is the fact that for almost any familiar object, another culture can be found which will give it a different meaning. And within a culture a good deal of latitude is allowable for choice of context wherein to interpret a presentation or an object (MT chap. 4).

The other-than-self in perception is the given element, the presentation the mind passively receives. Our response to this given is interpretation (PC §3). Interpretation is at first spontaneous or intuitive, then reflective. The line between these two levels of interpretation is indefinite and shifting (MT §48). As experience accrues, aspects of it become habitual and move from the reflective to the involuntary level. On the other hand, reflective criticism may well draw aspects of habitual interpretation into a light where they may be examined or changed.

Some of the factors of a perspective which determine how the interpretation (whether habitual or reflective) develops may be mentioned here. I refer to the more pervasive factors (to be discussed in sections to follow), such as interpretative principles, both spontaneous and reflective; context; context intention or orientation; disposition; projection; mythical investiture. These factors determine how a type of interpretation unfolds. They take their source in our sensitive field and yield access to objects. The last two, projection and mythical investiture, are operative throughout one's life and are effective at all the levels of interpretation. Prominent specialized contexts also exercise a pervasive effect upon perception, for a lively interchange between specialized and common contexts is constantly occurring and profoundly affects both. All these factors influence not only the experience of objects but also self-understanding as well as understanding of the over-arching context within which both self and object have their being. Our primary concern here, though, is to reach a grasp of object-experience. To this end we need first to examine perception in greater detail.

§23. THE ELEMENTS OF PERCEPTION

The self perceives; objects are perceived or are perceptible. The notion of perception, however, is difficult to develop, for virtually every item that enters into a philosophical view of perception has been repeatedly moot throughout modern times (PC pp.123f., 185; MT §4).

I want at the outset to distinguish the present view from the traditional empiricist theory as well as from more recent sense data ones. Both of these kinds of theory begin with rather remote abstractions — sensory stimuli, impressions, patches of red, and the like — which may have their place in a psychological theory but do not describe experience. Also, both limit perceiving rather narrowly to the operations of the five traditional senses and fail to include such important elements as visceral and kinesthetic feelings, synesthetic sensations, reactions involving the sense of balance, and also moods — empathetic, sympathetic, hostile and similar responses — as well as the fringe or horizontal awarenesses which Husserl, James and others have found to be parts of the total perception. Likewise, they ignore what many students believe they observe: that we are globally aware of the bodily schema; that is, we constantly sense the body participating in its spatial and temporal context as if we possessed a sort of psychic map of the self-in-position or self-in-action to which other perceptions are referred for location and orientation. A modified Kantian view will be less slanted; this view starts with a distinction between what is given and what the perceiver in some fashion adds to the given in the process of coming to understand it. The terms "presentation" and "interpretation" are utilized for making this distinction.

An illustration will be useful: consider a flash of lightning. Initially, I turn involuntarily toward the flash. Then, if I am an ancient Greek, I may murmur, "Ah, Zeus is demonstrating his power again; I hope I am not the fated target," or if I am a modern Westerner, I may think, "There goes a sudden discharge of static electricity, at this distance not to be feared." In either instance there is a two-part act: first a presentation, yielding what is to be identified and interpreted, and then an interpretation. The initial and spontaneous phases of perception are common also to animals, and animals make useful distinctions upon this basis. But there can be no doubt that human interpretations are different in kind in that they are carried to a further stage during which conceptual principles become determining. The difference between the two stages of interpretation is similar to the difference between signals and symbols as understood in many non-behaviorist theories of language.

Presentation, the first element in perception, is never present, as I have already noted, in pure form. Inevitably, some intermixture of interpretation is detectable (MT pp. 17f.). The etymology of "presentation" is relevant: the term derives from Latin *pre* (before) and *sentire* (to feel) and suggests a recurring flow of feeling, or a flow shot through with familiar (recollected) elements and intentions. My observation is in accord with this description. All presentation is representation. Even though what is presented may not be clearly identified, what is noticed or recognized still bears some analogy to preceding experience. Otherwise, it would not have been noticed. Thus we do not, in the strict sense, experience mere presentations; we experience objects, particulars , something of a kind, a thing having meaning.

In short, objects are experienced as interpreted presentations. I do not hear a meaningless swish, but the rain on the roof. Each such object is a figure against a ground and within a horizon. Still, the presentation itself can be approached by abstracting all the interpretative elements which can be recognized. Some philosophers have attempted to identify the presentation with the sensations stimulated in the sense organs. But I have suggested that this identification is suspect, being tied to the altogether questionable theory that there are exactly five sense organs which respond mechanically to stimuli impringing upon them from an external world. Explanatory beliefs such as this one can be suspended or bypassed, and with some practice the observer of perceiving can witness a stage wherein perception approaches perhaps rather closely to just that which is given, a field of phenomena, a field of perceptions prior to many of the identifications and distinctions which we have learned to make. It is prior, for example, to the distinction between inner and outer, between subjective and objective, which so much of Edmund Husserl's better known work was devoted to examining. Here we shall assume the soundness of his work and pass immediately on to the more usual problem for the experiencer: the way in which given presentations can be selected and used within the self's particular horizon appropriately to express, represent, mean, or refer to recurrent complexes of presentations, i.e., to "objects." This response yields the minimal sense of "interpretation." Thus the self uses recurrent presentations to refer, by means of interpretation, to objects.

Some commonly noticed meanings immediately attributed to an object are gathered from its background and from its horizon, for the object is related to other objects; it overlaps other objects in my field of vision, for example, or is perceived as moved about by them. Also, there are properties of its own which are not presented, yet which are part of its meaning as I experience it. The other side of this paper is the usual example; I do not perceive the other side directly but I sense it or "co-perceive" it; it is on the horizon or fringes of presence. The object, in other words, possesses outer and inner horizons as parts of the meaning with which I experience it. These horizontal meanings may be quite complex and help to give the object the kind of independence and concreteness which I sought to communicate in chapter 2 when describing the Saarinean Archway (§9).

The given, then, is the presented; interpretation is the active movement going out to meet the given or those aspects of the given to which one is sensitive.[2] Experience is seldom arrested at the more passive phase — presentation plus involuntary interpretation — although in some types of aesthetic experience it may be completed there. Usually, experience proceeds to the active phase in which the perceiver explicitly meets the perceived with his own practiced powers of adapting it to his world. Interpretation, then, is initially spontaneous, habitual, intuitive; later it is reflective and perhaps critical (PC p. 185f.).

The essential turn of Husserl's method of phenomenological reduction lies not, as is sometimes thought, in distinguishing between presentation and interpretation and then attempting to restrict consideration to the first or given element, the mere presentation. Rather, the famous suspension of existence (the epochē) is the non-use of a factor within the first interpretative phase. This is the factor which characterizes an object as standing (existing) unquestionably outside of, and independent of, the perceiver. The non-use of this universally presupposed and normally (for us) involuntary interpretative factor has the effect of lending experience a strange quality. It tends to reactivate the sense of wonder *that* there should be any object or experience at all and may lead to questions and problems relating to the function of the self in constituting and ordering its experience. But these questions are likewise encountered by other methods, including the present one. (I add that it is not clear to me whether the suspension of just this presupposed belief about existence or whether the suspension of any firmly held presupposition is productive of wonder. I suspect that the successful questioning of any tenaciously held basic belief — any part of one's mythical investiture — would tend to elicit awareness of the world.)

If we attend as exclusively as possible to a presented something, a *that* (say a flash of light), we observe it is rather like a question. The development of the experience offers something like an answer to the question. Recall that "experience" is derived from *periri*. The Latin verb refers to making a trial, an attempt which may fail; "peril" has the same derivation. Initially, an experience is something like a questioning trial. It asks *what* is the *that* presented. The first spontaneous and unthinking response identifies the *that* in habitual or conventional manner. "The flash must have come from automobile headlights over there." Reflective interpretation presses the question more critically and seeks to adjust the first response to other evidence, other knowledge, a more determinate principle: "There is only a lake over there; hence the flash may have come from a boat's search light." Thus the flash, as something definite, not myself, presented and interpreted in my space-time, fulfills the minimum conditions for being an experienced object, however brief its existence. Such interpretations approach closely to the Kantian sense of experience; they refer to empirical knowledge. But I do not want to use the term so narrowly; "perceptual experience" refers to an event in which an object or the self-as-object makes its being perceptually evident to the experiencing self.

It should be added that there is evidently a presentation of self in self-awareness. And this presentation, like any other, requires interpretation. Again, it should be noted that the self, experienced as both a flow of feeling and as a something, a presentation eliciting interpretation, does not entail that the self is in every way an object, as we noted in the last chapter. Even though in some instances this self-presentation may be experienced as like an object, such interpretations turn out upon examination to miss the self who intends; they miss the non-object to whom objects appear.

§24. ON SPONTANEOUS INTERPRETATION

We cannot but accept the given presentation, or that aspect of it which we are sensitive to and have selected, just as it is given, but this acceptance is not yet experience in the full sense. Experience waits upon the human use of the presented.

In human experience, many immediate or automatic interpretations of the presented vary from culture to culture and from person to person. Certain of them, however, appear to be universal. One of these is the immediate and intuitive[3] location of the presented in space, with respect to the observer's body by means of the orientation of the observer's eyes or ears. Another common involuntary interpretation follows from the way purpose and intentions affect perception.[4] The intention, for example, to find my lost spectacles so alters the context of perception that objects resembling spectacles stand out in strong relief, whereas objects unlike them become almost unnoticeable.

No less automatic is the recognition of similarities of one presentation to other presentations or to objects. No reasoning or conceptualizing process is necessary to convince me that the object on my desk is a book. I automatically recognize it to be so, for earlier perceptions of books have by now coalesced into an interpretative principle which I can bring to bear forthwith upon present presentations. Only upon quite unusual or artificial occasions would I doubt such an identification. The unity of an object and its difference from others, e.g., where the book ends and the desk begins, are similarly immediately read into the presentation. Certain other properties, e.g., sense of meaning (what the book is useful for), are more slowly learned, but they nevertheless come with practice to be immediate interpretations.

Still other properties, e.g., embarrassment, sympathetic and empathetic reactions, matter-of-factness, boredom, anxiety, indifference, wonder, impersonality, and others, belong to the way perception occurs. Perception always occurs in some such "way"; some feeling tone or attitudinal coloring is invariably present. These data are probably best identified as aspects of the involuntary and immediate phase of interpretation, but they affect the total. In particular, they characterize what I shall call the non-objective aspect of the interpretation; they tell something of what it is like to be that particular percipient at that time. It is also important to note that these data are absent in non-human actions or movements, e.g., in the "linguistic" activity of a computer. Also, in human beings some of these data may, upon occasion, be excluded from attention or may be interpreted in stereotyped or exiguous ways, as in the objective attitude of certain impersonal investigators. Of course, all of these feeling responses accompanying perception are changeable or correctible by a process in which reflective and critical interpretation play an important part (see §44).[5]

Now, all of these responses to objects provide information about the self as well as about the object experienced. Involuntarily turning toward the object localizes the object; it also localizes the self with respect to the object. This turning toward the object is often an asking, as it were, "*What* is it?", and says a good deal about the interests of the being who so turns. It says that his initial response is interrogative and interrogative about *this* — the flash itself — rather than *that*, the clouds or the trees in the background. Art and religion usually focus on this early phase of experience, the presentation as spontaneously or habitually interpreted.

Phenomenology, too, seeks its starting point in this early phase. Dwelling upon the later, more critical interpretative phase is the function of practical common sense, and finally of science and technology, and is often aimed at revealing the character of the object experienced with an eye to its use-value. The reference of perception to the thing perceived will be called its objective reference; its referring back to the perceiver will be termed its non-objective reference. The non-objective reference back to the perceiver can often be utilized to yield knowledge of the self (PC pp.49ff.).

Other matters of the first importance lie concealed in this initial phase of experience. For instance, factors are discernable in it which are determined by what I shall later call mythical investiture (§27). Other factors are determined by the context. Likewise, the difficult problems relating to intersubjectivity are doubtless to be solved, if at all, at this level. Is the other person an object? Certainly he is, in a sense. One perceives another person as distinct from and at a distance from oneself, and thus as an object. One can bump into a man exactly as one can bump into a table. (However, one does not ask pardon of the table as one does of a man, thus acknowledging the ambiguous character of the man's object status.) Also, a man is successfully taken as an object by the various sciences which study him or his behavior. Sometimes these studies, biological ones in particular, achieve considerable predictive value, and even when they do not achieve this value, we are assured and generally believe that they will eventually do so. This pragmatic assurance tends to persuade us that man is indeed an object among objects, or an animal among animals, as the ancient definition asserts.

Still, it would seem that even if a man is an object in some senses, there remains a very important sense in which he is quite unlike any object. And this sense is, at the least, that wherein his first and involuntary response to the other person is, or can be, unique. If one is said to respond to objects with an objective attitude, one directed upon the measurable and calculable or public aspects of the object, then perhaps it should be said that one can respond to other human beings non-objectively, or that the non-objective response is (or should be) completed along with the objective one. We are familiar with this immediate non-objective response in the experience of empathy, affection, introjection, embarrassment, respect, and the like. Similarly, these particular non-objective responses may even be extended to objects; when they are so extended, objects are experienced as very like, or identical to, a person. The ancient Greek's personifications and deifications are examples of this extension, as is the poet's power to inject a strange quality or life into the worlds of his creation. Here is a secret of the life of myth and perhaps also of mythical investiture.

Is there anything in the presentation of a person which is not present in the presentation of an object? Both may be presented to the visual sense as patterns of localized colors and volumes and of contrasts among these volumes and colors. In addition, another person is involuntarily perceived to move, sound and even look and feel as I do; I spontaneously expect his gesture and his glance to be meaningful, just as mine are. That is, looking back on my perception of persons, I find that the presentation of another like myself is immediately interpreted as a person. The interpretation may seem to be based on analogy. But if anything is clear about human responses to other humans, I suppose it is that reasoning by an explicit and abstract analogy is not the basis for such responses. It would be more profitable, rather, to search for the peculiarity of the intersubjective response in the immediate interpretations accompanying the perception of a person.

Notice that an involuntary empathetic response is often made to the tensions and attitudes present in, but hardly consciously distinguished in, the behavior of another person. These evidences of tension are more or less inhibited gestures, involuntary but telltale movements described below (§44) as "small signs." Though largely implicit and muted, such movements are effective communications — communications, even, of a linguistic character[6] — to which a percipient can respond in kind and recognize because they elicit common and familiar feelings. If a person is hostilely or affectionately disposed toward me, I usually know it, even if I do not know how I know it. I know it, as I observe, because a like response has been empathetically initiated in me. An important mode of knowledge of the other is acquired by way of this kind of mimesis. Thus my awareness of the other is reached by forming within myself a kind of concrete analogy to the other, the basis for which is undoubtedly to be discovered in one's sensitive field. Such a mimetic or concrete analogical response is not merely an objective happening in the world. It is an immediate response of my own feeling and is sensed as a part of myself, as a cue to my own self-interpretation. Accordingly, I can interpret my own feeling as reciprocally affectionate or hostile.

Hamlet provides a more complex illustration. If, at the end of the play, the Prince were to come on stage and say "I am the self who played that role," we would understand what he meant. We of the audience, too, were Hamlets for a while. The libraries of Hamlet-interpretation are built upon this concrete analogical basis.[7] Interpretation of a person as a person through involuntary empathetic response to his unconscious gesture is probably no more mysterious than immediately understanding "pen" to refer to this writing instrument; a difference, however, lies in the fact that the former language has as yet been given no explicit grammar.

§25. REFLECTIVE INTERPRETATION

Perceiving need not stop with the immediate and spontaneous interpretation of the presented. The initial perceiving may become grist for reflection and considered interpretation. This secondary level and its relation to the first become clearest in the context of work, for it is easy to observe that in complex work, factors that have become spontaneous and immediate once were the reverse. The work environment thus allows us to view these two stages of interpretation in developmental sequence.

Work proceeds by the skilled application of tools to material. In general, a tool is an object used to mediate the direction of power of an organism's appendages in order to accomplish an end. According to this definition, chimpanzees who use twigs to fish termites out of a termite mound are tool users. Human tools, however, differ specifically from this haphazard substitution of a twig for a finger. Human tools are usually produced with other tools and are intentionally preserved for a specific use. More importantly, they are employed within a context or complex system of other cooperating tools, materials, and the like to accomplish intermediate ends, with an eye toward some remote end. I may, for example, use a screwdriver and pliers to tighten a screw on a mowing machine which is to be attached to a tractor, so it can be used to cut the grass in paths through the woods and fields in order to make them safe and enjoyable for afternoon walks. The general intention, which dominates this and other contexts and orients all human work, is the final end; perhaps *the* final end is man himself or his good. A subordinate but still moderately general intention determining this particular work context is the intention to cut grass. Within this context is the particular intention to repair the mower, and hence to tighten this screw. Prior to effecting this intention, the screw had to be selected and placed in the proper position for tightening. Thus intentions, defining contexts of increasingly narrow reference, direct work and effect its coordination.

Work — power purposefully directed toward effecting change in some object or objects — requires a series of fairly complex recognitions, problem-solving operations, and decisions, all of which parallel and direct the actual operations as they proceed. These mental operations may be understood to be the outcome of using a group of standard object-concepts, images, paradigms, subtle feelings, and muscular sensations that embody rules of operation belonging to the particular work context in question. These may be collectively termed the principles of interpretation for that context.[8] Such principles are chosen from among the elements constituting the context within which the object in question is identified or used. Clearly, the context from which particular interpretative principles are drawn must be prior to the particular principles and their application. We can raise questions about the meaning of marriage customs among the Zulus because we already have some experience of marriage customs. We can speak about measuring the distance to the sun because we are already acquainted with distance and its measurement.

The history of acquiring a skill so that one may execute a type of work is the history of acquiring the use of interpretative principles so that they pass from a relatively explicit or tentative apprehension to the point where they may be used without reflection, or, as an Aristotelian might say, used by habit or second nature. Our choice of the aspects within a total presentation to which we should attend in order to learn a technique is at first awkward and slow. Through practice we become sensitized to the appropriate aspects and manipulate them efficiently. This learning process is accompanied by a characteristic feeling tone which, in the happier instances, harmonizes with and reinforces the learning. Our recognition and responses become immediate and intuitive; we are no longer led astray from the work to be done by irrelevant elements of the presentation. Thus perceiving is disciplined and diversified into types or kinds. It will be useful to correlate these kinds of perceiving with contexts.

In the illustration above, I recognized the screw in part because I already possessed a good acquaintance with the context of household appliances and machinery, a context which counted among its elements the paradigmatic image or interpretative concept of a standard I had learned to use. I then had to match, so to speak, the presented objects with the interpretative principle and to select by hypothesis and testing from among the competitors for the correct screw. A practiced mechanic might have been able to select immediately, by a sort of automatic eye-measurement, a screw of the required length and thread. Entrance into a complex work-context like that of a physics laboratory is achieved only by long apprenticeship to the discipline of matching physical concepts with objects and operations sometimes already partly familiar in everyday life. At the beginning, a student can be shown the oil drop experiment for measuring the charge on an electron, but he does not see what to the physicist may be obvious. He does not yet possess the interpretative concepts which would be the knowing-what-to-look-for.

Observation further indicates that the capacity to recognize and utilize objects in the common life-environment develops in a similar fashion. Thus my preconceived image of the Saarinean Arch formed part of the operative context within which I could compare the given presentation to principles, and recognize it as the thing it was. No doubt this image also quickly took on the characteristics of a standard image or principle in its own right and helped me to pass judgment on the ambiguity or non-ambiguity of the perception. As in the instance of a specialized worker's context, an essential element of the common life-context of all of us is a stock of object-images and convictions about object-properties standard within a culture. They show us what to attend to, what to ignore. One comes into possession of this stock of standard objects and convictions by way of the trials and disciplines of everyday life. Such interpretative principles or standard images may not be precise concepts, but they function accurately enough to identify particular presentations as objects of this or that sort, in this or that situation or condition.

For example, a strange object comes into view. My noting of its characteristics is the effort to identify it further by means of seeing it through that member of my stock of object-images which at first it seems most nearly to resemble.[9] My ambiguous or non-ambiguous perception, which, as we have seen, is linked with the distance of the perceived object, is likewise determined by comparison with such a standard object and calls attention to the fact that part of the standard character of the object is a conventionally determined optimum situation for viewing or identifying the object. In a perception, ambiguity or its lack, and distance or its lack are judged by comparison, so to speak, with the standard object-image. The ambiguous, ovoid, ribbon-thin, greyish-colored object was compared with my arch image and thoughtfully identified as the Arch seen from a considerable distance.

The stock of standard interpretative principles indispensible to anyone either perceiving or involved actively or contemplatively with objects, may, upon encountering an unusual situation or problem in the course of experience, prove inadequate. Then the appropriate interpretation is missed; consequently, the person involved must settle either for failure or for critically examining his interpretations of operations and perhaps changing them. Upon the latter option, a dialectic is engaged which may eventuate in the discovery or clearer expression of interpretative principles. Later (in chapter 8), we shall devote some time to a consideration of this process.

For the present, we note that principles of interpretation, when considered apart from the actual process of interpretation, can be designated, conceptualized, defined, and discussed no less than perceived objects. Indeed, they constitute a class of objects, ideal objects, of primary importance for modern cultures. The square root of two is quite as objective for us and our engineers as the rope triangle was for the Egyptians and their surveyors. We need not enter now into the controversy concerning the kind of reality to be attributed to these ideal or conceptual objects. It suffices that objects can be observed to exhibit common characteristics, and these common traits can be named and defined. They thus become definite ideal objects, although separated from the concrete contexts in which they are perceived as the properties and characters of particular objects. Ideal objects can, therefore, be founded in perceived objects. When these ideal objects are used as principles of interpretation, it is useful to distinguish those among them which are secondary or derivative from those which are primary. The latter are termed "categories." Categories, then, are basic principles of interpretation, or primary intentions. We shall return to the study of these basic principles in chapters 6 and 7.

The abstraction of ideal objects or principles (what Husserl termed the eidetic reduction), practiced in the three preceding chapters, is one of the crucial philosophic operations. For one thing, principles, meanings, *logoi*, when explicit and abstract, render possible a more sophisticated and skillful use. Then learning and reflective interpretation proceed more efficiently and expeditiously. For another thing, principles are more open to criticism, correction, and reformulation when they are separately entertained. Recall that the Demiurgos of the *Timaeus* (29A-E) had at the beginning of his creative effort to decide whether to look to the created or the eternal patterns in making the world. He chose the eternal since they were the better. We, too, have constantly to make a not dissimilar decision. Although we may not appeal to the criterion of eternality, we do appeal to other analogous criteria, for we recognize that some principles of interpretation are carelessly made or imagined. The reflective interpretations utilizing them, consequently, become confused, distorted, misleading, or outright false. Other principles lead to excellent interpretations.

We have already recalled the comparison of the Aristotelian to the Newtonian theories of falling bodies, of the phlogiston to the atomic-molecular theories of heat, of the Ptolemaic to the Copernican theories of the heavenly bodies. And we might compare the Epicurean theory of man to the Platonic, or to be more modern, the Skinnerean model to the Jungian. The question concerning the properties possessed by the good interpretative principle is too large a question for more than passing mention here. We note briefly two types of such properties.

The better interpretative principle possesses certain intrinsic characteristics. It is relatively simple, clear, self-consistent, and consistent with other interpretative principles. In addition, it answers to a number of criteria associated with the objects to which it is referred or which it is to interpret. Thus the good interpretative principle is relatively rich in explanatory power; that is, it refers to many objects, perhaps to objects seemingly unrelated to the initially interpreted objects. Also, it exhibits pragmatic excellence; that is, it "works" and exhibits predictive value. It suggests further profitable interpretations. And it tends to render experience more precise and determinate, and also to unify or to articulate experience more explicitly or in greater depth and scope. These logical and pragmatic criteria of interpretative principles have called forth much study in recent times. Here, though, a note of caution needs to be struck. Despite the importance of abstracting and weighing principles, equal emphasis should be placed upon the recognition that reflective interpretation, however sophisticated, is closely related to spontaneous interpretation. Indeed, the two do not differ in kind.

Of course, reflective interpretation takes place in a context explicitly dominated by an intention, whether specialized or common, and proceeds by something like a comparison of the standard interpretative principles of that context with presentations or with the object to be further interpreted. Still, success in acquiring a technique is marked by the passage of interpretative principles from the stage where they are compared reflectively and explicitly with their objects, to the stage where they or many of them are used immediately and involuntarily. Reflective interpretation thus tends to become spontaneous. My point is that skillfully abstracted and explicit principles are still the same principles as those implicit in the living processes of use.

Consider the fine art of gardening. Here the context-intention is the intention of producing vegetables for nourishment. Among its principles are recollections and images of earth for cultivation, gardening tools, seeds or seedlings, and so on. The neophyte gardener progresses much faster if he has conceptualized these principles of interpretation, for then at the beginning of his career he can consult a gardening manual to decide, say, which tool to use in order to prepare the soil. He quickly learns to make the correct selection quite without thought. Then his decision initiates a series of gardening acts which are comparable with those described in the gardening manual. Eventually he becomes independent of the manuals and instructions and their more or less explicit principles, for these principles have come alive in his hands and eyes. He has become a gardener.

Notice that we loosely speak of "comparing" the concept, image, or rule with the object or activity. The essential function is the *seeing* that the gardener's procedures conform to the rules and suggestions set forth in the manual and are subordinate to the general intention of making a garden. In general, interpretive principles are two-sided. On the one hand, they are noematic; they are concepts, rules, and even images which may be compared with objects, written down, or preserved in manuals and thereby formalized. On the other hand, these principles are noetic acts, e.g., a conceiving, a subjective process of judging or producing a concept, rule, or image (a *logos*) which, further, may direct or infuse activity. Husserl observed the universal correlation of these two, noetic and noematic, conceiving and concept, imaging and image. No image is produced without an image-forming act. A term like "interpretative principle," then, is ambiguous; it refers sometimes to a formed principle, sometimes to the act of forming or using a principle, sometimes to a principle intended, sometimes to the intending of a principle.

This act of intending, e.g., of forming an image or a principle of interpretation, is usually felt to proceed from a self, a sensitive field. Wherever there is the effect of a subjective act, there we expect to find subjective activity which enacted it. The self or sensitive field must be at least as complex as the acts proceeding from it, and its possibilities must be far richer than its effects. Some knowledge about the self can be gleaned by observing its formative activity. Euclid's geometry, for example, may be taken as a treatise upon certain kinds of abstract spatial configurations and objects. But it may also be regarded, non-objectively, as an activity and a part of the biography, more properly the autobiography, of Euclid himself. It informs us that he was rather good at a certain kind of reflection. It tells us something about how he thought and what he liked to think about. It also indicates something of the way he received and used that which was presented him. When Edna St. Vincent Millay remarked, "Euclid looked upon beauty bare," she may have had in mind something of the world which, through long proximity to the mathematician, was by way of becoming his native world. Perhaps it is worth observing that the poet, the novelist, and certain kinds of psychologists would be apt to take note of this non-objective reference of Euclid's work; the mathematician, the scientist, the technologist would turn more naturally to the objective aspect. Human limitations, together with intransigent competition, seem regularly to drive men to this kind of compartmentalization. It takes both, though, to make a Euclid.

§26. CONTEXT, DISPOSITION, AND PROJECT

Perception, we have observed, is diversified into kinds. Characteristically different sorts of perception dominate different specialties, different cultures, or different epochs of history. In a given kind of perceiving, certain elements of the presentation are habitually noticed and are given preference over other elements. I shall say that a definite kind of perceiving occurs within a correlative context. The discussion of context, disposition, and project and their structure will offer the occasion for distinguishing different types of perceiving and for raising the question how the reigning types of perceiving are selected. Discussion of this latter question will require us to consider the nature of world.

Some attention was allotted to the topic of context earlier, and distinctions were drawn among the center of reference of a context (the self or some self function), orientation, and distance relative to an object (§11). Here it should be remembered that context intention, like any intention, originates with the self and is oriented toward a specific object or kind of object (cf. §53 below). The context intention determines which interpretative principles are thought to be pertinent, which irrelevant, or which inapplicable. Also, we recall that interpretative principles drawn from the context are used to categorize objects which are in the process of having their nature and function determined with respect to a particular context intention. Distance determination illustrates this usage.

Thus, a context is a related group of experiences and possible experiences; it is the source of interpretative principles, organized around a context-intention, prior to and directed upon the appropriate objects. Practical illustrations of contexts are offered by the specialties, physics, chemical engineering, and their like, as these are ordinarily recognized. The context, for example, of mechanics is dominated by the scientist's intention to see and understand objects in terms of relations among physical bodies (masses). The more specific orientation of this context from the time of Galileo until that of Newton was to define mass and discover the basic laws of its behavior. This context-intention was actualized by means of its interpretative principles or standard images and concepts. The interpretative principles for Newtonian mechanics were, first, contemporary common sense and involuntary ways of perceiving objects, then in addition, the four philosophical principles, eight definitions, and three laws set forth by Newton in the *Mathematical Principles of Natural Philosophy* (1687), all of which define mechanics and guide perception to apprehending the (mechanically) measurable and calculable aspects of presentations. These principles were used to bring presentations into experience as physical objects, objectively apprehended.

Changes in the factors which determine the structure of a context will allow one and the same presentation, a tomato soup can for example, to be perceived in various ways, viz., as a useful container, an object of art, a cylinder having certain mathematical properties, a sample of a chemical substance, a mass-point in physical space-time, a waste product of the affluent society, and the like. I am not proposing here a casual exercise in shift of point of view. To grasp what is meant by change in the way of perceiving, consider the following situations.

Suppose you are visiting a friend in his laboratory or atelier; he addresses you in the laboratory:

He: "What are you doing with that tomato soup can?"
You: "I'm going to throw it into the garbage."
He: "Please don't! I have to find its center of gravity for the experiment I'm running."

Or in the atelier he might have said:

"Please don't! That's one of Plato's most beautiful figures and part of the still life I'm painting."

So you are caught in sudden confusion, look with embarrassment at the thing in your hands, and replace it.

This change in the concrete way of experiencing a thing points to what is intended by reference to change of context. Presumably the presentation, the given element, remained the same, but garbage in everyday life is not necessarily garbage in the laboratory or atelier. That which changed when the object experienced was altered was the interpretation, the presentation remaining (presumably) constant. A presentation enters experience through interpretative activity. Interpretation occurs always in specific contexts. The context opens the percipient to certain aspects of presentations and provides principles for interpreting them as objects of an appropriate kind. Thus only through man, or through some being who can make interpretations or give meanings, can a world of objects, of interpreted presentations, come into existence.

The contexts in general use at a given time, those which have formed the average adult's habits of perceiving and experiencing, are neither fixed nor arbitrary. One of the basic factors determining which of the many contexts are taken seriously and which ignored or rejected can be profitably specified here. This factor I shall term "disposition." When persons actually share certain context-intentions and use or attempt to use their interpretative principles, then they are possessed of a disposition favorable to those contexts. They move easily into them and can act within them.

A disposition is a definite way of feeling or valuing. One who either involuntarily or upon reflection regards a tin can as a mass point obviously values the physical context and shares the feelings and valuations of physicists. He uses, or favors those who can use, the interpretative principles of that and similar contexts and approves of their operation. If he can shift over to the artist's context, then he replaces the physicist's disposition with another, so far, ideally, as the two do not conflict. The fact probably is, though, that the average specialist in the physics of modern times often does not shift easily into the artist's context.

He shifts more easily into contexts resembling the physical in both intention and interpretative principles. Thus he is more readily disposed to sympathize with the chemist than with the painter. We say, therefore, that his disposition is scientific or objective. Thus one's characteristic ways of perceiving are a function of the contexts toward which one is favorably disposed. As context-intention is to a single context, so disposition is to a related group of contexts. A disposition thus determines a context of contexts.

I introduce the notion of disposition because it actually describes an aspect of anyone functioning toward a context of contexts. Dispositions favor the development of certain contexts, are neutral to some, and are outright hostile to others. There is such a thing, too, as a common context, and the disposition toward it a whole nation or even a civilization may share. For everyone must learn to perceive and operate within the everyday life of his time. However recondite one's daily work may be, one must get to work in the morning and return home in the evening through a world shared with others. But the needs of a time also provoke the development of specialized contexts. Inevitably, practitioners in specialized contexts learn to perceive habitually through the interpretative principles of their specialty and often tend to evaluate all objects and events as if they lay properly within the orbit of their particular disposition. Such a prejudice may become persuasive and widely shared when the specialty in question is prestigious. Specialized contexts thus influence the common context and may induce a notable change in the latter.

In consequence of the dialectically developing relation between the common and the specialized, a quite characteristic mode of perception and type of disposition may be developed by a people. We remark that their lifestyle acquires particular and easily recognizable traits, or we may conclude that they have developed their own culture, their own world. Civilization has been defined as the concerted effort to direct life toward common ideals and to interpret behavior according to common principles. When the common life of a people acquires this idiosyncratic character, I shall say that these people are engaged in a project. A projection, then, is something like a context of all contexts whose governing intention and interpretative principles are distinctive, pervasive, all-inclusive, and mostly implicit. But a projection, as I am using the term, is not yet a world. It is more like the structure of a family of cultures. I doubt that such a structure has ever been rendered fully explicit, although philosophies done in the grand and universal manner do seem to aim at giving full expression to a possible culture.

A projection, being the widest but usually the least noticeable large context, the one within which all other contexts and groups of contexts are fitted and objects are perceived and used, calls for especial note.[10] I choose for illustration a culture different from our own, the Sonjo, a tribe of East Africa whose life is taken to resemble closely the life of stone-age man, and will briefly describe some of their views on agriculture.[11] This illustration also exhibits the function which I shall call "mythical investiture," but this function will not be discussed until the next section.

The Sonjo hold that the earth is their mother, and the grain she produces is her gift to men. The mother should not, they believe, be wounded by man-made instruments used for killing. But their current instruments used for killing are generally imported and are made of iron. Hence they conclude no iron instrument, e.g., no iron hoe which overdeveloped peoples of the West are willing to donate, should be used in cultivating the earth. One should, rather, use what the earth herself has produced. For "ploughing," therefore, they use only sticks whose sharpened ends have been hardened in fire. Likewise, it seems fitting to these people that mainly the female should be concerned with helping the earth to bear her produce. Thus after the men have cleared a field, women prepare the earth, sow, tend the plants, and reap the harvest.

Of course, the process of cultivating the earth is attended with rituals and religious consideration of the appropriate time for ploughing, planting, and the like. But the primitive mind makes no sharp distinction between the symbolic character of certain acts and their causal effectiveness. The notion of abstract cause is not among the interpretative principles of this projection. The symbolism of the wooden stick as distinct from its use in loosening and aerating the earth is a meaningless distinction to the Sonjo. Probably the whole process of cultivation should be regarded as a ritual, punctuated here and there by ceremonial acts of dancing and other observances which are parts of a single and whole action. The dominating intention is indistinguishably to worship and honor the earth mother and to provide nourishment for man.

The projection of this mythical world and the agricultural beliefs and practices following from it seem absurd to the practical Western agronomist. He grows bigger crops more easily and does not waste time in unproductive religious observances. But his projection is radically different. Naturally, he finds it all but impossible to impart his more successful (by his measure) and more scientific interpretative principles to the Sonjo; they are unimpressed and are no more disposed to accept his beliefs than his hoe. We must conclude that such objects as seeds, earth, and harvest are experienced differently by the Sonjo and by the agronomist. How is this difference to be understood? The difference here is nothing less than a difference in total projection. We may speak of the two as the mythical and the objective (or technological) projections.

Ernst Cassirer and others who have attempted to understand the myth-making mind in modern Western terms are more or less agreed that it is characterized by a sense of the nouminous, a feeling of the uncanny, which is "projected" into the object or situation upon which attention is directed.[12] This projection surrounds the object or situation with "mana," a sense of unearthly power understood and felt to be *in the object*. The mythically reacting person, accordingly, feels constrained to act and react as he believes appropriate in the presence of this divine and personal power. The image of the god, or the sense of his presence, and the object perceived tend to coalesce. The belief in the real power of such mythically endowed or invested objects is so profound that they seem to acquire magic effectiveness. A talisman of this sort can kill or cure the believer.

Granting that Cassirer's account of mythically thinking people is perceptive and accurate, we may still doubt that there is any basic or structural difference between their experience and ours, or between the "way their minds work" and the way ours do. Now, I suggest it is not so much that they are victims of projections and myths and we are not. We, too, can invest objects mythically. The difference between them and us may merely be that we and they are disposed to make different overall projections. This view at least offers a simple — if incomplete — and uniform hypothesis.

In the course of life, one can acquire the disposition to use a certain totality of contexts, which determine certain kinds of interpretation rather than others. Thus the Sonjo's projection results in a mythical and religious world; the agronomist projects an objective world.[13] Just as the experience of a "Z" as a mythical being is the result of a mythic projection, so the objective experience of it is the consequence of an objective projection. This observation is not a tautology; it points to the dependence of one dimension of meaning upon another; it points to the dependence of the contexts of experience upon the kind of projection with which one goes out to meet the given. An object, an interpreted given, always refers, however obscurely and involuntarily, not only to specific contexts, but also to the over-arching projection and its inclining dispositions within which the percipient lives.

Thus a projection is a structure which first gives shape to the presented; it is a widely shared structure within which beings can be manifested in a distinctive way. This account of the perception of the world in a definite and describable way fails, however, to render cultural prejudice intelligible. It fails to explain the tremendous power of the conviction that just *this* habitual way of perceiving, acting, valuing, understanding — in short, of living — is correct, for it alone brings us in touch with reality, whereas others flounder or fail, for they are in touch only with a "mythical" realm which is only subjectively — in the pejorative sense —valid.[14]

§27. MYTHICAL INVESTMENT

A projection is a totality of contexts, and its associated disposition is something like the result of the dispositions of its component contexts. Perhaps the remarks made in the preceding section about projection have suggested that the term is only a surrogate for "culture." But the suggestion is not quite correct. In most of its uses, "culture" is the richer term. A projection is the common structure of a family of cultures. A culture ("cultural world") exists concretely in the minds, traditions, habitual behavior, and language of a people; thus it is more than an abstract structure. Especially to be observed is that a culture is held with extraordinary strength. Nothing in the notion of projection or disposition, as so far developed, gives any hint of the nature or source of this strength nor of the conservative character of culture. Still, it is well-known that some projections acquire so profound a hold upon large numbers of people that those projections are considered to be obvious common sense, whereas others are regarded as historical fossils or as barbarous, ridiculous, or mad proposals.

The strength of the hold which the common intention of a culture has upon those who share it can best be expressed by saying that it and everything closely associated with it are accepted as if spoken by a god or some transcendent authority. Also, I observe that it is extremely difficult, almost impossible to divest oneself of fealty to a culture and its intention, to whose manner one is born. One cannot jump out of one's cultural skin, as the saying goes. I do not, however, intend to speculate upon the nature of the force with which a culture is held but wish only to describe its function and effect.

For the most part, the basic convictions of a culture operate involuntarily, determine the immediate interpretations of presentations, and strongly incline toward certain reflective interpretations. But they are not easily accessible. Even evidence which seems — to an outsider — to go counter to cultural beliefs is usually ignored or else reinterpreted so as to harmonize with these beliefs. Thus the steam which serves a steam engine is interpreted by some primitive tribes as a particularly active and powerful god. Such reinterpretation is always possible, for a culture, like a project, is an all-inclusive context, and *ex hypothesi* all that is, finds an appropriate place within it. These properties — strength, tenacity, and conviction of sufficiency — belong to the faith with which myths are held. Basic cultural beliefs partake of the nature of myths; I shall, therefore, refer to such a widely and tenaciously held project as a "mythical investiture." A culture, then, is an interpretation of a mythically invested project, and investiture is a kind of erotically held belief, a faith, a product of persuasion.

The Sonjo's beliefs about agriculture, mentioned in the last section, offer a good illustration of mythically invested beliefs; the agronomist's assumptions offer another. I shall also speak of world as exemplified in a family of cultures. And the cognate family of possible cultural projections, when mythically invested, would be a world project or simply a world (a total project, like the Western European world as we have known it since the Renaissance). World, then, is a most inclusive projection which has been mythically invested. Cultural world is the embodiment of world in a culture.

Let us approach these notions from a slightly different perspective. The distinction between myth and what I have called mythical investiture is important but is usually blurred and hence merits a further elucidation. Myths are often described as stories expressing a view of the world, of man's place in it, and of his origin and end. They are about world-making powers visualized as human and are told or enacted so as to arouse effectively a sense of the noumenal and of their own unquestionable truth. For men today, they may more informatively be described by an application of a common notion of symbol. Let us say that a symbol (X) is a part of experience that includes feeling, emotion, attitude, imagery, or thought (Y), through which X refers to another part of experience (Z). Thus the symbol, X, refers by means of Y to Z. Now, when X is a rather complex story concerning personified powers of world-making, governing, or destroying (or the like), and when Y runs the whole gamut of human responses,[15] and when Z is the environment as colored and partly determined by one's characteristic attitudes, valuations and ways of feeling, perceiving, and thinking, then X is a myth about Z. When the environment or totality of objects is thus unified in an all-inclusive interpretation, this interpretation becomes a representation of that vaguely sensed but determining totality we have called world. World is the primary determinant of interpretation. It is communicated by the activity of mythical investiture. The phrase "power of world-forming" has this activity in view. A culture is a concrete embodiment of a world.

Myth utilizes persuasive personifications and other rhetorical devices to identify the believer and to relate him to the world embodied in his culture.[16] My term "investiture" refers only to Y when Y determines the world, the way the world appears. Y, that is, is a whole of operative principles of interpretation. It is the total "readiness" for experience, world in the noetic sense. Z would then be the investor's world in the noematic sense. Z would then be the investor's world. Mythical investiture demands complete commitment to the projection communicated by the myth (X). It is one's total response (Y) to a total world (Z). World thus becomes a determining element in every context, in every perception, and operates largely at the level of spontaneous response. Since they are determining elements in the experience of objects, world and culture are hardly to be thought of as objects in the usual sense; rather, they are among the all-pervasive sources from which anything acquires an object sense or, for that matter, any other sense. (Later in this book, I want to relate this determining function of world to what the tradition in philosophy has called "being, cf. chapter 9.) In sum, world is the first medium through which being is sensed; hence it is the primary determinant of one's relation to the beings (objects) of experience. It is ordinarily an unquestioning acceptance of a form of being/non-being, one/many, true /false, good/evil, and same/other which relates self to the self and to the other essential items (see chap. 9.).

That not only myths in the usual usage of the term can be mythically invested is an important observation. Convictions involving non-personal powers may likewise be invested. Probably any projection can come to be held in this manner. A good recent illustration is Marxism, once merely a projection. It was a philosophy, an intellectual view referred to the world, to society, and to labor as a theory is referred to its data. In certain groups, however, a little after the turn of the century, more than the intellects and dispositions of a few philosophers became involved. A whole people turned away from its ancient world of blood and soil and, undergoing a radical change, mythically invested this projection. Marxism then came to be referred to all the activities of life by means of the Y in our formula. It came to express the total response to a total world; that is to say, it became the undoubted and superior truth for which its adherents were willing to kill and be killed.

A projection, then, offers a view of the world, an anticipation of experience and of its value. Mythical investment is the unreserved acceptance of this offer. But such an acceptance is not unalterable. "Radical change" is precisely a change in the self or in society of the dominant investiture. The significant global changes in the life history of a person or of a nation are always the changes which have taken place in its mythical investiture.

Looking back over Western history, an observer might agree that the following were at different times mythically invested and, to varying extents, remain so to this day: to live in peace with the gods and with fate; to live in harmony with the great awe-inspiring powers of nature; to re-establish within one's own soul the image of the Christian Trinity; to utilize natural energies as efficiently as possible for the greatest good of the greatest number. It will be useful to place the last of these, the modern mythical investment, in perspective by means of a brief sketch, perhaps not wholly imaginary, of its development.

I pick the matter of mythical investment up at a point where the early philosophers were concerned with the nature (*physis*, source, birth, life) of all things. All things were said to be composed of the elements available to the apprehension of anyone — earth, water, air, and fire. In attempting to understand these early thinkers, one must beware of the trap of cultural self-mirroring. One must beware of regarding them as early empiricists who had the misfortune of living before Sir Isaac Newton, but who were, nevertheless, hard at work anticipating the British genius. Rather, one must recall that somewhat earlier the four elements were gods, and though the early philosophers had left aside the divine personalities, the four elements still retained much of the gods' uncanny power.[17] The early Greek philosophers seem to have been interested in deciding which of the four elements was the more fundamental.

But that is not our interest. We note, rather, the properties of these elements. Earth, Gaea, the mother of all, is heavy and damp; earth provides a basis which protects and supports man with its produce and his buildings with its solidity. Water from the heavens — Zeus was associated with rain — fertilizes the earth and brings forth her fruits in due season and order. Air is spirit, the breath of life, which can be formed into speech, and winged like Hermes, expresses aspiration to divinity. Fire is divinity itself, that which moves man and illuminates the world; once it was embodied in Dionysus, the god of wine and inspiration, later in the sun god, Apollo. Man, of course, has a share of each of the elements. His body is earthy, his animating soul water and fire (blood), which enables the spirit (air) to communicate with the gods and to think (cf. PC §3). A good deal of evidence points to the pervasive sense of the sacred which penetrated early Greek feeling. This sense of the numinous was a common possession. No question but that the four elements were its carriers. This sense of the sacredness of *physis*, of its elemental parts, also of man's need to live in harmony with these powers, is the form which mythical investiture then took.

In general, primitive or mythical experience is infused with a sense of the numinous quality of the world. Later experience seems to have grown away from this awareness. Earth, water, air, and fire are taken with theoretical seriousness by Aristotle, and composed, according to his physics, of two pairs of contrary qualities which have mathematical-like relations to each other.[18] Christianity marks a further limitation and a channeling of the early mythic investiture. Christians and Jews are the religiously jealous people of history. Their god could bear no rival. Accordingly, the Greek daemons or spirits, fiery beings who peopled the air and bore messages from the gods to the people of earth, were branded by the Christians as demons, beings of the under-earth. Milton's Hell is ruled by Beelzebub and other non-Christian spirits and deities. The sense of the sacred was redirected by Christianity exclusively upon certain objects. This burning bush, not just any fire, is the abode of Yhwa. Not the whole earth but just this plot of ground is cut out and set apart to serve as a holy place. Not in some indefinite time, in *illo tempore*, did the god live and have his being, doing good for man, but at a certain historical moment, namely during the reign of Augustus Ceasar. Not any bread or wine is a gift of god, but only that which has been consecrated by the priest according to the ritual set forth once and for all.[19]

This specific and disciplined directing of the mythic sense of the sacred (the Y of our formula) insured a gain, no doubt, in intensity but also a loss in pervasiveness. No doubt, too, this careful channeling of mythic power avoided the excesses depicted in Euripides' *Bacchae*. At the same time, the gain in intensity seemed to entail the development of a vast and increasingly political and worldly institution to protect the objects and circumstances which retained this intensified power of the sacred. The medieval Christians still preserved, though perhaps often in a weakened state,[20] the sense of a world created by God for man, a gift manifesting his handiwork, and used as a vehicle of his power.

But with the success of the Protestant Revolution, all sense of the earlier mythic investiture of the world, of the great natural beings of earth, water, air, fire, finally seemed to disappear. Nature, like man, had fallen completely from grace. The medieval use of symbols, the suffering man-god, the goddess mother, were rejected. The sacraments as the privileged, worldly channels of the divine power were refused. The consecrated bread and wine, so it was said, were nothing but ordinary bread and wine over which some unintelligible words had been mumbled; their rational religious use lay only in the emblematic common meal, celebrating the brotherhood of man. The medieval mythic investiture was withdrawn from the basic elements of the world.

Protestant Christians attempted to redirect investiture upon an otherworldly god grown somewhat abstract and upon an exacting morality based upon a sense of guilt. But even here, since a de-sacralized and fallen world offered no means of communication, a mystical leap of faith was required to make contact with god. It was not difficult to move through deism to a point where Newton's *Principia* — eventually without the "scholia" — became the sacred word. The earth (as well as water, air, and fire) became an aglomeration of material particles having only primary qualities. This view became known to some historians of philosophy as the neutral world. In this projection, there were no colors, no odors, no sounds, no values, no moral worth, no beauty. All these were regarded as merely imaginary, subjective, vaguely "projected" upon the externally existing reality. This extended reality itself was objective and measurable matter and motion.

This was and is the world of "impoverished reality." Its being was exhausted in the movements of minute masses in the infinite void of quality-less but measurable time and space: a mechanism in a machine shop. Thus the stage was set for the entrance of technological man and his culture. As yet only a few men of modern times have exhibited the Lucretian power to invest mythically this mechanical cosmos; one recalls Lord Russell's essay, "A Free Man's Worship." But such testimonials are rare. Men today do not live by them. Has, then, the power to effect mythical investiture been lost? Has it given way to "superior" psychic operations? Or is it merely transferred to other objects?

The power of mythical investiture is tantamount to the power of forming a world to which one is spontaneously and totally committed. A tradition becomes possible only under the firm grasp of such an investiture. Such an erotic power belongs to human being and cannot be lost. One is enduringly a worldly being since one is a cultural being, just as one is always a language-using being, even when silent. If these observations are true, then the power of mythical investiture cannot have been lost in modern times. This investiture and the correlative modality of objects must have been transferred to something doubtless more complex than the neutral universe just mentioned, although the neutral cosmos may remain a part of the modern investiture. One would, therefore, expect that a little probing would reveal that men in modern times still do live by a myth. To discover it, one has only to determine which objects, events, and traits are spontaneously regarded as either those unquestionably belonging to man or those toward which he unquestionably should strive. These are the objects, the traits, upon which life itself and its preservation and increase depend. These inviolate and indefeasible objects may not be sensed with the awe and wonder associated with religious and mythical things; they are, nevertheless, generally held with a reverence easily detected by the anxiety provoked in the average scientist as well as the average man when they are questioned or challenged. For when they are questioned or challenged, then the whole world seems to be falling away.

To display a little more clearly the function of world in determining common interpretations of the given, an illustration will be useful, and the modern Western world offers the appropriate one. I suggest that the characteristic of modern times in the West is that its people have mythically invested the following: the nation state, which is (ideally) structured by equal laws holding among equal citizens; a secularized and humanistic moral code, which should hold among individuals, enabling them to live free, peaceful and productive lives; reason, which is the capacity to be educated so that one can not only lead an orderly social life, but also, in the happier cases, contribute to understanding and subduing nature; science, or the application of mathematical reasoning to data acquired by objective observation and measurement; Progress,[21] conceived as the rational development of techniques of control over nature and society, continually achieving, thus, the betterment and divinizing of humanity.

I am suggesting, then, that the nation state, humanistic morality, reason, science, and Progress are the modern counterparts of earth, water, air, and fire. These factors express in greater detail the primary intention to harness natural energies for the greatest good of the greatest number. Such are the factors of the project-intention which form our world and give it a distinctive character and a communicable and powerfully persuasive direction (cf. MT p. 197). It may be questioned whether all these factors in all their senses are coherent with each other. If not, no doubt one of them would end by dominating the others and forcing their current meanings to conform to its own. The dominant one can be expected to be the one which appears at some given time to be most essential to realizing the primary intention of the projection.

These factors determine which aspects of which presentations will capture attention and which will be ignored. They determine which convictions and dispositions will be sought out and cultivated and which disowned. If reverence, or the mythical investiture, of these elements were to become annulled or weakened, our world could collapse, like ancient worlds before it. Though certain aspects of the modern world have been brought into question, the issue is not usually radical. It is usually accepted without question that our world's basic intentions are fully worthy of our allegiance and reverence. The normal questions concern, rather, their implementation. We ask, to take one instance, whether our schools really teach students to rely upon and to use their reason; perhaps another type of schooling would accomplish this task more effectively. But we will not risk our security or challenge our foundation to the point of genuinely wondering whether reason, as now usually understood and cultivated, is an appropriate recipient of mythical investiture. On the whole, we remain unquestioningly true to the Cartesian spirit.

Along with this orientation of contemporary reverence, there goes a characteristic way of viewing objects at the level of unspecialized common sense. Perhaps the best way of describing these objects is to note that they are abstract and metaphysical. By calling them metaphysical, attention is directed to the conviction that they are basic and standard. Terming them abstract serves to emphasize the contrast between contemporary objects and objects as perceived or interpreted in other projections, such as the medieval Christian, the classic, or the earlier Greek. In these latter, the object is comparatively concrete; to it are attributed not only presented qualities but also all the experienced values and significances the interpretative myths affirmed to be there.[22] To the Christian, for example, any object is created for man by God and bears within it the mark of God. The Christian seeks to understand the object as bearing that mark and uses the object, thus understood, to convert his mind and himself back again to his source and his destiny.[23] Also, a person advanced in the Christian discipline, e.g., a monk, was only living the life the ordinary Christian understood and would probably admit he should be living. Thus the specialist in the Christian life was not a specialist in the modern sense. He and the average medieval Christian belonged in the same common world, viewed objects in the same way, valued the same discipline, hoped for the same fate.

The object in the modern world, on the other hand, is shorn of many of its perceptual qualities and other once-experienced or experienceable significances and values. Rather, the modern mythical investiture finds or localizes in the object only or primarily the object's meaning for science and its use for technology. Modern man tends to look to the sciences to define objects for him. Thus his principles of interpretation are exiguous and tend to be precise and technical. His objects tend to be specialized, abstract.

A science defines an object for its use initially by abstracting from, or leaving aside, properties of the common and more concrete object which are irrelevant to the scientific procedures in question. Or as the matter may also be expressed, the scientist is trained to select from presentations just those elements or aspects amenable to treatment by his techniques of observation, measurement, and calculation. Scientific culture, embodying the views and values of the modern Western world, enjoin him to do so. An object for mechanics, for example, is a mass having location and momentum. If a bomb were dropped from a plane, or if the pilot fell from it, both could be shown to describe the same curve and attain the same acceleration (neglecting friction) in a given time-interval; that is to say, as objects they would be equivalent for physics. Physics must abstract from the humanity, or the non-objective character, of the falling pilot.

There is nothing surprising about this limitation. An object is always an-object-in-a-perspective; here the perspective belongs to the physicist. The unusual element lies in the disposition to take the physical object in a metaphysical sense and as standard, not only for scientific contexts but for other contexts as well, including the common one. One can, thereupon, seemingly ignore the physicist's perspective since it presumably belongs (or should belong) to everyone. Although the details of the physicist's objective view of the object are inaccessible to the non-specialist, still the physicist and his like are those to whom the modern world has learned to look for technological success and Progress, hence for the preservation of life and for its betterment (in the current sense of betterment).

Technology and its progress have thus increasingly become objects of mythical investiture; hence views like those of the physicist and the chemist have invaded common experience and largely determine the way objects are perceived and evaluated for current common experience, as well as for special experience. Thus, for the typically modern mind, any object is matter, externally existing, localized in isotropic, homogeneous space and in clock-time, and is (relatively) independent of the observer. Properties which really belong to it are measurable and calculable; their behavior is predictable, being determined according to mathematically expressible rules. The trained capacity for viewing objects in this manner is designated as "objective" and is evaluated very highly by everyone. In fact, it is popularly believed that the scientist thinks objectively, and hence correctly, about everything, and that everyone ought to aspire to the same skill. Such are some of the meanings given to the object under the mythical investiture of the project of natural science and technological Progress.

To the extent that science and technology and their progress have in modern times become the primary mythical investiture, even human beings tend to become nothing more than objects, subject to scientific analysis and technological manipulation. That people have become such objects (i.e., "human resources") to many politicians, military men, physicians, and laboratory investigators is easily documented. That they are also becoming such objects to ordinary men is suggested by the widespread favorable reaction to Lieutenant Calley, officer in tactical command of the My Lai massacre.

My purpose, however, is primarily to emphasize the dependence of object-interpretations not only upon presentations to be interpreted, but also upon world and its cultures in which interpretative principles are selected and used. The modern technological culture and world offer the handiest concrete illustration of the kind and extent of the dependence of culture and civilization upon the world. Despite the finality with which modern Western culture tends to view the scientific and technological world, no doubt it is well to remember from time to time that indefinitely many other worlds are also possible, and some one of these worlds could guide interpretation with equal convincingness into quite other channels.

Terminating this section with some brief but pithy phrase expressing the essence of world would be altogether appropriate. Essence, in the traditional sense, however, describing a definite class of beings by indicating their genus and differentiae, is hardly ascribable to world, the most inclusive concrete determinant of experience. For in what still more inclusive genus or locus would it be placed? Perhaps we might say that world is in being, but being is even more elusive than world. Nevertheless, in order to specify its meaning, we may look back over the preceding account and extract some of the important properties of world.

World is a mythically invested projection. As a projection, a context of all contexts, world is (ideally) a unified totality. As mythically invested, this projection is actually embodied in the intentional structure of men's living. It is a kind of faith. It imparts a characteristic style to all men's preferences, thoughts, and actions, and directs their development, although it, too, undergoes change in the dialectical interaction with peoples and cultures. Hence world is also an open-ended totality of intentions. As such, it is a dynamic form uniting self, others, and objects, or persons, society, and nature. In addition, we observe that world is embodied in cultures and is communicated by means of world symbols, for instance, by means of myths which intimate to a person or a culture its identity and orientation, its origin and its end. World thus rescues man from the merely animal. It is, finally, the basic pervasive determinant of interpretations. The basic determinants are most difficult to elicit from the several spontaneously functioning levels of one's culture. But they may be imagined to be characteristic, concrete embodiments of the primary apprehensions (being and non-being, one and many, good and evil, true and false, same and other). Let this description stand in lieu of a succinct definition of the essence of world.

§28. WORLD SYMBOLS

A world is a unity of intentions, the context of all contexts, a mythically invested projection. A culture is one possible exemplification of the structure and orientation of a world. Thus a world can be embodied in many partially different cultures. This embodiment of the structure and orientation of world in its member cultures and in the people who belong to and communicate the cultures is not merely an adventitious growth. It is, in an important sense, the response to powerfully effective symbols, world-symbols, I shall call them. These symbols represent, continually call to mind, and powerfully inculcate the ideas and ideals which have been mythically invested by a people and which belong to their world. A particularly forceful symbol of this kind for Western-world cultures is the Christian symbol of the crucified god. A more recent such symbol is the embalmed body of Lenin in his glass coffin with the red flag of the USSR waving (spiritually) above it. Elsewhere I have suggested that the Cyborg, that electronically contrived union of man and machine, could be a candidate for this symbolic status in the fully technological society (MT p. 152f.).

The function of these symbols is rhetorical. They summarize and review the mythical investment constituting the world to which a given culture belongs. They are the persuasive means of inculcating the feelings and beliefs of a people and hence of forming, uniting, and directing their attitudes and aspirations. Such symbols are objects of an unusual sort. Within a culture they are more or less universally interpreted as expressing and preserving the highest ideals. They body forth a world in communicable form and have only to be exhibited to inspire awe in the faithful. As it might be said, mana clusters about them. They belong to the rhetoric of the world and of religion.

Less specifically expressive than the world symbols mentioned above, but no less important as a part of the speech of the world to man, are great objects of art. Mana often collects no less effectively about them, perhaps even more so for being less attached to partly explicit meanings associated with a somewhat local time and place. Objects of these kinds, ritual objects, world symbols, great works of art, belong to a quite special class, the class of mythological objects; they form a class apart and are set into strong contrast both with the objects of everyday commerce and with the impersonally considered objects of the sciences. These objects invite a special study. In this study, however, we can do no more than recognize their existence alongside the objects of common experience on the one hand, and on the other, the specially defined objects of the sciences.

In sum, then, an object offers a number of dimensions of meaning as it emerges in the experience of man, the being who gives meaning. An object, a particular being in time, begins as a presentation and is interpreted on spontaneous and reflective levels by application of interpretative principles. The appropriate principles are initially determined by the mode, whether specialized, common or mythological, within which the interpretation proceeds. These modes and contexts occur within a wider projection, and are rendered persuasive by a mythical investiture which underwrites, as it were, the disposition to select certain types of contexts and to reject others. Objects thus become accessible to us through presentation and interpretation and through the determinants of interpretation: world, projection, disposition, and context. All these factors are present in possibility in our sensitive fields. Since great variety is possible within each of these factors, there is no wonder that cultures, which are embodiments of these factors, are discoverable in comparable variety. The experience of objects has, in the course of Western history, run a gamut from the primitive ritual object, heavy with magical powers (objects functioning as world symbols which harness and direct the energies of a people), to the object of common and everyday experience, and finally to the abstract, scientific object defined for laboratory and technological usage. Interpretations of the significance of the self likewise fall into these three kinds.

Such are the extremes of mythical investiture and such also are the varieties of the kinds of experienced objects and persons. This variety suggests something like a rough-and-ready scale for the measurement of person and object-experience. Toward one end, the non-objective dominates; toward the other, the objective is predominant (cf. §52). No doubt the ideal of human wholeness requires that one should remain in touch with both extremes. Thus the object of common experience would be situated somewhere toward the middle of this scale. Today, though, common experience has drifted in western cultures toward the abstract extreme. And the techniques directed toward knowing and controlling the environment and other people are far more assiduously cultivated than those which envisage self-knowledge and self control.

§29. LIMITATIONS ON THE EXPERIENCE OF OBJECTS

This doctrine of the interpretation and experience of objects cannot properly be labeled a cultural relativism, despite the fact that a number of expressions used may seem to suggest such a relativism. There are several non-cultural limitations inevitably placed upon experience.

We have observed that experience is made up of the interpretation of presentations. Now, that which is given, the presentation, is given precisely as it is. One cannot change it by wanting or imagining it to be different, whether "one" happens to be an individual, a nation, or a culture. Nor need interpreting it change it; interpretation gives it a meaning or a use within the percipient's projection. Clearly, there exists considerable freedom in identifying and using presentations and objects. An object appears differently, for example, in different contexts. Indeed, any object is rich enough to be patient of indefinitely many interpretations. Still, any meaning attributed to a presentation or object may fit it well or poorly. The truer, the more appropriate meaning, we must believe, will eventually win out, thanks to common sense and to the various techniques of verification allowed by one's world. Though the given is subject to many interpretations, the given itself places a limit upon the kind of interpretation to which it is subject (cf. p. 125f).

The contexts, projection, and mythical investiture which a person has acquired and which serve to interpret the presentations given, may themselves appear to be culturally relative. Perhaps the interpretative powers themselves are affirmed to be culturally relative, or perhaps only their use as developed in their history is thought to suffer from this relativity. Upon examination, however, neither alternative can be maintained.

The powers of interpretation are powers any being must possess in advance of experience, at least in possibility, in order to qualify as human. A non-human being cannot experience objects in the sense in which objects exhibit the dimensions of meaning explored in this chapter. There is no cultural relativity in these basic powers. To the contrary, cultures are relative to them. No doubt different cultures select and exploit different possibilities while leaving others dormant. Dormancy, though, is not non-existence. Possibilities must be already possessed before they can be selected for development or rejected as irrelevant, dangerous, or merely passed over in ignorance.

The ontology of man is the study and analysis of the powers characteristic of human being without reference to the physical or biological organs, the psychological mechanisms, or cultural institutions and the like, by which such powers are either realized or not realized in particular cases. The sciences which propound theories about such organs and mechanisms exist within contexts which utilize these powers, whether or not they are made the topic of an explicit examination. An ontological study of human being would display the limits of human being and determine what kinds of cultures he can and cannot enter into while at the same time persisting in his own being. The present chapter only approaches this study. Here I wish merely to call attention to these powers and to the kind of limitation they place upon the perception and experience of objects.

Let us speak of the "readiness" of the human being in the several respects he can act and be peculiarly human (MT §25). A man, a being having a sensitive field, is "ready" for the perception or experience of objects in space and time, for self-experience, and for the experience of others — in advance of the actual experience of these beings. Such experienceable beings fall within his ontological horizon and within his perceptual possibilities. The gamut of object-perception runs from the awe and fear created by a flash of lightning to the objectively conducted and carefully calculated experiments in the electronics laboratory. It makes sense to say that one can either perceive or not perceive in these ways. One's ontological "genes," to speak metaphorically, permit in principle these kinds of perception, as a dog's ontological "genes" reject them wholly.

The readiness, the power, to experience a presented "Z" as an object obviously cannot be gotten into the laboratory and weighed or otherwise measured (as if it, too, were an object), in order to acquire the data which would enable one to subject it to a science, and to exploit it. Nevertheless, this readiness is limited (see §51). Human possibilities are not infinite nor can they be varied according to whim.

Although this readiness cannot be gotten into a laboratory, it can be actualized in time and history. It is exhibited in different ways in different times and circumstances. Noting and comparing some of these differences will show that different aspects and dimensions of human power come upon the stage in a regular manner as circumstances and environment vary (cf. PC, chaps. 2, 3, 4).

The growth of the power to perceive and consider objects in the way now called objective has coincided with, is in fact correlative to, the growth of the natural sciences. But this development is not a sudden change projected into history by Galileo, Descartes, and other thinkers belonging to the Century of Genius. It was gradually prepared and seems to parallel a loss of the power to perceive and consider objects wonderingly and non-objectively. The spread and fragmentation of Christianity, no doubt, was a factor in this development. There is, in short, a relation between the events of the Renaissance and the emergence of the objective mind, Christianity standing as a sort of intermediary between mythically thinking and perceiving primitive man and objectively thinking and perceiving modern Western man.

Though the power of human perception is a very flexible power, a particular kind of perceiving can be brought into existence only after the historical preparation has been adequate and when the mythical investiture and the available contexts solicit it. The perception of objects cannot be termed merely culturally or historically relative. A way of perceiving is the product, rather, of a dialectic between human powers and past and present history as they operate in a kind of question and answer fashion upon that which is presented. The outcome of this dialogue is an interpreted environment, an intelligible ordering of the essential items, a human scene where men can live and work and where they can judge the outcome of their interpretations to be either true or false (cf. p. 203 and chap. 9).

Notes

1. The arch "in itself," or any object understood not as in someone's perception but as "in itself," may doubtless be understood as the sum or unity of all the possibilities of perceiving it. Or again, the possible perceptions of an object converge upon or point to the object "in itself." This opinion cannot be elaborated here. But I develop some views on converging and pointing and the related ontology in the last chapter of this essay.
2. There are, no doubt, levels in this process of selection. The sensory organs are selective by reason of their position and structure. The eye, for example, is not sensitive to ultraviolet or infrared but only to frequencies between these extremes. We also note that the sensing apparatus is selective in consequence of feedback and other arrangements of the nerves. In addition, there are habitual and reflective bases for selection. We shall be concerned with these later. Also see §52 on the temporal structure of meaning giving.

3. The term "intuition," often used in this connection, is ambiguous; sometimes it appears to refer to the pure presentation, sometimes to the presentation plus involuntary or habitual interpretation. I shall use the term only when this ambiguity is harmless or unavoidable. Also cf. chap. 2, note #3.
4. Phenomenologists often divide intentions into those that are passive, the involuntary and habitual ("spontaneous") ones, and those that are actively conscious ("reflective"). I shall adopt this terminology (cf. PC pp. 185ff.).
5. The view of perception developed here is quite different from the more generally familiar one of philosophers who wish to explain (rather than describe) perception within an empiricist and scientific context. For this latter view, see the article "Perception," in *Encyclopedia of Philosophy*, ed. Paul Edwards, 1967.
6. That gestural behavior is to be construed as a kind of natural language, I take to be obvious. But should some support for this view be needed, I mention the following. The meanings of gestures have to be learned; these meanings vary widely from culture to culture — a certain movement of the hand which means "goodbye" to an Italian means "come here" to an American. When one gains control of gestures, one can make them lie; I can, by facial expression and movement communicate great interest when in fact I am egregiously bored. Likewise, I can be mistaken in my understanding of another's gesture. Gesture can often be substituted for sentences. Finally, gestures, like linguistic expressions, can be ambiguous, ironic, literal, and the like. A gesture language, however, is not self-referential and self-critical as a language in the full sense is.
7. It could be observed that Hamlet would have no need to appear in this fashion. His death rendered the meaning of his life complete and evident. In this respect, the death of his father was quite different; it was an incomplete act, or so Hamlet interpreted it. My point, however, does not concern aesthetic value but communication, communication by means of dramatic participation or mimesis.
8. Much of the usual study of contexts has been confined to statements and examinations of their abstract interpretative principles. Context intentions and dispositions (to be mentioned later) have been slighted. And categories or basic interpretative principles have been treated mainly from a rationalist viewpoint. See chaps. 6 and 7 for further discussion of categories. See Aron Gurwitsch, *The Field of Consciousness* (Duquesne Univ. Press, 1964), pp. 318-25 for a discussion of contexts.
9. This power to see, to become quickly aware of resemblances between presentations and one's stock of standard object-images, is surely an essential human power. See MT, chap. 4. See p. 75 below.
10. We live and operate within a context of contexts. A context of contexts is a

close equivalent of the phenomenological notion of horizon, only the latter exploits the metaphor of an observer at the center of a landscape. The observer's horizon is structured around a center, limited in extent, vague near the edges, "belongs" to the observer and moves along with him, but overlaps others' horizons. One's horizon utilizes a portion of the common world, but world, as the term is used in this essay, is more than a horizon of horizons; it is more like the horizon of many possible cohering horizons and is unquestionably believed to embody Truth itself. See §27. And see my *Socratic Ignorance* (The Hague: Nijhoff, 1965), chap. 5.

11. Cf. Robert F. Gray, *The Sonjo of Tanganyika* (London and New York: Publication for the International African Institute by the Oxford University Press, 1963), pp. 36-39; 105; 126.
12. Ernst Cassirer, *Mythical Thought* trans. Ralph Manheim (New Haven, Conn.: Yale University Press, 1955), p. 75 and passim.
13. The term "world" or "life-world" is given several senses in philosophical cosmology. One of these senses refers to the most general unity of intentions manifested at a given epoch. Used in this way the term is similar to my "projection." The term is also used to refer to a total projection which is mythically invested (cf.§ 27) and is superordinate to my term "culture." I shall occasionally use the term in either of these senses as well as in more usual senses. The context will indicate the meaning (PC pp. 186ff., 222f., 292; MT §4D, pp. 104f., 192-4).
14. A projection which opens the way to certain kinds of experience — and closes it to others — also opens the way to correlative kinds of error. Two kinds of error will be briefly mentioned in this note.

Elements in a context may be disharmonious with the presentations they are intended to interpret truthfully. The phlogiston theory of heat proved to be an error of this kind. The belief that the moon is a perfect sphere was, for the age of Galileo, another. Was the Aristotelian view of qualitatively differentiated space another such error? I do not think so. The Aristotelian projection as well as its interpretative factors are very different from the Galilean. Space can be qualitatively differentiated in one context and qualitatively undifferentiated in another, without contradiction. Whole contexts can, however, be at variance with the presentations intended to be interpreted in them. A paranoid's context exhibits such systematic error, but the paranoid's context lies within a more general projection which includes paranoia as a systematically erroneous but meaningful possibility.

A second kind of disharmony is produced when a projection leads to pragmatically successful understanding of its objects; yet ironically such success may become too great. The disharmony in this instance stems from the persuasive power of a successful context. If the context is so successful in interpreting a large class of presentations, it may be assumed or inferred to be equally successful with others as well. Thus an effective science or technique may come to dictate an entire projection or to determine an entire culture. Failures are interpreted as deficiencies in technique or as minor discrepancies in theory which will surely be corrected in due time. Thus errors or difficulties are systematically concealed. The error in this case is not the paranoid's error, though it may share some characteristics of the paranoid's. Nor is it merely an ordinary instance of hasty generalization. The generalization achieves dominance because it acquires the all-encompassing power of a projection. There is nothing outside it which could question it, and everything within it is interpreted, *ex hypothesi*, in harmony with the general projection. Nevertheless, there are always innovators, revolutionaries, unreconstructed critics and ironists who participate only partly in their own culture and can endure the thought of radical change.

15. Responses here will include those associated with the archaic brain, that brain-like organ atop the spine shared by all vertebrates. Some physiologists have concluded that at this level of psychic operation, the distinction between internal (individual) and external (worldly) is not yet made.
16. Perhaps the more usual use of "myth" still refers to X as just described, but under the circumstances where Y is something like a minimal or even condescending response and Z is the environment colored and partly determined by a very different set of attitudes and beliefs. Such a myth has outlived its effectiveness; i.e., it is no longer "invested." Effective or invested myths are normally not recognized as myths.
17. Cf. F. M. Cornford, *Principium Sapentiae, The Origins of Greek Philosophical Thought*, ed. W. K. C. Guthrie (Cambridge University Press, 1952).
18. Cf. Aristotle, *On Generation and Corruption* 2. 2-6.
19. Of course, the early Greeks made distinctions between the more and the less holy and elaborated rituals for approaching the more holy. But I am alluding to the fact that the Christian world made a different and a sharper distinction between the holy and the worldly (secular).
20. I have in mind the Christian teaching that the world is a place of exile and of trial. The saint, however, learns to perceive the world as related back to its creator. But few are the saints.
21. "Progress" will be spelled with a capital when used thus to refer to an element in the modern mythical investiture.
22. A view of the difference between the concrete and the abstract will be developed in chap. 9. For the present, let the more concrete object be the one to which the greater number and variety of qualities are attributed (cf. MT pp. 228ff.).
23. Cf. St. Bonaventura, *The Mind's Road to God*, trans. George Boas (New York: The Liberal Arts Press, Inc., 1953).

VI

Categories and Paradoxes

§30. ON PRINCIPLES OF INTERPRETATION

Heidegger has remarked that a science is mature to the extent it can undergo a crisis in basic principles.[1] The same is true of philosophy and philosophers. Each is mature to the extent each can utilize crises as the occasion of return to fundamental principles (*archai*) with a critical mind and with the insight and courage to begin anew. In this chapter, we shall inquire into *archai*, whether they are uncovered in crises or in other ways. What are the principles we use in making interpretations? What is their structure and origin? Are some more basic than others? Are there alternatives to the ones we commonly use?

Once again, consider briefly an interpretation. The usual first stage is all but automatically accomplished by most of us. "There," one might say "is an inviting recurrence, something I need to identify or to understand better." The arresting recurrence is quickly placed in the class of discrete, persisting beings. The next step, identifying the being, is often more difficult. The operative cue is the being's similarity to things with which we are already acquainted. This reflective step, therefore, requires getting it into a context in which we already have some knowledge. Our prior knowledge of objects and kinds in this context provides the basis for making analogies of the unknown thing to objects at least partly known.[2] These analogies are (or provide) testable clues. Thus the large curved shape on my horizon: a parabola? No. An inverted catenary? Yes. An arch—the Saarinean Arch! The testing here in memory and imagination is quickly accomplished, and is hardly crucial. More interesting is placing it appropriately in a mythological context. Still more interesting is the critical problem whether the electron is to be placed in the context of material bodies (§35).

In the case of the Arch, the first recognition of its shape and size brought, so to speak, the figure out of its ground. From that point on, analogies to other shapes and to arches were easy to make and to test. Movements to more general principles — e.g., to the general structure of any conic — were unnecessary. This latter movement, though, is sometimes required, as it was in the instance of identifying the electron, or (by Einstein) in the instance of identifying matter (as the ratio of energy to a function of the maximum velocity). Even this last crucial instance reached only relatively basic principles. We, though, being concerned for an earlier beginning, pursue a grasp of first principles, principles necessary in any context.

We have, in fact, been engaged in various aspects of this inquiry since the beginning of this book and have now reflected upon several illustrations of rather important kinds of experiences: of space, of time, of self, of objects, even of the world itself wherein all are shaped. Such experiences have been presented as interpretations, spontaneous or reflective, of something already given or presented, whether in feeling, sense, imagination, memory or intellect. And these interpretations have been seen to fall into definite modes and to be used in many different sorts of contexts. Even so, interpretative principles would be unmanageably various were they not somehow reduced in number. This reduction is effected by distinguishing the non-derived from derivative principles. Thus we begin this investigation having in mind the distinction between basic and derived principles. To this distinction we add another: that between formal and non-formal (contentual) elements in principles of interpretation.

The task requires that we discern within the act of interpretation (within a perspective) the factors rendering it possible, and that we discover the origin and structure of these factors within the sensitive field. We shall find that the indispensible elements of this act are the categories, the basic and formal principles of interpretation from which other principles are derived. Therefore we may think of this chapter as directed toward understanding the structure and origin of categories. We shall discover that different kinds of categories are related by being placed at different points along a continuum of categories whose unity lies in their similarity of structure and in their common origin (§53), the categoreal matrix, finally being. We consider categories which are basic and formal and also categories which are only relatively basic, that is, are basic for some definite sector of experience (e.g., categories of the object or categories of human existence) and we shall take note of the relation of these categories to other derivative principles of interpretation.

Being and unity, Aristotle remarked in the Metaphysics (4. 1804a) "fall immediately into the genera or categories (gene)."[3] The Greeks of Aristotle's day were generally inclined to regard other ways of thought than theirs as barbarous, hence as unworthy of consideration. And Aristotle looked upon preceding philosophy and its principles as leading up to his own in the same way that childhood leads to adulthood. It is tempting to suspect that the lack of other and major competing ways of thought and their categoreal systems was responsible for Aristotle's conviction that his own set of categories was the sufficient, and, in fact, the only mature expression of being. Kant, too, though for different reasons, shared the same untroubled satisfaction with his categories. In recent times, however, all grounds for this contentment have disappeared. We are keenly aware that other cultures and their ways of thought and interpretation are as effective as our own. Interpretative power always operates within a particular world, culture, society, and a particular historical epoch. It is something like a talent which can be disciplined in different ways. The ancient Greek saw lightning as a fire cast by Zeus, whereas we see it as a discharge of static electricity. Either of us could be killed by it, but we would die for different reasons.

When different cultures are analytically examined, the principles by which their members thought and experienced their world may gradually be discerned. The purpose of one branch of anthropological study is precisely to engage in such a discernment. The present study is different. It is not interested in listing or describing different or competing sets of ontological or other principles. It is concerned mainly to grasp the nature of the perceiving, interpreting activity as such. In particular, it will be concerned to understand the structure and origin of primary principles of interpretation. Then by means of this understanding, this study will expect to discover the interrelation among abstract, everyday, and ontological categories, to display some of their modes of operation, and perhaps to discover their origin.

Are the differences among cultures and worlds so great as to destroy the possibility of a general study of categories? Granted that the average American's categories are different from those of, say, the average Greek of the Golden Age, may there not be something similar in the perceiving and interpretative activity which eventuated in their quite different interpretations? May it not be possible to discover a kind of categoreal matrix from which various sets of categories may be drawn? Obviously, there do exist many uniformities in human experience, thought, and interpretative activity. Indeed, at the level of common experience, very considerable similarity among the categories of a large number of Western cultures can be empirically established. Still, the observation that categories can vary markedly from world to world or from one historical epoch to another must guide the present study. At the same time, we shall expect the present study to find a common origin and common elements of structure for all categories, no matter how various in other respects.

This expectation is reasonable, for after all, experience is human and must exhibit the character of all things human. For example, experience is commonly of things in space and exhibits a temporal character; there must be recognizably recurrent elements (objects) in it, and commonly it is said to "belong" to me, the actor and observer, who utilizes his powers, his human being, in the formation and organization of his experience in a manner characteristic of his world and culture. It would seem probable that a further study of categories, their structure and origin, would reinforce our awareness of the effectiveness of other cultures and their different worlds, so that we would be compelled to ask once again how, exactly, being falls into diverse genera and categories.

Let us, then, return to the beginning. Where, though, is the beginning? Aristotle's remark suggests that a beginning, *archē*, is being. Let us follow his lead, not out of exaggerated respect for a long tradition in philosophic thought, but rather because the indispensible function played by the verb "to be" in Indo-European languages suggests its essential place in the essential human activity, speech and thought, and strongly suggests, therefore, its necessary place and presence on the wider horizon.

Being, as we have noted, has often seemed to be either too empty, too vaporous, or else too rich and complex to be grasped; hence attention was first directed upon its constitutive aspects or parts. In medieval times these constituting parts were said to be one and many, truth and falsity, good and evil, same and other, and similar transcendental notions. As noted earlier, these qualitative parts may be imagined to be present in being somewhat as the several colors are present in white light, as qualitative parts. These elements of interpretation, however, are in their turn indefinite and hardly more easily grasped than being itself. Besides, they seem to ignore the person, the philosopher, who somehow expects, at least since the Renaissance, to find himself in some sense at the beginning of his thought. Perhaps, then, the qualitative parts of being (one/many, good/evil, truth/falsity, and the others) are qualitative parts of our own power to be, to speak, to act, to experience. This expectation leads us to anticipate finding these qualitative parts, the indefinite notions, at the basis of all our experience.

A reference to the theory of intentionality will help make this contention persuasive. Observe that being and non-being, one and many, same and other are not exactly intentions. We do not ordinarily intend being or unity or sameness, as such. The effort to intend being as such, for example, inevitably ends in a vague nothing, a being in general, or a specific being, neither of which is precisely our meaning. Being in the present sense is, rather, a (qualitative) part of any intention. Let us consider, then, how these empty, even vague, yet necessary notions are related to the intention of a definite object.

When I intend the object in my hand as, say, a pen, I intend it as a being in present time and space, not as an illusion or a memory; it is many (its point, clip, barrel), yet a unity of these parts functioning together; it is the same as itself and as other pens, and other than, say, pencils; it is good since it writes easily, and evil in that it is a poor instrument for digging; it is true (utilizing the sense of truth recovered by Heidegger) in that it appears as itself, by way of my sensitive field; non-true in that my intending it as a writing instrument conceals from me its other ways of appearing. Also, it is true in the sense that the object in my hand corresponds correctly enough with the pen-image I have formed over the years (so that the pen-image serves as the appropriate interpretative principle in this context). Thus this object, indeed any object, is intended as possessing meanings (*logoi*) which are something like specializations of the primitive apprehensions: being, unity, truth, goodness, sameness and their opposites. Hence we do in fact find the qualitative parts of being at the basis of all our experience.

The indefinite terms being/non-being, one/many, true/false, and the others mentioned are themselves without content; the content in the above illustration consists in the references to my pen. Without much alteration, other pens, even any pen, might have been made the content. With still further alteration, the content might have been any instrument. Beyond any instrument is the object in general, and beyond that only indefiniteness where content has, in effect, disappeared. But this indefiniteness is not a mere nothing; it bears a reference to form. Indefinite terms, in a way still to be investigated, are involved in the noetic acts by which I perceive this object as my pen. That is, the notions (although empty of content and therefore indefinite) of being, unity, many, same, and the others refer us to the ways our perceiving and reflective powers have of organizing what is presented. The notions refer to indispensible parts or functions of any noetic act and are exhibited in the noematic result. Later, these indefinite notions will provide us with the key for understanding the categories. For the present, I note that both the classical tradition in philosophy and its modern inheritors can accept the suggestion that if the philosopher were to have only one thought, that thought would be the thought of being. Let us take this cue and seek to follow it to the beginning of the act of interpreting and thinking. Along such a route, the categories, our basic intentions, may come into view.[4]

We referred in section 17 to the experience of placing the mind in a state of diffuse awareness where recognition of objects, the contrasts and tensions among them, is allowed to fade into a somnolent and uncritical receptivity. I take this state of mind as one kind of beginning. Perhaps there are other simplified states of mind, but the one suggested is sufficient and is easily experienced. I take it as the thought of being in a very undifferentiated sense of that term, one including sensation, imagery, memory, feeling. Elsewhere I have called it the flow of feeling (MT, §8). The phrase "inherited conglomerate"[5] seems not inapt and suggests the relatively unorganized collection of recent and older mental acquisitions to which I refer. Here the mind merely accepts the presented flow of feeling, presentation, and imagery as it comes and does nothing, or only the unavoidable minumum, with this presented material. Now, the movement from this state into the waking world of objects is ordinarily too rapid in the average adult to be suggestive.

Let us, therefore, imagine the awareness of an infant at an age when he has not yet learned to distinguish among objects and scarcely to distinguish between himself and the not-self, for his "self" has scarcely yet taken form. We shall imagine that his state of mind resembles a kind of waking sleep. Yet, and especially for the infant, this state may not be quite peacefully somnolent. The diffuse background, not yet organized, may be sensed sometimes as comfortable and secure, sometimes as vaguely menacing, threatening to swallow up the obscurely aware self. It is indeterminate, confusing, and can be overwhelming, a phantasmagoria of presentations which may issue in almost anything. This diffuse awareness is the matter of perception, a matter which has received only the minimal organization, shaping it only as something "there" scarcely other than the perceiver, yet an other which is, somehow, "mine," just because it is sometimes menacing to a minimal self.

Normally, the way of meeting this menance and cancelling the threat begins by focusing the glance upon some part of it, some repetitive unity, some provocation for recollecting presentations in a definite manner. Then, by distinguishing this recurring unity from the background, the perceiver recognizes it as persistent, or the same thing. Or again, an element in an infant's environment may attract his efforts to grasp it; perhaps if it disappears, it will survive his impotence to grasp it and be recognized and grasped upon a later occasion, thus becoming both a persistent something and a something different from the infant himself. Also, its disappearance, its non-being, serves to render definite its appearance, its being. In any event, this process of separating out and recognizing or recollecting recurrent figures or beings eventually replaces the indeterminacy of the initial environment with a collection of familiar figures,[6] an achievement, for where the familiarity is greater, there the threat is less.

The final achievement is the giving of recurring or permanent form to elements within this minimally formed phantasmagoria of presentations. This forming or synthesizing function is accomplished in perception. There are many theories about this power. Aristotle believed that perception yielded direct access to the form or sensible species of objects, and that from this species the intelligible form or species could be abstracted. Kant's analysis reverses this relation in an important respect. He concluded that sensation contributes only the matter of perception, the formal component originating in the mind. Of these two theories, an objectivist and a subjectivist one, the more objective one (Aristotle's) found difficulties in accounting for the varied ways in which the same object is perceived, whereas the subjective view has difficulty in accounting for sameness in different perceptions. Plato's theory is more complex, more picturesque, and at the same time potentially more adequate. He held, in respect at least to sight, that one component of perception comes from outside, the ray of the sun reflected from the object, while another, the visual ray, issued from the eye (*Thaet.* 156D-7B; *Tim.* 45Bf). When these two rays mingle and marry, then there is perception of the object (MT pp. 103ff.).

The full-blown analogy of light to meaning runs, in my opinion, as follows: as the visible light of the sun is composed of all colors and shades, only some of which are selected, organized, and reflected to us by a given object, so the ray in the eye is being/non-being whose formal "colors" are one/many, same/other, etc., selections from which can be used for discerning some formal (or recollected) aspect of the intelligibility of given presentations. Thus the object selects the colors and shapes to be reflected into the eye; then this reflected, colored shape selects the interpretative elements "within" the eye, whereupon we say that the object-presentation communicates a particular meaning both possible and appropriate to that visual presentation. Now, it hardly matters whether with Plato we imagine that the stream from the eye begins at the eyeball and meets the light rays somewhere in space, or whether with the moderns we suppose this stream begins somewhere back in the brain or nervous system and meets the light rays in the eyeball. The point is that as the undifferentiated light rays are selected by the object to reflect its own shape and color — just the visual presentation of that object — so the undifferentiated stream of possible interpreting principles, of meanings that issue, so to speak, from or in the eye are in turn selected by the visual presentations, with the result that the presentations are interpreted as just that object sensed, against that ground, and in that context. The infant may not have many particular principles to bring to bear upon his presentations, but he has the primitive apprehensions of being and non-being, one and many, and the like, enough to initiate the dialectical and growing process of perception. (The sketch on page 25 pictures this concept of perception.)

The interpretation of presentations by interpreting principles is said to be like a marriage, for a marriage is the bestowal of a status and unity on two otherwise discrete people. The two persons acquire, thus, a new meaning; they form a family and are brought as an essential organ into the social body, responsible for their offspring. The act of meaning-giving, forming a new type of unity, is the element which marriage and perception have in common. Perception is an act of meaning-giving which brings a relatively independent unity of presentation and interpretation into the body of experience; the offspring of this act are particulars of a definite type.

Nor is this marriage without eugenic possibilities. Note that the metaphor offers a relatively independent factor (presentations) and a relatively dependent factor (interpretative principles) and their combination in a marriage or participation. This determinately variable union indicates the possibility of a discipline whereby the two factors can be regulated as measured by some common standard (scientific, common sense, aesthetic) which yields the same otherness in being (the enduring, separate identity) which section 21 found to be essential to an object.

The perceiving process understood in this manner is something like a reenactment of the cosmogonic marriage between Gaea, earth, and Ouranos, sky (cf. §3 and MT §4), only here Gaea is the rich but undifferentiated stream of meanings or interpreting principles which issue from or in the eye, and Ouranos is the determinate and limiting stream of light and shape reflected from the object. The result of this marriage is an interpreted presentation, the perceived particular, whose appearance is made possible by the opening ("chaos," our sensitive field) between the parents. The act of separating the parents is the mythic way of describing the ontological freedom intrinsic to the interpretative act, e.g., the freedom, the power, to perceive in this or that manner, in this or that context.

These mythological and Platonic accounts of perceiving may be brought up to date by briefly referring them to the phenomenological doctrine of intentionality.

This doctrine is best known in Edmund Husserl's version, developed in *Ideas* (*op. cit.*) and elsewhere. According to this version, the stream from the object, what I called presentations, is present as *hylē*, the matter of perception. The stream from (or in) the eye, the intentional stream, is analyzed by Husserl into two factors. One is the noetic activity which originates in consciousness. This is the activity forming *hylē* into meanings. The second factor is the issue from this activity: the noemata or meanings as such. The Platonic marriage of the two streams, the presentations and the noemata, is called by Husserl a sense bestowal or meaning giving. By reason of this bestowal the object becomes experienced as just the specific object which appears.

Husserl's metaphor, sense bestowal, has suggested to some of his interpretors various subjectivistic and objectivistic excesses. In fact the noema should properly be regarded as actualizing certain meanings which, among others, the object of reference supports. Thus consciousness is not idealistically regarded as originating or somehow producing the object. Nor is the independent object-in-itself perceived. This latter, whatever it is, may be regarded as consistent with indefinitely many possible meanings, some of which may be actualized by a perceiver. For perception is apprehension of meanings or of objects as meant. Meanings, however, are human products, not to be encountered in objects-in-themselves nor in nature apart from a human context. Meanings do not grow like berries on bushes. Rather by means of this remarkable noema, this meaning-of-the-object-as-perceived, I experience the actual existent object as bearing just this meaning or being an object with just this sense.

Of course the meaning given can be mistakenly bestowed. That is, the object can be erroneously perceived. Then the mistaken meaning will not prove to be concordant with other perspectives upon the object or with other experiences, other noemata. I may, for instance, endow the shadow in the corner with the meaning 'bear.' But if I shoot this 'bear,' I hit only the shadow.

I do not develop the phenomenological doctrine of intentionality in detail, only sufficiently to help fill out what has been said about object, interpreting, and interpretation (interpretative principles), but this reference complements the mythological and Platonic accounts and helps to point to the self-as-perceiver, just as a series of different noemata may point to an object.

Worth especial note is that no ground in this view of perception remains for supposing that some preferred modality of perceiving is in and of itself truer or superior to others. In the commonsense mode, for example, a piece of gold can be perceived as valuable and useful for the purchase of groceries just as truly as it can be perceived as yellow or heavy. Or in the mythological mode it can be perceived as a noumenal symbol of royalty just as truly as a chemist perceives it as a highly ductile metal. The decisive question is whether the synthesis — the marriage — of presentations of the object with the interpretations by the percipient is sustained in the several contexts and circumstances of the perceiving. The object itself is endlessly rich and is patient of indefinitely many perceivings, of many identifications, uses, and relations.

There are some psychologizing philosophers who have thought that the interpreting principles (images, etc.) are discovered "in the mind" much as the eye discovers objects, whereupon the mind takes note of the resemblance or its lack between the principle and the object-presentations. When the correspondence between the principle (e.g., an image) and the presentation is close, then the perception is said to be correct or true. No such reification of principles is intended here. The principle selected by the presentation *is* the perceiving. The marriage metaphor should correct any inclination to reify principles. Besides, neither Hume nor anyone else has discovered an observer in the mind who perceives the correspondence (or its lack) between reified principle and presentation (or object).

Characteristic of the process of perceiving is recognizing and recollecting recurrent unit elements in the flow of feeling. Perceiving is sensing *again*. It is the process of collecting and bringing together into object-unities the otherwise menacing, cloudy, and changing presentations. The resultant objects may eventually be more or less systematically classified or related to each other by family resemblance. Thus a vague and perhaps threatening background of fluctuating shadows is replaced by sets of definite and interrelated objects. Clearly, this process is one in which both the man and the object, the interpreter and the interpreted, make their distinctive contributions. I shall give the name "perception" to the activity which limits the flow of feelings, the flood of presentations, by gathering its similar and recurring elements into unities which may be still further analyzed and interpreted. Perception is re-presentation. As such, it is the process of forming a stable object-environment. Necessary factors in this formative process are the principles of interpretation. These principles may be either unexpressed or expressed. In either instance, they are active (noetic) principles, continuously effective in the act of perceiving or meaning-giving.

The objects which come to populate the real world are the resulting perceived (or perceivable) and experienced particulars. They are things subsumed under universals; they are interpreted presentations, presentations which appear together with their meanings (*logoi*). We call them phenomena; each is one of a kind. As we have already observed, the kind, the *logos*, is the (noematic) issue from interpretation, and each phenomenon may be grouped under its own kind or kinds. But when the universals (*logoi*) are regarded in their function of actively collecting and separating off groups of similar presentations, they are being considered noetically, as active principles of interpretation. This interpretative power, realized in any functioning principle of interpretation, is one of the essential components of that sensitive field through which we gain entry into a human world of spatio-temporal objects and selves, with other persons our co-interpretors.

Several kinds of interpretative principles have been mentioned up to this point; I summarize briefly. A principle of interpretation is any concept, imaginative possession, memory acquisition, paradigmatic image, etc., which can be used in the identification and interpretation of a factor or an item of experience. Thus my memory image of a mocking bird is used to identify and interpret a spot of singing color on the bough. The "spot of singing color" is, of course, already an interpretation of presentations. The interpreting image or principle and the interpreted spot are linked by a bond of similarity to which my context-intention has rendered me sensitive. The selected interpreting (noetic) principle is the perceiving.

Sometimes principles of interpretation are conceptualized; that is, they are criticized and defined with some clarity, as the concept "bird" would be defined by the ornithologist. Still others are inalienably concrete: compare Keats' nightingale or "l'Oiseau Prophète." Some principles are basic; some derived. The basic principles, those not derived within some context, are the categories of that context. Thus we might speak of the categories of typically human experience (cf. §37f.).

Earlier in this section we were led to ask whether there are any categories basic to all contexts. If so, we concluded, they must have no content, nothing which is peculiar to any context; hence they must be entirely formal. And we suspected that such formal categories would be closely related to the indefinite notions, being, one, same, and the like, which belong to all contexts. It is evident, however, that the indefiniteness of the transcendental notions would have to be in some fashion neutralized and limited if they are to be used in the structure of categories. Our effort to effect this neutralization would be advanced if we were to acquire some understanding of the origin of categories. We broach this topic in the next section but will not conclude it until the last chapter, if even then.

§31. ON THE ORIGIN OF CATEGORIES (PRELIMINARY)

Given a man in an environment and a world, a necessary task lies in dealing with that environment and with the obstacles it places before continued existence within it. Like the infant already alluded to, we are inclined to tackle the matter by splitting the environment or the problematic situation up into events and objects, and kinds of events and objects. We proceed further by splitting these into parts, properties, accidents, aspects, and functions, each of which can be treated over again as object. As Bergson remarked, perception atomizes the world; it also collects the atoms into complexes that belong together. Perception is analytic and collecting. (We may say that the analytic act issues in the object's discreteness; the collecting act issues in its unity [cf. §20].) Categories of object experience are determined by the lines of the first and basic cleavages.

That the process of collecting and analyzing proceeds in a relatively regular fashion is altogether obvious. That is, it proceeds according to principles and rules. The child who succeeds in distinguishing the ball from the grass in which it is lying can use this experience to make the distinction more easily a second time, and then can apply it when the grass is replaced by a flower bed or by the pebbles of a driveway. He has acquired a rule for distinguishing such objects, an important interpretative principle.

An interpretative principle is rather like a habit of behavior. It arises from the sensitive field as an element in consciousness, rendering a certain kind of action possible in the same way a rule of operation is "in" the knowing hand and practiced eye of an artist. Such a principle can be abstracted and communicated or related to other principles (though it need not be).

The principle used in distinguishing the ball from its environment is derivative of a more basic distinction between spatial figure and ground, and this, in turn, from a still more fundamental contrast between same and other. The most basic of such principles we shall regard as categories. The categories thus specify the lines of the first and primary cleavages into which we split the environment so that we may enter it and come to know and use it. Categories in the noetic sense effect these cleavages. In the noematic sense, they record the effects of such divisions. A fundamental division, separating power from the direction or use of power, is represented among the categories by the modal distinction between objective categories and the categories of freedom or existence. And there may be other such distinctions. The grand difficulty of understanding our continued existence in the world seems, thus, to be divisible into many smaller problems of dealing appropriately with objects, persons, properties, aspects, inter-relations, and functions into which the environment has been divided.

Any list of categories in common use offers kinds of beings or objects which persist in their sameness or identity, are other than other beings, are localized in their own places and times, and undergo modifications in quality, in quantity, and in relation to others while remaining one and the same. The very general and formal categories I shall develop here are rendered more specific and limited first by the world within which they are developed (we shall return to this topic in § 39), and secondly, not only by the presentations which the interpreter happens to receive, but also by the interpreter's intentions (including context-intention), by the kind of problem which calls forth his interpretative efforts, and by his accumulated past experiences and generalizations from these experiences. At present, attention will be directed primarily upon the formal nature of categories rather than upon presentations or other content.

Let us begin with a preliminary consideration of the source of our basic principles of interpretation. I take it as obvious that categories are neither bequeathed us by some benevolent or malevolent power, nor are they always our own arbitrary inventions. Kant asked the question about the source of categories, at least incipiently, and noted that one category in each group of three was produced by a kind of mutual limitation of the other two of the group.[7] But he had nothing to say about the source of the two originating categories beyond noting that they had long been in use. Doubtless he is correct; some of his categories are basic, some derived. The interesting matter concerns the origin of basic categories. I want to indicate a way of understanding their origin in certain of our apprehensions and their development from this origin. This development moves by a process of limitation which perhaps recalls Kant's view, only this limiting process is not exercised upon still more basic categories but upon something non-categoreal. These non-categoreal sources of categories I call indefinite notions.

Interpretative principles which are genuinely basic and hence categories in the proper sense cannot have definite content, for such content would be already the product of prior categorizing, and the categories generated from such content would not be basic. Basic interpretative principles, then, must be formal, empty.

Kant held that his categories are already formal, their content being derived from another source, viz., from sensibility. But Kant needed some means for guiding the imposition of formal categories (or categoreal acts) upon their sensory content, otherwise the imposition of the formal categories upon their content would have been arbitrary. Kant found this guide in the temporal schemata of the imagination. A separate doctrine of schemata is not necessary if it can be seen that the formal categories in question are presupposed by actual experience. For the actuality of experience entails its possbility, or its transcendental validity. And the categories are the functional parts of this possibility. I doubt, though, that any specific set of categories (like Aristotle's or Kant's) could be justified by the suggested procedure. I shall be content to show that an indefinite number of categories of a given type and constructed in a specified manner are possible. The categories actually selected from this matrix will be a function of other and non-formal factors (cf. §33).

My suggestion concerning the origin of categories begins with the sense of power-to . . ., impotence-to . . . associated with, emphasized by, modified by, or cancelled out by elements in the flow of feeling, sense, imagery, and memory of our waking life. We witness in this sense an awareness of human possibilities, at first an indistinct awareness, to be sure, but one destined to become increasingly determinate. Our examination has already discovered a complexity in this sense of possibility which once was expressed in the transcendentals, so called, of the Greek and medieval traditions. The sense of power or impotence refers us first to a power to be or not to be, to be present or absent. The sense of being or power is further particularized by the remaining transcendentals, one/many, same/other, and the others, which are analytic of being.[8] These transcendental apprehensions, global apprehensions of our own possibilities, are primitive and indefinite.

The next step is to understand how these most primitive and least definite apprehensions can be specified according to some rule to the point they can be given relatively precise contents and be made effective in the enterprise of interpreting our experience. In the very nature of the case, such an attempt cannot proceed by an application of clear-cut ideas and conventional techniques. For just this reason, it is attended with paradox.[9] I wish now to specify as well as I can the primitive and indefinite notions containing implicitly the origins of categories, then to suggest a way they may be derived which will account for the formal structure of categories and will neither ignore the paradoxes involved nor surrender to unintelligibility.

At the beginning we find what may as well be called the notion of being/non-being. It is exemplified in the welter of presentations, imagery, and feeling — the idea of being mentioned in the preceding section — and imparts some minimal form to our environmental responses at even the lowest of accessible levels. The other transcendentals elicit other aspects of the rich and fertile idea of being, for these other notions are only slightly less indefinite than being/non-being, and they do express characteristics of any being which can fall within our experience. Any being is one in some sense, many in some sense, good in some sense, not so in others, and so forth.

The presence of these notions in opposing pairs is nothing captious but represents a generalization of our habit of recognizing a definite thing by way of its contrast with what it is not. Thus a part of the definition of "four" is that it is not "five"; an object becomes distinct to perception by way of contrast to its globally perceived background, and our own identities develop definiteness by being distinguished from that which is different from us. We shall, therefore, look for the formative elements of interpretation in these initially indefinite notions, notions of which we are hardly aware, nor do they ordinarily form the topic for thought; they are, nevertheless, essentially present in any perception and in any intention or thought and stand in contrast to their opposites. We shall take these notions as intuitive apprehensions, or as partial and primary intentions which are traits of our sensitive field, always present in the stream which issues from or in the eye — to recur to Plato's metaphor — and which function in the selection and interpretation of presentations, forming them into perceptions of objects. Categories understood as the basic kinds of interpreting acts take their origin in these indefinite notions sensed within our awareness of power-to . . ., impotence-to. . . . And the most comprehensive of these indefinite notions is being/non-being.

The origin of the categories, then, lies in being, just as Aristotle suggested, though we may not mean by this term quite what he meant. Contentless and formal categories, those which are to be discovered in all contexts, begin with being/non-being. But they cannot be identified with this or any other indefinite notion, for categories are definite, basic principles of interpretation. Perhaps then, they are, or contain, a structure of several such indefinite notions.

§32. ON THE STRUCTURE OF CATEGORIES

But what kind of structure? The function of this section will be to form a concept of the primary noetic acts immediately or derivatively effective in any perceiving, thinking, or experiencing.

I find in Plato's writings the suggestion that the structure of a basic principle of interpretation is to be sought in the opposition of indefinite notions or apprehensions. This structure can be understood as a paradoxical compromise and a mutual limitation of opposing indefinite notions. This supposition of a close relationship between category and paradox is nothing new. The insight was displayed especially clearly in the *Parmenides*, but elsewhere also, e.g., in the *Republic*. We shall offer an illustration of a paradox and of a category formed on the Platonic model and then venture a generalization concerning the formal structure of categories and other interpretative principles. It should be emphasized that we turn to Plato, not in order to determine what he meant or did not mean, but wholly for the purpose of finding what light his writing may shed upon the categories.

In *Republic* 523B-525D Socrates observes that the middle finger of three unequally long fingers presents a puzzle to thought, for it is larger than one finger and smaller than the other. The paradox lies in the one finger having confusingly opposed properties; it is both large and small. Now, I suggest that the notions of largeness and smallness may be thought mutually to limit each other. The middle finger is not merely small; it is smaller than the larger finger. And the larger finger is not merely large; it is larger than the adjoining finger. For some purposes, the determination "larger than" is sufficient. For other purposes, though, a difficulty may be found in the fact that the finger's smallness (to consider only one of the opposites) may be limited in indefinitely many ways; that is, there are indefinitely many possible fingers both smaller than the larger finger and larger than the smaller finger.

The next step taken by Socrates is to show that the confusion engendered by a finger being both large and small may be cleared up by the art of quantitative measurement. In order to execute this measurement, we first separate each finger from one of its properties, in this instance a quantitative property, its length, and replace each finger by its (abstract) length. So now the length of each finger can be measured by some equal and common unit of length; then one of these fingers, the middle, will appear to be larger *by so much* (i.e., by so many units of length) than another, and smaller *by so much* than the remaining fingers' length. Here the intelligibility (*logos*) of the finger is located somewhere between extremes, and these extremes, larger and smaller, are quantitatively specified. The middle finger can then be located in the class of things just so long. And the other two fingers are analogously placed. Thus the appropriate sense of largeness as opposed to smallness is selected by the art of measurement. Relations among the fingers can now be expressed in ratios. Here the lengths of the fingers are no longer simple opposites; their opposition has been translated into determinate ratios, so the paradox seems to have disappeared.

In fact, though, the paradox is only postponed, for in the operation of measuring the fingers by the standard length, exactitude was not achieved; in fact, it was not achievable (as Plato pointed out in *Phaedo* 74A-75B). In determining the unit length on a finger, an error would inevitably have been made which would render the unit measured on the finger either too small or too large, a fact always determinable by still more careful measurements. Also, it might be noticed that the numerical side of the quantitative unit (the one which measures) is paradoxical in its own right, being modified by contrary notions. The unit is at once larger than some numbers and smaller than others. Thus it is both large and small; its identity, too, is brought into question, but the question can be quickly resolved by determining through counting how much larger or smaller it is than some given number (and the rational integers of the number system are, so to speak, already measured).

We note, then, that the original problematical thing, the finger as described in opposing terms, is at least relatively clarified, for its confusing character is transferred to the unit and techniques of measure. Then, when an analogous technique is brought to bear upon the puzzling aspect of the unit and the techniques of measure, a still greater clarification can be achieved. Here the process of clarification is applied to preceding results of the process. Although this example illustrates a process of interpretation (see chap. 8 of this study), it does not, of course, reach basic principles or categories. The *Parmenides*, however, seems to offer something like a generalization of this procedure and does carry the paradoxes involved back to basic notions.

The conclusion of the first part of the *Parmenides* may be summarized by saying that the possibility of a science or of philosophic discussion depends upon there being something that retains intelligible identity apart from its changing and other-wise unclear illustrations, although the young Socrates understandably has difficulty in grasping the relation of this intelligible meaning to its many illustrations. In our example, the unit of measure and the numbers do retain their relatively clear-cut meanings apart from the initial confusedly related fingers. But as has just been suggested, this one identical and clear-cut unit of measure, too, tends upon investigation to become paradoxical. Still, an important point is that the measure, the theory, be distinct from its illustrations, or that the self-identical and invariant synthesizing element be distinguished from, yet seen along with, the flux of circumstances it is to unify and explain, for when the mind is enabled to "see" a *logos* or an invariant form along with presentations, then a curious thing may occur: the presentations appear as structured by this invariant form. The presentations thus acquire meaning and become as intelligible as — but no more intelligible than — the unifying *logos*, finally the category. They become "ones" of a more or less intelligible kind, phenomena embodying a *logos*. We may think of this process as gathering or synthesizing the presented flux (the content) in the form of a unity which is relatively clear since it is separated off from other similar unities.

Parmenides 137B-166 approaches somewhat closer to discerning the elements which constitute such a unifying principle. The first hypothesis (137B-142B) is an effort to determine what can be said about a unity which is only one, a one divided off and completely isolated from any object or relation which might compromise its unity. As will be recalled, the dialogue concludes that nothing at all can be said about this abstract unity. The notion is completely indefinable when isolated and separated from any kind of relation or embodiment. It is mere oneness, an identity which is simply identity apart from every other property; thus its identity is beyond our grasp and beyond analogy to anything we know; if it were analogous to or related to any object or situation through which it could be understood, it would not be completely isolated. We may recognize in this isolated one, this bare notion of identity, an element which, if modified by being restricted or partially denied, is always present in a category.

The second hypothesis (142C-155D) considers a one which is part of a continuum termed "being." It is a denial of the separation of one from being. This continuum is composed of parts, but they are not divided according to any rule nor differentiated according to an order. Here the one has become "ones," an indefinite many which may be collected in any fashion or united in any arbitrary manner whatsoever. Of this continuum of one and being, all predications can be affirmed or denied. Evidently the parts ("ones") which compose this continuum have no permanent identities, hence neither this continuum nor its parts are intelligible. Again, though, we may recognize in this notion of an indefinite many (not yet precisely identified) another element which, if partially denied, is always a constituent part of a category.

The first isolated "one" is beyond the grasp of our intellect, which can proceed only by collecting and comparing perceptions or objects and noting similarities as well as differences, e.g., comparative largeness, smallness, and the like.

The second "one" is below intellect, so to speak, for no order can be perceived among the shifting similarities and differences within the continuous parts of this amorphous being; their identities do not persist long enough to be collected into groups. These two notions appear to be extremely indefinite. But I suggest their indefiniteness follows from their primitive character rather than from their vagueness. Perhaps we have touched upon notions, which, however difficult to grasp in themselves, are always involved in perception or in intelligible discourse. These two "ones" of the first two hypotheses of the *Parmenides* seem to form the brackets, as it were, or indicate the bounds of the universe within which division and collection or determinate discourse can proceed. At least this supposition provides a hypothesis concerning the composition or structure of the formal component of categories.

I suggest that the way a universe of any kind is first delineated is a consequence of indefinite notions, such as one and many in the present instance, entering into some sort of mutually limiting relationship which defines a formal standpoint from which presentations, or other content, may be interpreted. Presentations provide the initial content; the one as limited by the many provides the prior formal structural unity, whereupon the interpreter sees or discovers this formal unity in the presentational or perceptual content.

We adopted in the preceding section the view that the primary intellectual powers of the human mind are two: viz., dividing and collecting. And in fact, we observe at every turn our quite fundamental power of dividing off or actively separating one kind of object from others, or parts or properties of objects from the whole; and then the objects or properties thus separated or divided off are collected together and apprehended as a whole, a manageable unit. The being and non-being of the mind seem to be most evidently expressed in just this power of collecting and dividing, synthesizing and analyzing.

This two-fold operation of the interpretative function of our sensitive field —our essential being — is exhibited in the generalized indefinite notions such as being/non-being, one/non-one, independent/dependent, good/evil, and the like. In their development from this origin, the fundamental formal structure of categories is determined. As the finger in our earlier illustration was both large and small, so any object is both being and non-being, any being is both one and many, both the same as some other beings and other than others; any value is both good and evil, and so on. The relation between these two opposites may be thought of as a mutually limiting relation. A being becomes determinate by contrast with what it is not. The unity of an object is limited to those senses in which it is not many. And its multiplicity is precisely its specific denial of unity. The good, or value, of a being is limited by just those ways in which it is evil, and vice versa. Just what the being, the unit, the value is, is another and additional matter (a matter of content). But the basic formal determination is such a limitation of indefinite notions.

In sum, *Parmenides* 137B-155D may be seen as exhibiting these two functions of mind independent of each other. The isolated one of the first hypothesis exemplifies the dividing function operating independently. The second hypothesis, the one which is being, presents the receptive or collecting function operating without restraint. Each of these hypotheses issued in unintelligibility. We are thus prepared for discovering that an intelligible hypothesis or concept will require that the two regularly function together. The myth of Ouranos and the dialogue tend to the same view. We take this view as pointing to the structure of a concept, an interpretative principle, or indeed of any product of the mind's operation, and expect, therefore, in any such product, to be able to separate the relatively unformed, contentual factor from the formal, organizing, and eventually directive factor.

Thus a formal concept which is both primary and intelligible (a category) is neither an isolated unity nor a one having all the properties of being without restriction (an undifferentiated many). In other words, one and many mutually limit each other and form that paradoxical unity of many which is a category. In its merely formal nature, however, a category is quite without content. But it is not for that reason merely nothing. It acquires content and can be used to impart structure to experience.

Plato offers an illustration of a category acquiring content in the third hypothesis of the *Parmenides* (155D-157A). The first step is to notice the introduction of the notion of time and change and the use of motion as an illustration (content). A moving being is not both at rest and in motion at the same time and in the same sense. One must deny predicating of it either rest or motion when these predicates are asserted without restriction. An object can be said to be both at rest and in motion only if these predicates are asserted in a limited sense; that is, each is partially denied. If the object is in motion, then it is not at rest at that time or in that relation. Such a limited affirmation forms a concept, a *logos*, which gathers a definite multiplicity under it by virtue of its power to exhibit the common unity or intelligibility of many particulars.

Perhaps we may be allowed to elaborate a little upon suggestions offered in the *Parmenides* (155D-155A) in order to examine the formation of another concept, the concept of change in motion (acceleration). Let us say the moving object is first at rest at time t_a and later in motion at time t_z; at what time, then, did it change and begin to be in motion? If slightly later than t_a — for example, at t_b — it is still at rest and again somewhat earlier than t_z — for example, at t_y — it is in motion, then the beginning of motion will be between t_b and t_y. If small increments of time are added to t_b and subtracted from t_y, the double series will converge on an instant, say t_{mn}, which will be a limiting moment, the very moment wherein the object at rest is ceasing to be at rest and is beginning to be in motion. This instant is the *exaiphnis*, the very moment of change itself. But clearly this instant cannot cover any span of time, for the thing cannot be both in motion and at rest in the same sense during a finite period of time, however brief. This definite instant of change in motion must be durationless, out of time; such an instant is more of the order of a concept than of a thing or a concrete moment. It is the concept of change in motion or of acceleration (or deceleration).

Unlike a former instance, where the paradoxical character of the length of a finger was managed by techniques of measurement, the category of motion and the concept of acceleration is rendered sufficiently definite without resort to limitation by a standard of quantitative measurement. The mutual limitation of opposed notions may finally be expressed in a definition which serves as a criterion of membership in the classes subsumed under the category in question. In much the same manner, another kind of concept might be specified in which the discrete object becomes continuous, the dependent being is independent, or the rather clearly viewed object is still partly ambiguous. Each such concept is defined by the blending of opposing notions brought into relation to presentations or to some other content within the context to which it is applied.

In the foregoing paragraphs I assumed the motion involved was physical movement from point to point through physical space, for it seemed that Plato had something like that kind of context in mind in *Parmenides* (155D-157A). The same formal category, however, can acquire other kinds of content. For example, the motion may be organic, the motion of growth and decay; an *exaiphnis* might be the change from organic immaturity to maturity. Or again, an understanding or motion in dramatic time might require this category; here an *exaiphnis* would be exemplified in the catastrophe and insight which brings one cycle of the movement to its end and prepares the way for another phase.

Consider another category, quality. Quality represents some sort of compromise between being present or absent in a substance. And specific qualities subsumed under a category of quality exhibit, as one might expect, the same kind of formal structure. Color (another non-basic principle) expresses a compromise between visual presence and absence. And specific colors, too, are similar compromises. Observe that a given color of the spectrum can be defined by two bordering colors which shade off indefinitely toward a common limit, the color we wish to define. Thus a concept of the color in question, a color perceptible in many instances, is delimited, as orange is defined between red and yellow. In this instance, as in the previous ones, we deny (a) that the type of color to be defined is identical with one of the boundary colors and (b) that the color is altogether different from, isolated from, its boundary colors.

Similarly, a definite musical note could be defined by relating it to two series of boundary tones, one higher, one lower, which converge upon it. And analogously, a species of plant or animal, a point in space, a moment in time, are definable. Aristotle, it will be recalled, defined the habitual kinds of behavior he termed virtues in a not dissimilar manner, by relating them to correlative excesses and defects. And finally, the approximating technique of measuring the finger by the unit length, which strikes a compromise between the too small and the too large, will also be recalled. We remember, too, our earlier utilization in chapter 2 of the visual clue to the nature of experienced space: this space is the class of the visually clear and the visually ambiguous; a particular distance is correlated with a particular compromise between clear and ambiguous.

In general, opposing or boundary notions become the component parts of a well-defined concept by a process of joint denial of the bordering notions. Such a concept can, then, perform two functions: (a) it divides off a multitude of similar objects from the prior, relatively indeterminate experience; (b) it unifies this multitude under a *logos* rendered specific by the process of joint denial just described. Certainly a most interesting feature of the *Parmenides* is its use of indefinite notions, one and being, which defined, as it were, the "space" (context) of ontology and within which arises the categorealizing and interpretative activity which constitutes a necessary step toward developing our world of objects, properties, and relations, located in space and time.[10]

We are now sufficiently prepared to give expression to the structure of a category. A category, a primary intention, whether emphasis be placed upon its meaning or its use, is, on its formal side, a compromise or a mutual limitation of two opposite indefinite notions which are the basic or general expressions of the collecting and dividing operations of the interpretative power inherent in our sensitive field. That is, a basic category is a formal or empty ratio of two opposing indefinite notions. On its contentual side, a category is any item or items of experience which can in some sense be both one and many, being and not being, same and other, good and evil, and the like. Categories having such content, though, are not basic except possibly as relative to the context wherein the categorealized content is to be found.

Let us turn next to consideration of some particular categories and to a terminology which will help clarify this view and illustrate the way a category acquires content.

§33. TERMINOLOGY FOR CATEGORIES

It will be needful now to develop three terms essential for the description of categories: indefinite notion, indefinite (or possible) category, definite category. These three terms will be sufficient both to enable us to speak relatively clearly about the formal character of categories and at the same time to preserve a salutory recollection of the paradoxes which categories involve and are designed to manage.

1) The indefinite notions are apprehensions we must have in order to form categories. They are the first specifications of our possible receptivity, our ways of seeing or sensing. It is as if we already possessed these indefinite or infinite

apprehensions and, by processes already indicated, turned them to use in the development and expression of categories. These indefinite apprehensions are the elementary and opposite notions whose synthesis, after the model suggested by Plato, constitute a possible category. Since well-defined terms are always terms classifiable within categories, and since indefinite terms have non-categorealized meanings, obviously these latter terms cannot be well-defined. The distinction between definite and these indefinite terms is important. It should always be possible to determine in a given instance whether a defined term refers to or describes a given object or idea, that is, whether the object, idea, or image does or does not belong within a given class. "Yellow" for example, correctly describes the objects in a well-defined class and is incorrectly applied to the objects in another. It is true or false to say that this wall is yellow, but to say that a mathematical equation is yellow or not yellow is nonsense. "One," on the contrary, as an indefinite term, can, in at least one of its many meanings, be truly descriptive of anything whatever, including itself. To say that this wall, or an equation, or anything else which can be named is a unity in some recognizable sense is meaningful. Each is also a multiplicity. In sum, categoreal terms are finite in their reference; indefinite terms are indefinite in theirs.

2) The meaning of a suggestion made earlier in this chapter is now more intelligible. The crux of the problem of understanding the structure of categoreal meaning was said to lie in grasping the movement from the (logically) earlier and indefinite notions to the finiteness and specificity of categories. This movement from the infinite or indefinite notions to the finite and formal categories is, in the first instance, accomplished by bringing two opposing indefinite notions into that relationship which has been called a joint denial of each of them. This joint denial is further analyzable into two acts, collecting and dividing, as has already been illustrated. The first act is an affirmation of their blending (collecting) i.e., of their continuous relationship, which is tantamount to a denial of the isolation of either one of the notions. The second act is a denial that either of the indefinite notions loses its identity owing to the denial of its isolation (i.e., a denial that the first denial is without restriction). Neither of the two opposing notions actually becomes the other. A unit of length is a unit of a quantitative multiplicity; quite different is the unity of an organism which is a living and indivisible organization of many organs. I will speak of "tensions" between opposed indefinite notions, for this word suggests a continuum of varying relations. This continuum is the indefinite or possible category.

An indefinite category, then, is the set of all possible tensions holding between one pair of opposing indefinite notions. It is a class of, say, many "ones" of all possible kinds. Such an indefinite (formal) category is a set of possible concepts. By "set" I mean, at the minimum, that the concepts thus specified are derivable by the operation of the two rules defining joint denial. By "possible" I mean that these concepts in any particular case are definite in principle, even if they have not as yet been exactly defined. Thus an indefinite category is the set of all possible formal concepts formed by jointly denying two opposed indefinite notions of each other such that if an X belongs in such a category, then it is not exclusively described by either of these boundary notions, but is identifiable by help of a formal concept which is a blend of both. The consequence of this relationship is that each indefinite notion limits the meaning of the other so that their infinite character becomes more definite.

Through a process describable in this manner, our primitive apprehensions take their first step toward becoming specific, intelligible, and useful in rendering other things intelligible. A multiplicity is understandable because it is also a unity; a unity is intelligible and applicable only if it is analyzable into many. We understand a being only if it is not another being yet is the same as itself. Non-being is intelligible only to the extent that it can be seen to be other than being. A truth is defined by way of its contrast with the relevant falsity. Indefinite notions, thus limiting each other, are ready, so to speak, for application to some kind of content.

(3) A definite category which can actually be used in specific instances, one with which we actually see or sense, would be a selection from the set of tensions between elementary notions which forms an indefinite or possible category. The selection is made by bringing, say, a particular one/many tension (a formal category) into relation with the presentations or objects intended to supply its content. The resultant (non-formal) concept or category may contain a series of increasingly specified sub-concepts useful in resolving the perplexity at hand.

Given a set of conditions for which a theory is to be constructed, or a *logos* to be discovered, what tension or definite relation between opposing indefinite notions is to be selected? Alternatively expressed, given a continuum of (formal) relations between two indefinite notions, i.e., a possible category, where is this continuum to be "cut" in order to produce a concept effective in the identification or organizing of presentations or objects? Here is a question of the use or intention the category is to serve. The answer is a function partly of the presentations or objects (matter or content) actually given, partly of the pre-existing situation and its context, and partly of the intentions of the interpreter.

Illustrations are everywhere at hand. An investigator, for example, to meet a need for determining the length of a finger, might cut the continuum of an indefinite category at the point where the many "ones" are all one centimeter in length; for counting apples, he would have cut the indefinite category where the many "ones" are all unit apples. The category would then be applied to interpret presentations, synthesizing redness, roundness, and the like into separate and countable unit beings, each of which is identified as an apple; these identifications are retained through time until the whole group is counted.

Such an application of interpretative principle is, of course, to be tried dialectically by reference to standards of evaluation appealing to teleological principles, and finally, no doubt, to the idea of the good. Perhaps, further, the idea of the good functions in its turn as an indefinite notion which together with its opposite, forms the indefinite category of value. A definite category of value selected therefrom may, when it acquires relevant content, operate as the ideal or standard, providing direction and a defense for the categories chosen for some particular task. The problem, however, of selecting an appropriate formal category from among those possible is complex; it develops by a dialectic not to be considered until the chapter 8. I wish at present merely to make the point that a definite category requires the selection for a purpose of a single formal concept out of a possible category.

In summary, joint denial and selection are our processes of deriving basic formal categories from opposing indefinite notions. This derivation determines the category's structure as a paradoxical compromise between opposing notions. The two procedures — denying isolation and denying indiscriminate blending — enable one to move effectively from the primitive apprehension of infinite notions to a series of more specific concepts, i.e., to the indefinite or possible (but still formal) category. A particular category is a single tension between indefinite notions selected from the indefinite category, partly under guidance of the end to be reached, and partly led by past achievements as well as by present presentations, and intentions, in order to fix and interpret the flow of presentations. Thus we are led to diversify and to render ever more determinate the inchoate idea of being/non-being with which we imagined the infant's experience to begin.

A category, then, may very well be a basic concept in the sense that it is not derived from definite prior concepts. But it is selected from a set of possible formal concepts and is derived from indefinite notions by joint denial. Atoms, orderly motions, the cosmos, begin logically in concepts. So do the things we identify and deal with in daily life. Basic concepts begin in a blending of opposed indefinite notions. Categories are, thus, basic but derived.

This view of the structure and origin of formal categories leads to two observations. In the first place, the technique of forming categories by joint denial and selection does not destroy or explain away the paradoxes involved. That a unity should not be applicable unless it is seen to be not a unity after all but a many, and that a multiplicity should not be understandable unless it can be seen to be a unity is a situation to perplex the mind that examines it. A basic concept we actually select represents a tacit agreement to ignore the paradox involved in order to make use of a specific compromise between the relevant indefinite notions. In times, though, of intellectual stress and catastrophe, as the history of science, philosophy, and culture demonstrate, the basic irrationality often becomes evident, and a way out of the difficulty may be sought by selecting another such compromise. The philosopher, then, as the thinker whose sense of paradox has been sharpened, should stand ready to perform the important function of helping to lead himself and others through periods of categoreal stress and change into some other compromise with paradox.

Finally, since history indicates that the categories actually used do change, it may be thought that categories are merely very general hypotheses and thus are subject to some kind of process of verification as if they were scientific hypotheses. In fact, many metaphysicians today who consider the problem of the categories associate themselves with scientists by referring to their study as hypothetical. They say that they are making a world hypothesis, the most inclusive of all hypotheses. Hypotheses, however, are specific concepts constructed within an area rendered limited and definite by the relevant categories, for they can be made clear and intelligible only within the universe defined by a set of categories. The philosopher, then, who is concerned to understand basic principles of interpretation cannot be making hypotheses about them. Rather, he is attempting to understand one of the conditions under which hypotheses can be made.

§34. ILLUSTRATIONS OF OBJECT CATEGORIES AND PARADOXES

In order to bring this view of the formation and structure of the formal nature of categories more within the realm of the familiar, I note briefly that Aristotle's categoreal schema exemplifies the characteristics which have been indicated, and indeed Kant's does also. The Aristotelian substance is explicitly said to be both being and non-being; quantity is both one and many. Only so can these categories be used to refer to the many (and only partly actual) substances, or to the many quantities and kinds of quantity with which we have to deal. Each of the categories is recognized to be a class of contraries. Aristotle writes concerning quantity, "It is the distinctive mark of quantity that it can be called equal and unequal" (*Categories*), 6a, 31-35). In addition, the definition of species is composed of genus, or that which is the same as the species to be defined, and differentiae, or that which is other than the other species of this genus; thus a species is a subordinate concept located between sameness and otherness. Aristotle, translating the same contrariety into other terms, pointed out that each species stands somewhere between the two extremes of privation and completeness (*Metaphysics*, 10, 1054d, 33-35).

Kant's contribution was to make the categories functional: he discovered in them noetic, or synthesizing, powers of mind. He also emphasized that aspect of their meaning we are now noting. His schematized categories are functions of unity and are receptive of the many, the pure or empirical manifold of intuition they collect and synthesize into various kinds of unities. This procedure certainly does not resolve the paradox of one and many, but merely, as one might say, activates it by means of the synthesizing and noetic power of the imagination and its schemata. And the fully categorealized and recognized object is anything but a simple unit entity, no less a strange thing (this combination of the *a priori* unity and the contingent many), than the *exaiphnis* of the *Parmenides*. I offer these observations drawn from the philosophies of Aristotle and Kant in order to strengthen the suggestion that the present account of the categoreal matrix offers nothing exactly new; it merely suggests that Aristotle's and Kant's categoreal sets can be drawn from this categoreal matrix.[11]

Considering a category from common and everyday experience would now be to the point. We might choose a familiar category, a category of experienced space, time, or object. But these topics have already received attention in chapters 2, 3, and 4. Another well-developed example of a concept belonging to common experience would be the Aristotelian understanding of substance, for substance is, formally, a concept of being and non-being; its content is limited to independent and recognizable things having properties in common with others. I dwell instead, though, for a moment upon a somewhat more primitive category, an infant's family. I have in mind a picture of the infant, or rather the infant-mother, surrounded by the others of his family. One may imagine the child's thought to move through some such stage as the following: one is to many as myself-mother is to the other familiar presences over whom I have less or no control. This interpretative principle, "family," is a rough one, no doubt, yet subject to refinement. It has received this refinement in Plato's *Phaedrus* in the grand figure of the family of gods circling through the heavens in perfect harmony around Hertha, their center. And again it received another kind of refinement from Euclid in his account of the perfect figure, a family of points equidistant from a given point. Expressed another way, one is to many as the invariant "circle" is to its values. Here the indefinite category one/many acquired limitation from its content in the field of geometrical points, as the others acquired their limitations from their contexts. I turn now to a more modern illustration.

Time, space, motion, and mass are often regarded as the categories of classical physics. It has become quite evident that mass, to select only one of these, is not a simple (i.e., non-composite) concept of a material unit. Nor is the unit-being (object) merely a compromise between such formal and infinite notions as being/non-being. It can be brought more closely within our reach by conceiving of it as schematized, i.e., as delimited within the rather general but still relatively indefinite notion of continuous/discrete. This recognition can be expressed by noting that mass, an ultimate physical entity as understood in the history of physics, is in fact the outcome of a decision concerning its discrete or continuous nature, its quality of being indivisible or divisible. When attention is concentrated either upon the discrete or upon the continuous character of the mass-particle, this definite character can become opened to question; its discreteness can be made to appear continuous, and vice versa. And in the dialectical movement of its history, these shifts have in fact occurred.

Dalton made this point with respect to the chemical composition of material objects when he argued that their continuously varying affinity for other chemical substances was only apparent. In point of fact the naturally discrete unit, the chemical element, is fixed in its weight, and each combines in fixed proportions with other atomic units. This externally fixed and discrete but internally homogeneous mass-particle was not a satisfactory concept either. It was too easy to ask embarrassing questions about it. For example, Dalton had nothing to say concerning the character of the interior of this particle, yet he might fairly have been asked about its composition. At the least, it is extended in space. Now, experienced space becomes mathematically intelligible to us when unified by geometrical concepts. But geometrical space is divisible and continuous. Hence this atom might be thought to be continuously divisible also. It will be unnecessary to recapitulate here all the arguments devised since Zeno's time to show that such a particle cannot be conceived of as either merely discrete or merely continuous. Perhaps, then, this particle must be understood somehow to be both discrete and continuous. That is, we must deny the unrestricted applicability of either of these predicates when used to describe the mass particle in space. The category of mass was, therefore, a definite compromise between these relatively indefinite notions. The later history of this category indicates that this compromise was not the only one possible.

Classical physics finally arrived at an adequate solution to its version of this problem: the solution involved arranging a somewhat different compromise between the two notions of discreteness and continuity. A definite quantity of that which resists change in motion, physicists held, is discrete in the sense that it is always clearly defined in position. Also, it is associated with a continuously variable force; consequently, its momentum is calculable at any moment. Mass, therefore, is a complex concept. It is discontinuous with reference to location in space. It is continuous with respect to time and velocity.

Within its limits, this concept was highly fruitful. Then it, and its associated techniques guided physicists to the discovery of new phenomena, e.g., the photo-electric effect, which suggested that the force associated with these particles did not vary continuously. Thus a crisis was provoked which led to a return to basic principles and issued in a radical change in theory. The outcome of this criticism has been to make the notions of discreteness and continuity more essentially (and at the same time more paradoxically) intrinsic to the elementary entity. For experiment shows it is in fact impossible to assign an exact (i.e., discrete) value both to the position and to the force or momentum referred to a microparticle.

Heisenberg's famous principle goes further and states, according to some interpreters, that it is theoretically impossible to determine both with precision. The two aspects of a particle then, its position (for which its discreteness is a necessary assumption) and its momentum (for which its nature is required to be continuous) are both essential to the particle. But both cannot be precisely described at the same time. If both descriptions are precise, then one is inapplicable. Two descriptions of this kind, both verifiable but both unobtainable simultaneously, are said to be complementary. The necessity for using these two descriptions strongly suggests the point I want to make, that the concepts from which such complementary theories are derived are more complex than they once were suspected to be.

The concept of mass is built upon a problem and is a compromise between opposing notions. The compromise is achieved by the joint denial of the opposing notions which enter into the composition of the concept. The crisis in physics associated with the formulation of the principle of complementarity was merely an occasion when the tension between the opposing elements of a concept commanded attention. My point is that all our concepts, even the most fundamental among them, exhibit a similar complexity or internal tension. Paradox, therefore, appears to be inherent in them. Moreover, as the illustrations adduced indicate, there may be many possible blends of the notions entering into the composition of a category. Those which have been elicited during the history of a science or a culture are selections from among indefinitely many categoreal possibilities. New data, new problems, new uses, elicit novel categoreal schemas which open up discoveries and unsuspected uses.[12]

§35. KINDS OF OBJECT CATEGORIES

Some useful points relative to categories can be made by classifying them with respect to their abstract or concrete modalities. The most sharply defined and abstract of categories are, of course, mathematical. In fact, classes of mathematical objects may often be described as partitioned. Classes are partitioned if and only if any two of them, placed in a single universe, mutually exclude each other and jointly exhaust the universe. For example, the class of circles is partitioned off from the class of squares. No figure is both. No Euclidean figure, that is, has sides which are both straight and curved.[13]

The application of mathematical categories to physical and other objects encounters non-mathematical difficulties which often can be managed by techniques of measurement. We can assign length, weight, and similar measured quantities to physical objects within definite limits of the too small or the too large. But special difficulties constantly occur. The question arose around the beginning of the century whether an electron is a physical object which can be measured in this manner. The question was settled by using Newton's laws as criteria. The electron was demonstrated to exhibit entropy, and so was placed in the category of physical objects. Now its momentum, diameter, charge and other quantitative properties have been measured. The same problem arises again today, though in a more difficult form, in regard to the neutrino.

The Cartesian metaphysical categories are modeled upon the mathematical; they are partitioned. Everything in Descartes' universe is either thinking or extended; nothing (properly) is both. With these exiguous principles of interpretation, Descartes undertook his metaphysical calculations. Little wonder he had to smuggle in other concepts (PC p. 72 and note #18).

Other specialties categorize and classify their objects with somewhat less precision. Consider, for instance, the shrew; is it a rodent or a primate? It can be placed in either family as seems convenient. The category of married persons is hardly more precise, since the unit-being, the married person, is not everywhere determined in the same way. Marriages are not made in heaven. Still, the category is definite enough for many practical purposes, the social-scientific, for example.

There are, in addition, "fuzzy" classes or sets. The notion of a fuzzy set is itself not particularly fuzzy; it refers to a class whose members exhibit the qualification for membership, not fully, but to some specifiable degree. The class of disabled veterans is in many contexts a fuzzy class, for it contains veterans who are not totally but only partially disabled. Thus a veteran who is only 60% disabled belongs only 60% in this class. Calculations can be performed on sets of this kind, but their usefulness in some of the social sciences has perhaps not been fully exploited.[14] Also, I can think of no philosophy which has as yet utilized the notion of fuzzy sets in defining its categories. But no doubt a future monograph will fill this gap.

Quite another kind of apparent fuzziness is exhibited in many categories commonly used in everyday commerce with objects in the world. Generally, these categories remain implicit. Merleau-Ponty, perhaps more than any other modern philosopher, has attempted to isolate and describe these categories. Consider, for example, the lived body and — if I may so name it — the lived mind. These are two distinct categories, although each is ambiguous. Each is partly and "in a sense" the other. This blend, strange to a Cartesian, is not merely the product of foggy and irresponsible thinking, but represents an effort to do justice to the experienced data with the language and concepts the observer has inherited and is obliged to employ if he is to communicate. The lived body acts not like a Cartesian machine but like a human body. The lived body is a unit-being (object) in time, limited by a non-being which excludes mechanical and predetermined behavior; the interpretative principle, "lived body," enables us to deal with bodies which are oriented and prethematically aware of their places and times, having a kind of implicit foreknowledge of the objects they are to manipulate, a foreknowledge which can be lost or distorted. This sense of body is close to that which Descartes criticized as childish and wished to expunge just because it included an element of soul (*anima*, cf. PC §8).

Likewise, the lived mind is a consciousness inseparable from a particular human body interwoven with its environment. It is exhibited by a speaker who unhesitatingly utters the appropriate next word in an as yet incompletely formulated sentence, as if concepts, language, situation, brain, and the muscles of his lips, tongue, and larynx were all inseparably engaged in the thinking-speaking process. Such ambiguous categories are scarcely useful in problems requiring translation into a calculus; nevertheless, they seem accurately to express operative categories present in common experience, in actual work, and in productive dealings with objects. These categories are perhaps especially useful in the arts and crafts, where the materials manipulated tend to appear to the artist as acquiring a life and exigency of their own, which render them all but one with the artist's intention.

Sometimes it is not easy to know what indefinite notions enter into the composition of a category of the object understood in this ambiguous sense. I offer as an illustration an object seeming to demand such an ambiguous category, the stone into which the sculptor projects or finds reflected his own vision and sensibility as he carves, for in this instance the stone may take on a kind of active personality. The stone is sometimes said (non-metaphorically?) to take charge of the sculpting, or at least to enter into dialogue with the artist. We may speak in this context of a mythical object-category. One might be inclined to recognize such a mythical object-category as a blend or tension of physical body and consciousness; these two are only relatively indefinite notions, and the tensions between them specify categories relative to special uses. We are on a sound course, I believe, if non-being and being, as understood in certain ontologies belonging to the European romantic tradition, be taken as the opposing indefinite notions which permit tensions of this kind. One must look to recent continental philosophers, to Heidegger and Merleau-Ponty, for example, to find serious studies of these categories.

On a spectrum running from the abstract to the concrete, these latter categories are evidently to be placed near the concrete extreme, in contrast to the clear and distinct mathematical and physical categories mentioned at the beginning of this section. This spectrum, then, runs from the mathematical and the physical, through the categories of common experience, to those which are concrete and mythical. The physical, mathematical categories are derived from common experience by removing some properties or aspects of the latter; thus these categories are reasonably classified as abstract, whereas the categories of myth utilize properties or aspects of common everyday experience, moreover adding to them. Thus the categories of myth may be held to be more concrete than the categories of common experience. No doubt the thinker using or devising a set of categories, for whatever reason, does well to consider the degree of abstraction his subject matter and his purpose demand. And he will place his categories appropriately on this spectrum (cf. §54), while not losing sight of other possibilities. Otherwise, he may find himself guilty of an irresponsible Cartesianism on the one hand, or of an inappropriate romanticism on the other.

Similar distinctions were expressed in the earlier chapters of this essay. Space, it will be recalled, is seen sometimes and for some purposes to be mathematical or mathematico-physical, but there is also a space of ordinary experience and a mythological space as well, as the discussion of archways indicated. A doctrine of categories is obligated to be as wide as the modes of possible experience. Convenient here is the Kantian notion of schema for designating the kind and degree of abstraction differentiating a mode of experience. A schema is the first and very general characterization of a definite kind of content. One of my illustrations ran thus: (one is to many as) one discrete being is to the (continuous) many as one discrete Daltonian atomic mass is to the many continuously varying in energy level. Schemata may be considered to direct one in performing the kind and degree of abstraction appropriate to some such mode of experience. They specify kinds of categories (cf. §53) and designate the very general context for some definite kind of pursuit.

Notes

1. Cf. *Being and Time*, p. 30.
2. See my *Socratic Ignorance*, pp. 124-8.
3. It will best suit my purposes here to work with an intuitive notion of class, genus, or type. Some of the difficulties of this notion are discussed by Fred Sommers in "Types and Ontology," *Philosophical Review*, 72 (1963), pp. 327-63. The difficulties he uncovers, and the resolution he offers, though important, are not particularly relevant to the present enterprise.
4. Linguistically inclined philosophers, with their quite different interests (these interests often are directed toward defending a nominalistic and naturalistic metaphysics), are disposed to follow another route to the categories. Professor Gilbert Ryle finds his clue in the misuse of language, which he terms the "type prank," or (later) the category mistake (cf. his "*Categories*" in *Logic and Language*, ed. A. Flew [Garden City, N. Y.: Doubleday and Co., 1953], pp. 281-98). He proposes to substitute different kinds of words for the subjects or predicates of acceptable sentences and thus to produce different kinds of absurdity. Then he proposes to track one of these kinds of

absurdity down to its lair among the categories. J. J. Smart, believing he is following Ryle's program, finds a difficulty (cf. his "A Note on Categories," *British J. of The Philos. of Science*, 4 [1953-54], pp. 227f). Consider the acceptable sentence "The seat of the chair is hard." Substitute "bed" for "chair" and an absurdity results, seemingly a category mistake, Smart says, and yet chair and bed both surely belong to the same category. Smart concludes that Ryle's program does not distinguish category mistakes sharply from other kinds of mistakes, and so does not offer a reliable way of discerning categories. (I must add, though, that since Aristotle's time, chair and bed have been regarded as species, not as categories or most inclusive types. Perhaps the error here lies in confusing a species mistake with a category mistake.) B. Harrison in "Category Mistakes and Rules of Language" (*Mind*, 74 [1963], pp. 224-34) works out a way of recognizing categoreal absurdity by reference to the physical pre-conditions for using linguistic rules. D. Hillman develops a method of generating categories by use of rules of phrase structure and Chomsky's transformation grammar, without reference to absurdity, in "On Grammars and Category Mistakes" (*Mind*, 72 [1963], pp. 224-34). Professor Willard Quine believes the categories, "a limning of the most general traits of reality," will emerge when the simplest and clearest pattern of canonical notation is discovered, cf. *Word and Object* (Cambridge, Mass.: The M. I. T. Press, 1960), p. 161. All of these ways of getting at the categories seem to be needlessly complex, counter-intuitive, and perhaps circular as well. Besides, all are directed toward categories understood as classification schemas, not toward categories understood as the noetic acts by which such schemas are produced. Also, all assume language as something already given and do not touch on categories functioning (noetically) to generate language.

5. This phrase comes from E. R. Dodds, *The Greeks and the Irrational* (Berkeley and Los Angeles, Calif.: University of California Press, 1963), chap. 7.
6. Cf. William James, *Text-Book of Psychology* (London: Macmillan, 1892), pp. 12f. Why is one set of recurrent presentations or objects more attractive than another? A difficult problem. See Paul Feyerarbend, *Against Method* (Atlantic Highlands: Humanities Press, 1975), chap. 10 for illustrations.
7. I. Kant, *Critique of Pure Reason*, trans. N. K. Smith (London: Macmillan, 1929), B111.
8. Cf. St. Thomas Aquinas *Concerning Truth*, Q.1, art.1 and Duns Scotus "Concerning Metaphysics" in *Philosophical Writings*, ed. and trans. Allan Wolter, 6th ed. (Indianapolis: Bobbs-Merrill Educational Publishing, 1978), pp. 3-13.
9. It is not useful to associate paradox vaguely with the non-orthodox. Neither in the present context is it to be specifically defined as contradiction, although some philosophers have attempted to do so. Contradiction is a spe-

cific form of opposition, a relation which can hold only between well-defined terms or classes. Here we are concerned with a stage prior to the formation of well-defined classes.

10. We have been dealing with two problems which some readers might prefer to have expressed separately: (1) the problem of constituting the meaning which is a category, (2) the problem of determining its reference or use. The intimate relation of these two problems can be made evident when note is taken of the two-fold sense of, say, "many" in the one/many opposition. On one hand, it is a component of the meaning of an interpretative principle; on the other, it refers to many objects. Or again, the unity which a category means is just the unity seen in the many objects which form its content and which it also denotes. The category expresses the *logos* of the "many" phenomena to which it refers. Consider quantity, which a large number of philosophers would regard as a category. It has a unitary sense: the measurable. Also, it is complex (many) in that there are, for example, many kinds of units of measure. In addition, the category refers to or subsumes the unit number, the meter stick, the pound, and the like, as well as quantities congruent with these units of measure. The complexity of meaning of the category arises from the fact that it does refer to indefinitely many kinds of such units. In this note the term "meaning" does not have the noetic sense often given it in the text.
11. For further ontological consideration of Aristotle's and Kant's categories see Joseph J. Kockelmaus, "Toward a Transcendental-Ontological Doctrine of Categories" in *Categories: A Colloquium*, ed. Henry W. Johnston, Jr. (Penn. State Univ., 1978), pp. 41-71.
12. According to a well-intentioned bit of advice, we are enjoined to look to the use of a concept in order to discover its meaning. I trust the preceding discussion will have demonstrated that this advice risks ignoring the complexity of a concept by directing attention primarily upon its many references and overlooking its unity. But the unity, the meaning, of a concept is precisely what tells us how to recognize an appropriate use. Thoughtful experiments, trial uses, may discover new meanings. And new meanings can point to unforeseen uses. "Don't look to the meaning, look to the use," is as short-sighted as the recommendation: "Don't look to the use: look to the meaning."

    Perhaps I should add that my references in this section to Dalton's revolutionary hypothesis was of course not intended to be biographical or historical. My point was that Dalton's atomic hypothesis, however he may have arrived at it, illustrates a new categorial principle exhibiting a new tension between its relatively indefinite component notions. Some historical particulars concerning Dalton's atomic hypothesis and the changes it effected in chemistry are discussed in Thomas S. Kuhn, *The Structure of Scientific*

Revolutions, International Encyclopedia of Unified Science, Foundations of the Unity of Science, ii, No. 2 (Chicago, Ill.: University of Chicago Press, 2nd. ed., 1970), chap. 10.

13. Professor Manley Thompson evidently thinks of philosophical-linguistic categories after this model. See his article "Categories," in *Encyclopedia of Philosophy*, ed. Paul Edwards (London & N.Y.: Macmillan Co., 1967).
14. Cf. L. A. Zadek, "A System-Theoretic View of Behavior Modification," in *Beyond the Punitive Society: Operant Conditioning, Social and Political Aspects*, ed. Harvey Wheeler (San Francisco, Calif.: W. H. Freeman and Co., 1973), pp. 160-169.

VII

Existential Categories

§36. CATEGORIES OF HUMAN BEING

When Oedipus the King stood upon the steps of the Palace and announced with unconscious and solemn irony to all present that he had decided to exile the slayer of Laius, whose presence in Thebes had angered the gods and brought a plague upon the citizens, he was giving forth only the concluding part of a complex decision. Prior to this judgment, he had already recognized himself as the happy father of a family and as the just King of Thebes, obligated, therefore, to rid the city of any dangers to his and to all other Theban families. Observe that his whole identity is bound up in this decision. To discover that he was not justly the king was already a deep political shock. To discover further that a radical error lay at the very basis of the decision in which he had identified himself as husband and father was the profoundest of personal shocks. The appropriate reaction to so astounding a discovery was to turn back in anxiety to the basic primary beliefs and motives which in the first place had led to his decision.

This experience of the shocked recognition of error concealing the meaning of basic principles and decisions, a recognition which sends critical thought back to its foundation, I have termed "archaic experience." Philosophy can appropriately turn its attention to the examination and appropriation of this kind of archaic experience, for the drama presents in an action what the philosopher finds to be a matter for thought. Our study of the structure of categories (*archai*) in the last chapter, however, was limited to the categories which are schematized to interpret object presentations and objects. They are not for the interpretation of human being.

Of course, a man is, in a sense, an object, and to a limited extent may be considered under the categories of the object. He occupies a definite space at a definite moment and exhibits the properties of mass, as well as chemical, biological, economic, and other objective properties. Also, in ordinary life he performs many menial and other tasks which can be executed just as well by non-human beings; he has long been used to taking the place of machines. In addition, though, he is a human being, and thus observably a non-object. His body is a human body enmeshed in the world, an element in a human dialectic and a manifestation of self-conscious awareness. He is the body-consciousness to which objects appear. That is to say, he is, or he carries with him, a sensitive field whereby presentations occur and are interpreted by application of his categories and derivative interpretative principles. Normally he experiences himself as the center and possessor of this sensitive perspective field and as owning a certain autonomy and directive power in relation to himself and to the objects appearing to him; he experiences others as like himself in these particulars. A man, therefore, is radically different from the objects which appear and which are dependent upon his sensitive field for their appearing. Thus, although a man may correctly and profitably be thought under object-categories in certain respects, in others, precisely those wherein he is most characteristically human, object-categories are materially inapplicable. Other non-objective categories have for sometime been used in describing and studying self-experience and specifically human behavior and human change. Here we question what some of these other interpretative principles are that they can be counted upon to render intelligible his non-objective nature, his sensitive field, and his typically human action. What interpretative principles, for example, would Oedipus probably have employed in order to render intelligible the events in which he had enmeshed himself and which issued in his dramatic change? After all, every separate and developed subject matter requires a set of principles designed to resolve its peculiar perplexities. Thus the categories and principles required by the physicist are not identical with those employed by the biologist, and both sets differ from those used by the economist, and so on. Here we turn our attention to the modally distinct categories useful for giving meaning to man as man, and in particular, for understanding and directing human change.

It might, nevertheless, be argued — in fact, up to Kierkegaard and Heidegger has unquestioningly been supposed by many philosophers — that the matter has already been settled and that no changes need be made in one's set of categories, merely because the user of these categories turns his attention upon the study of man. It has been assumed that the differences between man and other objects are all differences in complexity, not differences in categoreal kind. Still, it seems risky to suppose without reflection that the categories which suffice for the study of non-human objects should suffice also for the study of human being. Only a reified self could be expected to issue from this procedure. Human being's, however, know themselves immediately, from "within," from self-presentations. Consequently, they see themselves as standing in contrast to non-human things in very significant ways, if not in all ways. They embody a culture in themselves and in the societies they form for the protection and regulation of their lives. They are possessed of the unique power of laying out a sensitive field whereby objects, other persons and their own selves appear in characteristic ways, are divided into kinds, subjects, objects, and properties, and are then reunited into linguistically expressible complexes. They wonder about their lives and the world as thus organized; they incorporate their wonder in myths about their function and destiny. They are able, within limits, to direct objects and themselves toward ends of their own choosing. And they engage themselves in love relations with other persons and things. In these activities, human beings are altogether strange, unlike any object. They are non-objective as compared with the objective; they are the no-thing as compared with the something. And understanding them would surely seem to require non-objective interpretative principles appropriate for the interpretation of non-objective being.

The Procrustean attempt to force man into objective categories can hardly be inspired by anything other than a misplaced reverence for Occam's Razor or a misconceived awe of the more prestigious of the exact sciences. This attempt has issued in antinomies which recent philosophers have pointed out;[1] there is no further excuse for being caught in the hopeless project of capturing the human and the personal in the categories of the impersonal object. Experience of the human is modally *sui generis*.

Without more ado, therefore, I shall take it as evident that an unprejudiced examination of human life and its changes will reveal that we actually do use specifically human categories for self-interpretation. My purpose in this section will be to exhibit some of these categories and their structure.[2] Since the same mind is engaged in examination of the self as is engaged in the study of objects, the supposition that the categoreal matrix arising from the sensitive field should retain its formal structure in the two usages is scarcely surprising. But humanly relevant categories are unique and are modally distinct in their initial schematization. They are to be contrasted with such a quantitative schematization as that which we noted in the possible category continuous/discrete. Let us call this existential schematizing human being/non-being.

Again, we might continue to follow Plato's guiding suggestions in examining human categories. If so, we would probably turn to the *Sophist*, for it undertakes to begin with indefinite notions (being and non-being, same and other, motion and rest, one and many), and by specifying them, to develop a set of terms which will suffice for distinguishing the class of sophists from the non-sophists, with reference to the different kinds of linguistic images each produces. Our purpose, however, is somewhat different from Plato's, for our interest will be directed to understanding human change. Our needs, therefore, will be better met if we follow Plato's suggestions from afar. We shall, like Plato, begin with indefinite notions. But the indefinite categories actually utilized will receive their initial schematization from the necessary moments of human change. They will, in other words, be schematized and only relatively indefinite.

These five moments are related to the uniquely human character of the protagonist, to his process of change through decision, struggle, and insight, and finally to his need for being assured that this process is indeed moving him toward his true self. We shall see that the indefinite notions closely related to these five moments are being/non-being, same/other, one/many, good/evil, and true/

false. First, though, a general and preliminary discussion of these existential-dramatic categories will be offered.

§37. PRELIMINARY CONSIDERATIONS

All the categories which are implicated in human acts, and which formally constitute self-experience, may be viewed as variations upon two opposing relatively indefinite notions, human-being and human non-being. This opposition also refers us to the contrast between the non-objective and the objective, between the no-thing and the something, and suggests a series of possible concepts of the human which vary in the emphasis placed upon the non-human, natural, or objective component, in contrast to the emphasis placed upon the human, free, or non-objective. Human change is concrete and complex, however, and cannot be immediately considered under the tensions between formal indefinite notions (such as being/non-being) nor even with adequate specificity under the less abstract opposition between human being and human non-being. We shall, therefore, attempt to discern several relatively primary categories in a specific form, a form which allows the implicit paradoxes to emerge in close relation to the major involvements of human change and authentic time.

The categories I have in mind bear upon action and acquire and give meaning in their relation to alterations in men's character and identity. Now, the centrally important human change, according to a notable part of Western tradition, is directed toward the discovery of the self and the self's power to be or to become itself. But the effecting of this change is beset by paradox, for the self is both a directed power and a directing power; it is both given a meaning and meaning-giving. Or, as the tradition has said, man is both a natural and a non-natural being. The predicaments in which he finds himself follow from this central paradox.

The first step toward interpreting the changes a man must undergo makes use of a category I shall call the category of the protagonist. This category evolves from the recognition that a man is both determined by physical and other laws and is also free and answerable for the use of his freedom. His being lies at an indeterminate point between complete and fatalistic (or natural) determinism and an assertion of unrestricted freedom from nature, although these extremes are certainly not unexemplified in Western thought. Given such a category, a marriage between freedom and fate, and guided by the prevailing tradition of the Western world, we can identify the protagonist as a being who is able to pursue his own identity and the free use of his powers, but who encounters inner as well as outer obstacles in this pursuit, obstacles tending to limit or entirely override his freedom (cf. chap. 1, note #5 regarding the distinction between several senses of "freedom").

There are other paradoxes. A man is the same as himself, though he discovers this sameness by identifying himself with other persons or things, and he almost habitually makes alienating choices of that with which to identify himself. The society to which he is obligated often calls upon him to play roles or to execute tasks he finds to be stultifying or abhorrent. Often he finds the identity he has chosen and the struggles he has engaged in to have been altogether wrong and to have revealed only that he has misjudged his true self.

The next step, then, will be to discern the categories utilized in the pursuit of freedom through these paradoxes and obstacles. The movement to this end follows now, as it always has, a characteristic pattern. I shall mention this pattern here only briefly, for I have outlined it above (§ 16) and discussed it in more detail elsewhere.[3]

The pattern begins with a decision on the part of the protagonist, hero of his own drama and living his authentic time, to identify himself in some definite manner. As a rule, man being what he is, this decision is inevitably made in the shadow of hybris or of excessive or deficient confidence (or of excessive distrust) in his own independent but untested powers.[4] Then the action proceeds to a struggle, most often a losing struggle, to live according to the terms of this decision. It concludes with the dramatic action returning to the initiating decision, only with some new insight into its adequacy; usually the insight is negative and recognizes that the decision made by the protagonist was actually a hybritic misidentification of his true being. So the dramatic action (the non-objective dialectic, as I shall frequently call it), can begin again with a new and perhaps a more realistic decision. Thus the protagonist, in his pursuit of true self-knowledge and consciously directed human power, must possess three things: first, a category relevant to freedom; second, categories which will render decision, struggle, and insight intelligible and operable; and third, a category which will enable him to consider and evaluate his whole movement toward more complete and authentic being.

Each of these categories is necessary at some stage in effecting human change, and thus all are necessary for understanding it. This point should be made in a somewhat different manner before proceeding to a more detailed account. In order to make a decision at all, the protagonist must be in possession of the relevant freedom; also, he will require a language, a culture, and a tradition which will have schooled him to some skill in decision-making and also in some ideals of human life and, therefore, will have provided some hint of the direction in which the decision is to be made. This hint, indispensible to initiating the dialectic of human growth, is derived from the guidance and the models culture and tradition provide. Man, the political animal, is indefeasibly the product of his culture, as well as its maker.

The category involved represents a compromise between notions of the independent person and of cultural determination. In order that the protagonist should be able to struggle effectively to enact his decision, he must be a member of an ongoing society, one which will, for example, offer him alternative roles within which he can live, act and endeavor to be the self identified in his decision. Here the relevant category expresses a compromise between the notions of independent unity and individuality and of social constraint and determination. Then, in order to achieve the insight which marks the end of a dramatic action, the protagonist must have some sort of view of his place in the world, some cosmic picture of human life and its destiny against which to measure each particular insight and the good or evil character of the decision (or its success or failure) revealing the truth about himself. The opposing notions between which a definite category of this sort falls may be called the everyday and the mythological. And finally, the protagonist will have to think about the whole series of dramatic cycles through which he has passed and will pass. Does this life-movement, motivated by a drive to completeness, lead to a convergence upon his non-objective self-awareness, his true being? He will have to reflect upon the truth or falsity of the being he pursues and will, therefore, require a category which represents a compromise between authentic care for his self and carelessness of that self.

In sum, the protagonist will require a category located between the relatively indefinite notions of freedom and nature in order to understand himself as a possible protagonist in the first place. Then he will require categories of culture, society, and myth, and finally the category of authenticity needed to develop an account of the changes in character or identity which are to be undergone in an intelligible movement toward a true grasp of his being and of his own personal freedom. The relatively indefinite notions between which the latter four categories are respectively located are the following: person/culture, individual/society, mythological/everyday, authentic/careless (or inauthentic).

§38. THE EXISTENTIAL CATEGORIES

We begin the further examination of these categories by noting the way they are related back to, and schematize, the categoreal matrix, the opposing, formal, and indefinite notions with which all categories begin. I have suggested that the very general and formal indefinite notions we have already utilized in forming categories — being/non-being, one/many, and the like — can hardly be applied immediately in the analysis and understanding of human life. Rather, these formal notions are given a general content and direction by the several contexts just indicated above, and within which they are utilized. A model was offered in an earlier section (§35), where the formal indefinite category, one/many, was given an initial schema or generalized content, discrete/continuous, in order to develop a definite category of the elementary physical unit particle. Now, for existential usage, human being/non-being is also given an initial human orientation, a schematic content. The protagonist's possibility thus oriented is still his sensitive field. This field is felt as "power-to . . ."; it is first sensed as a certain freedom from necessity and instinctual determination. More positively, we may think of it as the beginning (*arche*) of a limited power to be human. For convenience, we shall denote this possible category by freedom/determination. Being endowed with this kind of possibility, the protagonist can embark upon the project of self-discovery and self-knowing with the consequence that he is enabled to understand and to direct his own powers in a more enlightened manner.

The first step in that project normally begins with the identification of oneself as the same as some type of person, a type which is other than persons of other types. Now, the guide in this decision is drawn from the possibilities offered by one's culture. Thus the culture, or some effective element within it, provides a content which gives the indefinite category same/other a general content (a kind of schematization) relevant to the need for identifying the self somewhere between a completely independent being and a ready-formed cultural ideal. Then, in obedience to this decision, the struggle to unify or coherently integrate many events with one's scattered powers is helped or hindered primarily by other persons. That is, the struggle takes place within an individual-social context which lends an initial content to the tensions between the formal indefinite notion, one/many, a content immediately relevant to the protagonist's efforts to integrate the many events in which he is involved into the unitary person with which his decision identified him. This schematic content I call individual/social. The insight in which the struggle for unity and identity culminates and which evaluates the initial decision is conceived within a context defined by a tension between the mythological and the everyday and lends a primary content to the formal indefinite category, good/evil.

Finally, the being which accrues to the protagonist in consequence of his repeated movement through this tragic cycle is sensed as either true or appropriate, authentically his own (as in the instance of Socrates), or as inauthentic and untrue (as in the instance of Macbeth). And thus the indefinite notions, true/false, are given an initial content, authentic/inauthentic, which narrows their formal generality further to the point where a definite category, useful in interpreting one's sense of the direction of his change toward his authentic being, can be envisaged.

Since everyone is engaged, willynilly, in the process of human change, everyone is actively involved in both the general paradoxes, being/non-being, same/other and the like, and the relatively more concrete but still indefinite principles relevant to the human context: freedom/determinism, person/culture, individual/social, mythological/everyday, and authentic/inauthentic. A person's interpretation of both his own and the general human predicament represents compromises either attained or sought between these conflicting notions. The possible compromises between these opposing relatively indefinite notions are the existential principles of interpretation.

Now let us return again, but still more closely, to the five existential categories to be derived from the several pairs of relatively indefinite notions just listed, and observe further the relation of the latter to the formal indefinite notions. The first of these oppositions, the human or free versus the natural, marks the extremes within which a concept of the protagonist and of his dramatic or non-objective dialectic is formulated. This possible category presents a series of tensions between the objectively determined and the totally non-objective. This possible category may be thought to refer back to the division between man and animal, crossed, according to a widespread bit of modern mythology, during a crucial epoch of our evolutionary past. This crossing was effected when the instinctual nature, still a major determinant of animal behavior, was separated from reason and choice, the primary means for directing human power and resolving the problems presented men by their environment and condition. The fact of this crossing represents man's willingness to take his fate as far as possible into his own hands, to be responsible for himself, and to appropriate his own powers. It expresses man's being and non-being, his limited power to use his reason and other talents to become an independent self.

What rationality is, how it determines decisions, the way and degree in which it differs from animal instinct or is freed from biological mechanisms are, of course, moot questions. Is human rationality and the freedom to follow it an exceptional creation originally given by god, or stolen from heaven? Is it the exceptional development of an organ or mode of behavior possessed also, though in less well-developed form, by other animals? Is it, perhaps, a dangerous over-specialization? Or could it be an epiphenomenon, a mere appearance and an illusion, so that, properly speaking and in spite of appearances and tradition, all is nature?

A concept of man or of humanity, then, contains among its constituents one of the many possible compromises between the extremes of total or unrestricted freedom and a thorough, natural determinism. The more closely the human being is assimilated to the natural or animal, the less his human or rational power appears to influence his behavior, and the less his will is thought to be free. On this basic matter, philosophers range in their opinions all the way from Sartre to the behaviorists, all the way from condemnation to unlimited liberty, to a complete surrender of freedom and dignity in the interests of an idiosyncratic notion of science and technology. These opinions represent the compromises between the opposing notions of the free and of the determined, between the human and the natural. Evidently, then, there exists a whole spectrum of possible views concerning the relation of the human and free to the natural. These views collectively specify an indefinite or possible category. Any particular philosophy of man would select one of the tensions within this indefinite category and develop arguments supporting it and excluding other competing categories. Thus it would establish a definite category, the category of the human, the category of the dramatic protagonist.

Three existential tensions related to the crucial turning points in the career of this dramatic protagonist are the sources of principles needed for an understanding of his growth into maturity and self-knowledge, and are the instruments he utilizes to give himself an appropriate meaning. The first of these tensions holds between the notions of person and culture, the lone and separate person and the collectively produced and commonly owned culture. Culture is often said to be to the human being what instinct is to the animal. Culture is a structure of convictions, values, and ideals — mostly implicit — characteristic of a people over a considerable portion of their history (MT pp. 108f., 237, note # 17). Culture is commonly relied upon to provide at least the initial answer to questions concerning the identity and use of objects, the identity and value of persons, the total career and probable destiny of man. The several arts, language, customs and other ways of communicating culture have over the millennia molded the savage to the forms of civilization. Certainly, in the more civilized and sophisticated cultures, an ideal of personhood has become important. The person in this sense lives his culture with a certain style and may achieve a degree of independence. He may even become that unsettling thing, an agent of cultural change.

Here, with respect to the question about categories, the issue is the formation of a concept of the human being in his collective versus his personal aspect. And here the concept finally developed will be one of the possible compromises between the claims of the isolated person and the claims of the collective culture to be the source of the motives and decisions animating productivity, whether of the artist or factory worker, whether of scientist, professional man, or of the man as person (e.g., the protagonist of a drama). Clearly, some culture and tradition are necessary if issues are to be debated and decisions reached. Equally clearly, culture can be permitted to take over the person's prerogative altogether and to make his decisions for him.

A primary decision concerns the identity of the protagonist. This identity, the sense in which he is the same person throughout many situations and episodes, will be formed in accord with ideals of personhood. But whence these ideals? Sometimes the person is said to be the source of ideals of personhood, which the culture then communicates. Or are these values instead originated by the culture and merely expressed in the individual person, his behavior, and his decisions? What identifies one? Does the person effect his own identification, or does he allow tradition or some vague public "they-self" to decide upon his identity and sameness? Or again, the issue may be thought to concern determination. Are we men primarily culturally (outer) determined or personally (inner) determined in respect to making decisions? Are persons the makers and masters of their culture? Or is the autonomy and creativity supposedly attained by some persons nothing more than another culturally determined illusion?

Again, a philosophy of man would attempt to select from the relatively indefinite category thus indicated (person/culture) some particular tension between these opposites and to establish this definite category as a principle for interpreting behavior. Thus the indefinite category same/other acquires a general content from the context related to a protagonist's need to make a decision concerning his identity. The relatively indefinite category, person/culture, should contain within its many possible tensions the definite category required for determining the sense in which the protagonist is just this individual person or actor. An illustration was offered at the beginning of this chapter of the identity decision of a famous hero. This hero, Oedipus, accepted responsibility for his decision; nevertheless, he was not without a sense of the fateful determination which had led him into his predicament.

Another basic opposition in the life of man is the individual/social opposition. Society is the whole institutional structure of roles, functions, and the like embodying a culture. It is the concrete framework within which individuals act and pursue their ends, where they struggle to unify and to be themselves, to enact their decisions, and to realize their ideals. As "personality" refers to the unique way a culture is lived, so "individuality" refers us to the special and particular manner of performing the roles, functions, and duties necessary for the survival and health of our social institutions. The individual in this sense is faced with the task of integrating the role or social function into his own economy in such a way as to serve his own needs as well as society's. Thus the opposition, individual/social, is closely related to the protagonist's struggle to retain the sameness, the identity, contained in his decision, and to reject the many elements which disturb or destroy this identity. We may think of the individual/social opposition as the indefinite category one/many, having acquired a general content rendering it relevant to this struggle.

Much of this unifying procedure is facilitated by the playing of standard roles. Individuals function in these roles. In the struggle to preserve his identity through playing the roles, engaging in the conflicts, working for the causes a society offers, the protagonist finds, by seeking to answer the claims both of the individual and of the collective, the occasion for unifying his experience in some relatively consistent way and in accord with his own ideals or ideals developed by his society. The manner whereby he resolves this social/individual tension will settle the way he accepts responsibility for himself and strives to carry his decisions into practice. The possible category of the integrated individual runs from the social orders characterized by extreme anarchic individualism (compare the romantic cult of personality which existed in Germany during the nineteenth century), to those totalitarian states where the individual is regarded as nothing apart from his role or his use value.

The habit in Japan of officially declaring certain individuals of remarkable achievement and mature wisdom to be "national treasures" represents an interesting orientation in that highly organized and complexly structured society toward valuing the individual intrinsically. Such persons have, in ideal at least, succeeded in freeing themselves from the mechanisms and stylizations of their society, while yet remaining functioning parts of it. They presumably possess a dominating sense of the primacy of their selfhood, while at the same time they acquiesce in playing appropriate social roles. Here we find them on the way to electing a compromise from the opposition, individual/society, and formulating a definite category of the unified and socially functioning individual.

Presiding over the last two types of categories just indicated is the opposition everyday/mythological, which renders relatively more concrete the formal opposition, good/evil. Notice that each of the categories discussed above presents an opposition between a more spiritual and a less spiritual extreme. Here the same alternative is presented. The selection between them can be made only in terms of an appropriate definite category, utilized in order to evaluate the outcome of the struggle concerning the protagonist's identity. Its application measures the protagonist's achievement in a single dramatic action and enables the protagonist to understand what grasp he has secured upon his unity, nature, and identity. The expected evaluation usually is negative, for the protagonist in his hybris and self-ignorance can be counted upon to make a mistaken (an evil) identification of himself, and thus to be obliged to enter in again upon the tragic path in pursuit of his true selfhood.

Finally, embracing the whole of a protagonist's movement toward his mature self over, perhaps, a whole lifetime, and expressing what might be called the protagonist's whole context-intention, his total intention to be human in his own personal way, is the category representing a compromise between authentic self-care and carelessness of self. And here the relatively indefinite category authenticity/inauthenticity records a degree of concern for the self's true being and represents a generalized content, giving the formal indefinite category, true/false, relevance to human life.

The first of the five relatively indefinite categories we have mentioned, the free human versus the animal, placed what many philosophies have concluded to be the more characteristically and maturely human, autonomous and responsible activity in opposition to the view that a man is necessarily under complete domination by his physical and biological nature. One makes use of this category in recognizing that one can (or cannot) make effective decisions, and in actually making such decisions. The second indefinite category, the person versus culture, is directed toward human activity, work, and self-understanding; it questions where a person's motivation and ideals originate and how he makes particular decisions. The third paradox arises in considering the function or role of the individual. It arises when the individual human being attempts to embody his decisions in action, and senses himself to be opposed to society or tradition, and their demands. Then he must clarify and settle the conflicting claims of the individual and of the collective with respect to which is to be the superior, unifying, and determining agency.

The fourth paradox and the indefinite category to which it gives rise (mythological/everyday), is clearly related to man's spiritual nature.[5] The drift of a considerable portion of Western civilization seems to indicate that the more spiritual value of each of the first three categories lies in the first member of the opposites as I have listed them. The free, individual person is or should be the greater value in comparison with the mechanical, custom-bred, well-adjusted social functionary. But this traditional consensus is not always easy either to define or to maintain against argument or the weight of average everyday public opinion, as witness the widespread collectivist tendencies at work in the world today, and the distrust of individual originality. The spiritual character I have attributed to the traditional consensus points to a definite principle of interpretation, in fact to an existential category. And this category, in turn, represents a selection from the relatively indefinite category defined by the opposition mythological/everyday.

But what of this selection of the more spiritual alternative? Is the spiritual character attributed to the choice of autonomy a mere appearance, or does it preserve a healthful grasp of some dimension, some being belonging as it were to another, perhaps noumenal, order? Is human nature nothing beyond the being which appears in everyday occupations? Or does it include a power of creativity, of insight, which becomes manifest only at exceptional moments or in exceptional persons? In respect to this opposition, the skeptic is at one extreme and the idealistic poet at the other. Each takes a position with regard to what he supposes authentic, or true, human being to be. The transcendental, formal indefinite notions, true/false, are here again rendered more concretely relevant to the human context. They become schematized opposites, authentic/inauthentic, and invite the selection of a definite category of the authentic with which to measure the whole course of the protagonist's life. Each, the skeptic and the poet, has mythically invested some compromise between the everyday world of the no-nonsense business man and the frankly otherworldly and probably religious visionary, and in so doing has applied a definite category of true and authentic human being. *Philosophy at the Crossroads*, for example, utilized a category of authenticity in evaluating what it called the Humian and Positivists developments in philosophy (PC §21), and also *Man and Technology* employed a category of authenticity in order to discuss problems related to the modern advance toward a completely technological society (MT §§37f.).

There may be other existential categories than the five I have indicated, but these suffice for understanding a very important portion of human change and its non-objective dialectic. These categories render intelligible the sometimes radical changes undergone by the tragic or comic hero. This tragic or comic movement is characterized by a shift in basic categories. Not uncommonly, the categories which the hero spontaneously employs begin by emphasizing the natural, cultural, social — the everyday — and give little thought to the self's true being; the categories toward which he works his way as catastrophic action moves in the direction of authentic being tend to belong to the other end of the spectrum. They are more human, personal, individual, and mythological. It is as if the action were pointing the hero, despite himself, toward executing the transitions he must accomplish if he is to come into possession of his human powers and achieve wholeness or authentic selfhood. Or so the tragic world seeks to persuade us, for it itself embodies a definite selection among the possibilities presented by the indefinite categories true/false, authentic/inauthentic.

Today's protagonist of the modern economic and technological culture develops differently. His categories depict him as a creature controlled by large, wonderous, and Progressive forces, a mass man, perhaps alienated, yet faithful under a prevailingly Protestant God to the institutions of the Land of the Free and the Home of the Brave, as they have frequently been hopefully depicted. Just this simple-minded hope provides the modern theater with an unfailing source of characters and topics. Arthur Miller's "Death of a Salesman" presents an altogether modern hero, who, we know ahead of time, possesses but little independence from the forces surrounding him. Accordingly, Willy Loman, with never an afterthought, follows the line laid down for men of his class by popular American culture. Careless of his personal and authentic being, he has automatically decided long before the play opens to seek financial success and to conform in every possible respect to popular standards. We see him flagging, an elderly shoe salesman still trying to persuade himself he is a real success, popular among the boys, and a fine example of American know-how. We see him pathetically eager to communicate this waking dream to his doubting sons. In the end, the dream becomes a nightmare; he cannot but recognize his economic failure and his abandonment by his erstwhile "friends" and cronies. Yet he cannot directly face his failure, and he resists any recognition of the hollow, average ideals which have guided him. But still, measured even by these everyday aspirations, his life is a failure, and he ends by committing suicide so that his wife can collect insurance. Measured by the standards he had so uncritically accepted, he is worth more dead than alive.

Clearly, Willy Loman's interpretative principles are all located well toward the natural or determined end of the respective existential indefinite categories. Indeed, so evidently are his categories thus located, that the reader or viewer of the play is forced to see the folly of popular categories and the need to locate interpretation nearer to autonomy if justice is to be done to human powers and if true human being is to be approached or even vaguely envisaged.

§39. THE RELATION BETWEEN THE TWO KINDS OF CATEGORIES

The behaviorist's and mechanist's principles for dealing with human action and human being were decided *a priori* to be of a piece with those needed for understanding nature. The strategy of this study, though, is to begin with human experience and to follow its lead; we have seen that it leads to two different kinds of principles, objective and existential. Eventually, the question has to be raised concerning the relationship of the categories interpreting the two modes of experience. The question seems initially to refer us to a difficulty reminiscent of the Cartesian mind-body problem (cf. §32). The Cartesian and much of later philosophy, however, first elaborated its two main modes of categories in order to meet another need, the need for a context in which the new science could advantageously be pursued, and it executed this task in a manner most favorable to physics. Then the attempt was made to force all experience to conform to these categories; of course the attempt was a failure. We, on the other hand, witness the intelligibility of all kinds of experience to one and the same mind, and expect, therefore, to discover a basic unity among all the categories.

Also, we initially sought in this study to discover not a specific set of categories acceptable to a particular culture and time; but rather, we attempted to discover the kind of concept a category is in relation to the kind of problem it was expected to resolve. We discovered a category to be understandable as a compromise, one among many possible compromises between opposing formal indefinite notions expressing opposing demands, the demand, for instance, for being both one and many, for being both an intelligible unity and a multiplicity. Thus our treatment has indicated that all categories are similar in that all are tensions between opposites, compromises between opposing indefinite notions. And these tensions are special expressions of the basic tension between being and non-being.

Unfortunately, however, we cannot terminate our discussion of the two kinds of categories by observing that these two kinds are related to each other through their common origin in being, for we have already admitted to possessing no adequate concept of this common origin. It may be observed, though, that philosophers have in the past often found an overall unity in one or the other of two extreme senses of being, the abstract or the concrete, constituting the two ends of the spectrum of kinds of categories (see §5 and §52). At the abstract extreme, the sense of being is pared down to the minimum (MT pp.219f.). Many philosophers prefer to begin thus. In imitation of mathematics and in accord with the intellectualism of the times, they prefer to utilize as few principles and operations as possible, so elect to begin in poverty and to build their way toward riches. Others, though, are inclined to begin with the richer sense of being, to articulate this sense and to refine it into the several concepts and techniques which an understanding of experience requires. This latter procedure is promising, especially since the human being and his existential categories can also be included in the richer and more concrete sense of being.

The speaking, thinking, acting self is surely of peculiar importance in any categoreal scheme. He is subject in the sense that he subjects other things, and in a peculiar sense himself as well, to language and to the categories his language expresses. In addition, this active self is a being which, according to tradition, is in some sense observable and describable, no less so than the objects falling within his experiential grasp. Clearly, this active self-function stands in special need of being appropriately described and understood, for its function is precisely the central function of experiencing. He is that unique being which possesses a sensitive field, the possibility of interpreting whatever is presented. Objective and existential categories are essential powers and interpreting functions of this field. Perhaps, then, the unity of these two kinds of categories lies in their belonging to one and the same sensitive field, the human being. If so, then we must press on to ask about the unity of this field. Does it manifest a unitary operation?

This central function can scarcely be made intelligible within the old, often naive, and well-worn frameworks of realism and idealism, for both of these philosophies are hopelessly stuck in blind alleys; they persist in attempting either to reduce the person to an object or the object to a person, and thus distort both. Phenomenology offers the more auspicious alternative, for phenomenology, striving to begin with an unprejudiced description of experience, prescribes that a complete description of an object requires describing also the perspective within which the object is viewed or experienced. An object is always an object in a perspective; it is always an object to a viewer. The old realisms and idealisms tend too easily to suppose that the point of perspection upon an object requires no special attention, or is sufficiently specified by current ideals of objectivity. Kant, though, observed that the categories are functions of the self, the transcendental ego, but this ego is formal, the consequence of his assumption that there is one and only one correct point of cognitive perspection, the objective or the Newtonian (PC p.150). Today, however, with the increase in historical knowledge and with the expansion in experience of other cultures, Kant's position seems simplistic. Though promising in principle, Kant's philosophy does not account for an X appearing as ϕ where ϕ is not a derivative of his categories. Still, it must be admitted that X can appear as ϕ to anybody, though only if the anybody concerned is able to occupy the point of perspection from which X does in fact appear as ϕ. And years of exacting discipline may be requisite before a given person can come to occupy that point of perspection.

The self exercises the function of initiating perspectives within which the object appears and is experienced, whether it appears as it is or in some other guise, or whether it appears from one aspect rather than another. The term "perspective" is a spatial metaphor, borrowed from the act of seeing objects which are at a distance from the viewer. In the present context, though, the notion of perspection is clearly not confined to its association with sight. It refers, rather, to the whole responsive and operative area set up around an experiencing being like a human being. The receptive functions are defined by the traditional five ways of sensing, and likewise by other means, e.g., by the sense of balance or by visceral feelings, mood, attitude, and the like. The objective interpretative functions are accomplished by using the principles of interpretation upon presentations or upon perceptions, memories, and images which are referred to the other-than-self. Here the perspected object does not and cannot appear to itself. But, as we have observed (in chap. 4), the self can perceive and interpret itself.

This power of initiating perspectives in which both objects and the perceiver himself can appear and be interpreted is the unique human function. And it can appear as a single and unitary function if it be understood as directed in two primary ways, directly upon an object or reflexively upon itself. Directed upon objects, the self extends itself and its rationality outward into the world in order to obtain a grasp upon and control over those things not itself. Directed reflexively, the self begins with itself as reflected in its own works and acts and then seeks insight into and control over its own powers in order, as is sometimes said, to accomplish its fate or to become itself. The sensitive field is one, but its areas and modes of operation are at the minimum dual. Thus the two kinds of principles suffice for understanding the whole perspective act, both its objective and subjective sides, both the object perspected or perceived and the act of perspecting. In this sense, the two kinds of principles form a functional unity of one and the same being, in one and the same world. Having at least these two kinds of interpretative principles, the human being can exercise his uniquely human functions; he can become that one being through whom he himself and other beings appear (MT § 8f.).

Objects are experienced within perspective fields opened up by the experiencing self. They are described and studied by means of the categories of the object. The experiencing self, on the other hand, who possesses or opens up the perspective field where it itself and objects appear, is described and studied by application of the existential categories. Each without the other is but half the story. Jointly, they make possible an account of experience and the experiencer.

No claim is made here to completeness in the discernment of the basic modes of experience. Thus I certainly do not assert that these two modes and their categories exhaust human possibilities. I have not, for instance, dwelt upon experience in the attenuated mode of the everyday. Also, there may be intermediate modes. Finally, I raise the question whether there may not be still another mode of experience, one perhaps appropriately called mythological, an additional mode distinguished by its own schematizing content and its own relatively primary categories. If so, then the schematizing or orienting notions could be something like divine being/divine non-being, and experience in this mode would be something like a receptive holding of oneself in the open to be acted upon by a superior power. But treatment of such topics belongs to the philosopher of religion and to the theologian. I do not feel myself able to do them justice, although the last chapter will approach them, and here and there I have alluded to them.

§40. ON CHANGE IN AND LEGITIMATION OF CATEGORIES

Categories, even the most basic of them, are constantly undergoing change. What is the origin of these changes? How determine their legitimacy? In this section, I shall hardly be concerned with the kinds of problems and changes sometimes tending (within cultural limits) to render categories and subordinate interpretative principles ever more evidently appropriate and effectively related to the presentations and objects they are to interpret, as measured by some currently accepted standard. We have already touched upon this objective dialectic and will return to it again in the next chapter. Here the topic concerns a more pervasive and elusive source of categoreal change.

The human interpretative power is various. We have observed that the formal structure of categories entails that indefinitely many variants of any particular category are always possible. Thus the structure of categories accommodates change, perhaps even invites it. Why is it, then, that upon a given occasion one categoreal possibility rather than another wins acceptance? The available variants are sufficient not only to accommodate all the kinds of interpretations which in fact have been made, but probably an indefinite number of others as well. Why have these other variants not yet been essayed? Which of them are acceptable? What directs the subjective and objective dialectic, or does it merely drift? Of course, some particular possibility must be preferred if a way for resolving a given problem is to be worked out. The question therefore concerns the ground for the kind of selection actually made.

The usual tendency today would be to search for such reasons within the characteristics of the culture, history, and environmental circumstances of the people who use the category in question. The problem would be understood to be resolvable by familiar techniques of objective research, data gathering, hypothesis formulation, testing, reformulation, and the like. Thus to understand why the ancient Greeks thought of lightning as a weapon hurled by Zeus, king of the gods, a modern researcher would investigate ancient records to determine with what other phenomena lightning was associated, how neighboring tribes pictured it, which linguistic terms expressed it, and so on; then he would draw inferences from these data in accordance with the rules of his science, and formulate an appropriate and testible hypothesis. This procedure, however, does not touch the question I have raised. I might also have asked why the researcher was inclined to make use of the techniques and canons of objective research. Many peoples have not possessed just these techniques and canons, yet have fared very well, though differently. The ancient Greek, observing the research scientist, might have surmised that the researcher proceeded as he did in honor of some odd god. Both responses, the modern researcher's and the ancient Greek's, are alike in that both offer illustrations of the use of categories rather than an answer to the question about the grounds for choice among categories.

My question may be rephrased in the language of this chapter. Why is a given possible category "cut" just where, in fact, it is cut in order to produce a definite category in actual use? Now, I shall not attempt to answer fully such a large question as this, but I think I can indicate the beginning of one kind of answer which is pertinent at this point.

We are returned to section 30 of the preceding chapter and to Aristotle's remark concerning the direct fall of being into the categories. Can it be that Aristotle was misled by a parochial confidence in the universal validity of his own categories? Can it be, perhaps, that being falls — to continue the metaphor — not directly, but through some medium, as it were, or in some fashion by which it is diversified and initially shaped for the particular categories into which it does, in fact, fall? I suggest that it does so fall and that the character of the medium is in an important way responsible for categories taking just the form which they do finally take. What, then, and less metaphorically if possible, is the character of this medium? What is the nature of the fall through it?

A first suggestion comes from the observation that categories are selected for a purpose. They are intended for use in solving a definite kind of problem, for throwing light upon some situation. Thus, like any conscious act, they are intentional. Hence we must look to our particular intentions and to our context-intentions to learn why we select the categories we use. But the same question may be asked again about context-intentions: Why these intentions rather than others? For an answer to this question, we may be directed to our culture.

Perhaps culture is that through which being "falls," and no doubt this "fall" into categories is a metaphorical way of referring to the many educational and character-forming influences by which a culture is created and communicated and which dispose its members to look for certain types of problems and solutions to them. But this supposition would explain nothing either, for a culture is one of those things formed by use of the categories. To give an account of the formation of categories by reference to culture is to commit a *petitio principi*. This circle is broken, though difficulties surely remain, when we recollect that a culture is an embodiment of world. The supposition I offer, then, is that being falls through world into categories.[6]

Here it will be helpful to translate Aristotle's figure of the fall of being into the terms developed near the end of the chapter 5 (§§26f.). We noted there that a project is the widest context within which a people conducts its life and thought for a period of its history. Thus a project consists of the formative elements defining a family of possible cultures. We also noted that such a total project can, under appropriate circumstances, become mythically invested; that is, it can become endowed with that emotional and believing power which leads on to its widespread, unreserved, and generally uncritical acceptance. A project thus mythically invested we called "world."

World is a form relating the self to itself, to others, and to the environment of nature. It has been called the totality of intentions, the horizon of horizons, that within which any kind of encounter occurs. In our language, world is the totality or unity of our sensitive projective field. As a totality, we can never be more than partially and paradoxically aware of it. As a project, categories may provide the basic terms adequate for describing it, but as invested, world exceeds the categories. As involved in the formation of categories, world is not an interpreted object or a presentation to be interpreted but an omnipresent quality of, and a determining element within, interpretation. Our partial and paradoxical awareness of it is displayed in world symbols, myths of totality and finality. These symbols are both elements of and signs of totality. They are hints, suggestions, matter for thought, rather than the products of deliberate thinking.

Elsewhere I have suggested that important world symbols are; for the ancient Greeks, the man-goat; for medieval times, Christ or the union of divine and human substance in the one person; and for contemporary times, that technical marvel, the Cyborg, an intimate union of man and machine. Each symbol told men of its time who they were and to what they should aspire. Each established the union of the human with what the human sought as the source of power to be itself. Each symbol sought to embody and to convey this essential aspect of world. World is the first definite form in which being in totality is manifested to us. World is what first diversifies being in a characteristic way apprehensible by us and, as it were, disposes us to certain kinds of interpretations and renders others improbable or unthinkable.

World in its relation to perception is for the most part operative at an involuntary level. It is unconsciously lived and manifested in a number of related cultures. Consider the cultures to be found, for instance, in the modern Western world, e.g., Christian, Enlightened, Romantic, modern American, modern French, and the like. Each such culture displays a different facet of the total project men have mythically invested. Each molds and is expressed in every item of a people's language and behavior. Every thought is thought within one's cultural milieu and is colored, though not necessarily determined, by the inclinations, beliefs, values and prepossessions of the world expressed in that culture. It is possible to become at least partly aware of some of the inclinations and beliefs of one's world as expressed in one's culture; indeed, the effort to become aware of the world and to subject it to certain kinds of criticism is part and parcel of living the philosophic life.

We express these points by admitting that we are and must be inhabitants of a culture and that our culture is precisely that through which we are able to make contact with the objects of experience in just the definite and limited ways we do experience them. World as expressed in a culture determines generally how we live in the environment, how we tend to act in it, how we are disposed to think about it, how we tend to conceive of ourselves and our fate. This *how* is given concrete expression in the categories chosen for interpreting what is presented to us. That is, one is predisposed in selecting categories by the world one inhabits. Or as it might also be said, being falls through the world and its cultures into categories. Conversely, categories provide an important part of the basic means through which one's world is experienced and known.

Evidently, I can never experience lightning as the ancient Greek experienced it, even though through sympathetic study I may come to understand the Greek better and better, and be enabled to answer more questions about him. But I can never genuinely sense a streak of lightning as a projectile hurled by an angry Zeus. The ancient Greek and I belong to different worlds, and I can never really possess or mythically invest the categories of awe-inspiring personal powers which possessed the ancient Greek. I come too late for Zeus.

Categories change, for time guarantees a gradual change in the world. The varying problems presented by the physical and social environments, the events of inner and outer history, insure such change. Philosophy takes its inception precisely in the attempt to interpret such crucial alterations and transitions. I have attempted to offer illustrations of such interpretations in the two books mentioned in the preface to this book. Here I add that the primary place this change leaves its mark is in the basic principles of interpretation, the categories. When, through the effects of time, a well-used set of categories proves to be unreliable, inadequate to develop the felt and needed resolutions to puzzles, or to guide through the maze of problems, then men are driven back upon more basic, more archaic apprehensions, to those we have termed the indefinite notions, and thereupon they seek to discover — and sometimes do discover — an unrecognized or unused categoreal possibility, a capability hitherto dormant in the world, one which will open the way to renewed dialectic and fruitful management of the new problems. Philosophy is the interpretation of archaic experience (unless it degenerates into a scholastic cultivation of well-worn techniques or into a repetition of routine schibboleths). It is a return to *archai* and to the world where categories have their source; it is the archway through which one enters into a new or renewed cultural kingdom.

A sophisticated doctrine, a mature culture, must remain open to this kind of basic criticism and possible change. Einstein's rethinking of the conventional physical concept of time in his special theory of relativity is a classic instance of this openness to categoreal change. Marx's rethinking of the concept of work and his conclusion that we need to aim not so much at understanding the environment as at changing it, offers another illustration. Oedipus' reconsideration of his own identity and of his relation to family, society, and environment of inherited values and beliefs provides still another example of this kind of change. Problems, crises of these kinds tend to force us to abandon the old categories which produced them and to return to the indefinite notions, to being and non-being, in whatever way one's world permits this return, and to essay new compromises with paradox, new categories which provide for interpretations that may once more bring a measure of unity and definiteness into one's life. A first step, therefore, toward understanding the grounds for changes in categories is to aim at an understanding of the world (or of some portion of it) within which the change occurs (PC §§6-9 and 16-18).

Being falls into objective, existential, or other categories, not immediately, but through the world which inclines us to be sensitive to one way of life, one general type of problem, one kind of solution rather than to others. The categories exhibited at any epoch of history are, at least in part, the consequences of an interplay between the categories already possessed and new problems, of a sensitiveness to novel situations, to newly discovered demands.

Is there no other source of change in the categories by which we live our lives and think about ourselves and our environments? One might suppose that being itself, which informs the categories, may have something to do with their changes. Is not the being, diversified by opposing transcendentals, falling through world into categories, an origin? Does it not possess traits of its own which partly, at least, determine the categories into which it falls? Alas, though, there is not even the beginning of an agreement upon the meaning of the term "being." Perhaps the two ends of the spectrum of kinds of categories mentioned in sections 5 and 51 suggest the variety of senses given the term. At the abstract end of this spectrum, "being" receives virtually no meaning. It is useful as a copula. Beyond that, according to the authority of Hegel, Nietzsche, the several kinds of positivists, being is so general and vaporous a word as to be quite empty of meaning, quite without traits of its own. According to other authorities, being denotes the power of world-making. It is the richest of words; indeed, it is so rich and unique a term as to be unmanageable by everyday methods. No doubt, being does have traits of its own, but traits well beyond easy discovery, traits apprehensible, it is said, only to a thinking scarcely to be found among the recognized activities of philosophers belonging to the Western world. Such thinking belongs more properly to a kind of poetic receptivity, or even to a kind of religious experience.

Further speculation, hence, upon the traits of being in this sense will not be appropriate here. Perhaps these traits belong with the additional mode of experience mentioned at the close of §39. We shall for the moment rest content in thinking about being as the origin of categories, as that which gives possibilities, and as the power directed toward world making and world change. This power is also, I suspect, what we glimpse when some crisis, some archaic experience, forces us back upon our basis. We shall return to consider this power more directly in the last chapter.

At this juncture, though, it may be appropriate to note that the Renaissance witnessed a change of the world order which has culminated in the present technological culture (PC chaps. 2, 3, and §51f.), and may eventually end in "technism," my name in *Man and Technology* (cf. pp. 204ff.) for a completely technologically ordered and oriented world. Man's sensitive field evidently admits the possibility of technism. To realize this possibility, we have only to elicit and use the appropriate interpretative possibilities and to allow competing possibilities to lapse into oblivion. In *Man and Technology*, I argued that life under technism would stifle the movement toward radical change of self (see below §44f.), and prevent it achieving further movement toward its end (see below, §51.). The present study thus provides a point of perspection for the prospect opened up in *Man and Technology*. We are led, therefore, to consider at least briefly the question of the legitimacy of the perspective recommended in this study.

The possibility of returning from any point of experience back to the origin (the *archai*), suggests a way of viewing the categoreal doctrine developed in this and the preceding chapter. For correlative to the several modes of experience are their objects. The relation between these two, objects and experience of objects, can be expressed in a manner recalling the Kantian transcendental deduction.

The *Critique of Pure Reason* undertakes to demonstrate that certain very definite principles and their constituent categories determine the possibility of all legitimate experience and knowledge and therefore necessarily apply to all objects. Of course, Kant's categories and principles were limited to those necessary for a Newtonian universe, and the kind of phenomena thus rendered possible were hardly those of common experience; rather, they were the phenomena of physics (PC §30). Here we begin, after our descriptions of the essential items, with the conviction that indefinitely, many categories and sets of categories are possible and are even, to varying degrees and for different purposes, valid. And we seek to establish a relation of interdependence between the categoreal matrix and objects for all modes of experience.

Let me summarize briefly the train of these thoughts. There are in fact two tasks: the primary and ontological one of envisaging the legitimacy of the categoreal matrix, and the secondary one of showing the acceptability of a particular set of categories within a particular mode of experience.

In chapters 2 to 4, four of the essential items (objects) as experienced were described. We decided they were in essence as follows: space is otherness (the condition of separateness); time is sameness in spatial being (endurance); object is unified (identifiable) temporal sameness in being; the self is unified sameness in being whose temporal and linguistic consciousness is the place of the primary truth process. These four receive their characteristic orientation from the world where they originate and to which they are (dialectically) related, for world is the determination of the primary sense being is to have for the cultures it subsumes. It is important to see that the description of the objects of experience cannot dispense with the transcendental notions. We may say that objects are conditioned upon these factors of being.

Now, the principles actually conditioning experience of these essential items may be traced back up the line of their derivation, through proximate principles to schematized categories, and eventually, as we have seen, to the opposing transcendental or indeterminate notions constituting the categoreal matrix. Thus the interpretative stream in the eye or in the mind (pp. 127-9) is most briefly and properly characterized by the transcendentals. But so, as the preceding paragraph concluded, are the objects themselves. Thus if I may use Kant's phrase, the conditions of the objects of experience are the same as the conditions of the experience of objects — a result hardly surprising, yet when the tortuous process of experience and interpretation is considered, hardly obvious either.

We have in these observations a basic legitimation of our interpretative operations. The further and secondary legitimation involves more or less familiar ways of testing for the (secondary) truth of our conclusions, opinions, and beliefs. These several methods are functions of the particular world and mode of experience within which the testing is undertaken. Thus in the contemporary Western world there exist the several ways of verifying or disproving scientific hypotheses. There are practical tests for supposed truths on an everyday level. There are ethical standards which measure our existential status and achievements. And I would suggest the need of some technique of mythological exploration as a means for passing judgment upon the desirability, and effectiveness of world symbols. In this study, however, we go no further than to make passing mention of these testing procedures.

The criticism of technism advanced in *Man and Technology* involved both primary and secondary kinds of truth. This criticism maintained that technism would end by identifying a worker (at whatever level) with his role. To that extent, the worker's experience of objects and of himself is limited; his opening upon the world is artificially circumscribed. And the constriction is maintained by persuasive world symbols which successfully insist that the categories in force are indeed the only acceptable (i.e., scientific) ones.

But surely a philosophy or a culture ought to do justice to all forms of human experience. In opposition to technism, the present study emphasizes that human experience does, in fact, come in more than one mode. Also, it derived the basic interpretative principles from the transcendentals of the tradition without, however, intending to suggest that these transcendentals exhaust all possibilities; there may be others. My point was that the categoreal matrix composed of these and perhaps other transcendentals is just the general human possibility of experiencing, knowing, and acting (cf. §4). This matrix seemed to me to be generous enough to embrace probably all possibilities and thus the whole ontological basis (the sensitive field) of human experience. Accordingly, preceding chapters were able to show that the essential items — space, time, objects, self, and world — were indeed rendered experienceable and intelligible by the use of categories drawn from this matrix.

A brief recapitulation of this whole view is now in order: the transcendentals, primary strands of possibility belonging to the sensitive field (I hesitate to speak of a "flow of possibility"), intersect with the flow of presentations and feeling, producing (as by a marriage) the flow of interpreted presentations or particular phenomena, upon which we may reflect in order to discover the *logoi* of the phenomena, having the identity and properties that myth, common sense, and the sciences find in them (see diagram on p. 15).

Notes

1. E.g., Walker Percy, *The Message in the Bottle* (New York, N. Y.: Farrar, Straus, and Girous, 1975), chap. 10.
2. A similar endeavor, but with results different from the present one, has engaged several contemporary writers, among them Erich Fromm, *Man for Himself* (New York: Holt, Rinehart and Winston, Inc., 1947) and *Sane Society* (New York: Holt, Rinehart and Winston, 1955), and, of course, Heidegger.
3. E.g., in my "The Sense of Tragedy" and "The Sense of Comedy" in *The Dictionary of the History of Ideas*, ed. Philip Wiener (N. Y.: Scribner's, 1973). Also see MT, §22 and below §51.
4. See §16, p. 100ff. MT §15.
5. An interesting derivative version of this category of the mythological is applied to more or less personified objects; we have described it as the mytho-

logical object category (§5). It is defined as being somewhere between the object taken in an ordinary, everyday sense and the object felt as endowed with symbolic value, personal attributes, or the mana of religious significance. Compare, in this respect, a pair of crossed sticks placed for peas to grow on, and the cross made of charred wooden beams near the entrance to Coventry Cathedral, England.

6. 'World' is used here in the active (noetic) sense, equivalent to the possible or actively structured sensitive field or to the total, "readiness" of a person for experience. It is occasionally used (noematically) to refer to that which such a (noetic) activity effects, a project or a mythically invested project. But the ambiguity is not harmful and is frequently useful. 'Category' is subject to the same ambiguity.

VIII

The Dialectic of Interpretation

§41. ON THE HISTORY AND MEANING OF DIALECTIC

We have at this point, and for this study, answered the question, How do we attain access to objects, to self, and to others? We have sufficiently clarified what it means to say that this access is obtained through presentation and interpretation, through perception and experience. Many other questions could have been elicited from the account provided so far, but had to be left in the background. For instance, we might have asked whether other clues to space and time than those we utilized would have led to different concepts (different essences). We might have asked, What is the character of abstraction by which we move from the more concrete to the less concrete? (In other words, is the technique of subtraction of properties an adequate account of this movement?) We might have asked in greater detail than we did about the nature of a context. And so on. But we limit ourselves to two further questions, the topics of the next two chapters. By what method or way does interpretation proceed? I shall answer in this chapter that it often proceeds dialectically. Toward what end does interpretation proceed? In the next chapter I want to explain what is meant by saying that it proceeds toward being.

The term "dialectic" refers us to a process of interpretation. It names the operation by which interpretative principles interact with presentations or objects to be interpreted. The outcome of the process is perception and experience. Experienced objects in space and time, the experience of self, others, and the like thus acquire new meanings. This outcome, the renewed experience, can be used over again as a principle, a paradigm, in yet further interpretations.

To suggest, though, that principles, whether existential or objective, come to be related to presentations and objects by a dialectical process may seem to be a waste of words. For dialectic has had so complex and varied a career that any attempt to disengage a useful meaning for it might appear at first glance to attempt to carry water in a sieve. Still, a closer look does suggest a generic meaning which has been fruitfully expressed in several specific forms. Effort directed toward discovering this generic meaning and toward distinguishing several of its particular expressions will throw light upon an essential human activity, the activity of applying principles for the interpreting or forming of experience.

In its beginnings, dialectic was a logically controlled conversation. The Sophists of the golden centuries developed it as a method of verbal attack and defense, using it sometimes as an intellectual game, sometimes in earnest political and legal combat. With Plato and Socrates, though, dialectic lost much of this aggressive and hostile character and became an instrument for the loving inquiry into truth, a method, moreover, which seemed to shape the souls of the inquirers in the image of the truth into which they inquired. Hints concerning the nature of dialectic are offered in, among other places, the *Phaedrus*; according to this dialogue, the philosophic souls imitate the celestial gods and circle around the intelligible fire in an ecstasy of insight; thus, as the *Timaeus* (47C, 90C) expressed it, the circles in the inquirers' heads came to be modeled upon the circles of the cosmos. By way of this celestial dialectic, these souls grew more divine.

A more ordinary dialectic circles around one topic and develops its intelligible aspects until its implicit principles have become explicit and can be evaluated or changed. Quite naturally, Plato hailed dialectic, both in the earlier form of elenchus and in the later form of collection and division, as the philosopher's instrument and technique *par excellence*. On the contrary, Aristotle believed it not to be a means for increasing the precision and scope of knowledge, but rather to be futile or at best probable reasoning. According to Kant's usage, dialectic cannot add to knowledge at all; instead, it is an illicit and illusory use of cognitive powers in the attempt to extend knowledge beyond the limits of possible experience. Then Hegel sought to restore its ancient reputation and use, and succeeded in exalting it almost beyond recognition. His dialectic, as embodied in the movements of history, seemed to become the footsteps of Deity in time. Then followed the Marxian waltz of man and technology into the heaven of a classless society.

One may wonder whether, in this see-saw history, these uses of dialectic have retained anything in common, or whether they have not been caught up in the dialectic process itself and have been made to undergo a sea-change. If the term does retain any meaning common to these varied philosophies, it probably refers to a process of the mind progressively attempting to clarify its categories and other principles and to interpret presentations and objects, itself, and other persons. The varying estimates of its meaning and value appear to stem from the recognition that the mind easily misuses this instrument and produces seductive illusion instead of clarification. Dialectic is a dangerous instrument. Upon occasion it encounters catastrophe; when it does, those engaged in it may be thrown reflectively back upon more basic beliefs in their endeavors to extricate themselves from conflict, frustration, and confusion. The Devil, according to Milton, is an excellent dialectician who excelled in precipitating catastrophe.

Most of those things with which the Devil is concerned turn out to be things not well-understood. So with dialectic. One of the difficulties preventing its acceptance lies in the fact that its manner of working has not always been clearly enough grasped. With the aid of a simple mechanical model, a view of the operation of dialectic will be offered in this chapter which should help remove some of the tarnish from its name.

Dangerous or not, a defensible historical thesis is to hold that a fairly stable meaning has been associated with dialectic throughout philosophical history, even by those who fear its use. The meaning I have in mind, illustrated in the situations, conversations, and writings usually called dialectical, is this: that a result of the dialectic at any stage can become a principle of interpretation determining the process at a succeeding stage. I mean to say that one factor of this process is directed toward the future, toward a state to be achieved. But the process is not simply future-directed; rather, its future-direction retains another factor, a grasp or memory of its past accomplishment, so that the possibility to be actualized or explored in the present can be selected in the light of an apprehension of the difference between past achievement and future goal. Dialectic, then, is a process directed in part by its own outcome. It might be said, in a certain sense, to be self-corrective. But we need to move more deliberately toward an understanding of this account of dialectic through an analysis of different kinds or species and through illustrations of the process itself.

In this study, it might be supposed that the primary dialectical interaction would occur between formal categories and pure presentations (content). As a matter of fact, though, neither formal categories, nor pure presentations, nor the initial interaction between them is experienced. There is no content in a pure or formal category; therefore, nothing is there to experience. Formal categories are, rather, factors in any experience (cf. §§3, 24). Also, presentations cannot come to us except with some form. The perceiver's situation in space already imposes some form, some distinctions among objects, the distinction, say, between the central and attracting object, those surrounding it, and those altogether peripheral. More than that, though, our complex sensory organs automatically make interpretations before they send messages to the mind and to consciousness, and these messages are organizing, forming. Thus, though it might at first appear that there are two kinds of matter to be interpreted — that which has had no interpretation at all, and that which has already received some (e.g., spontaneous) interpretation — in fact, only the second kind is to be reckoned with. Again, presentations are always re-presentations.

It is important, likewise, to observe that in the dialectical process the distinction between form and matter or content becomes relative. If, that is, the process begins with a certain matter (content), and moves to inform this matter with a certain form, then this informed matter becomes the matter for the next stage of the process. (A number of examples of this process will be provided in later sections.)

Dialectic, then, refers to a process of communication by which experience grows. As experiencing beings, we always find ourselves already in the midst of this process. We are, that is, aware of the interaction of feelings, images, recollections, and concepts any of which may function as principles of interpretation (form) and be directed upon other presented objects, events, persons, and the like (the matter or content) in order to produce further interpretations. By this process, things become familiar, and familiar things are overlaid with other identities, values, imaginings, beliefs, and knowledge, for once presentations have received some interpretation, some identification, they may be given all sorts of additional meanings.

Perhaps we must merely assume that pure uninterpreted presentations are initially interpreted by formal categories. In fact, I see no alternative to this assumption. But that we are unaware of any such initial stage of interpretation bringing these two pristine and pure factors together seems evident and verifiable. Even hypothetical reconstructions of early infantile experience indicate no such initial stage. At every phase of actual awareness, our flow of feeling, presentations, imagery, and memory, exhibits some organization, some testimony to prior interpretation. It is as if the dialectical process had always already begun. Formal categories and pure presentations, then, may come to be related through dialectic, but in every instance of experience they have already been so related.

Although the initial phase of the dialectical process does not fall within our purview, we can observe the progress of dialectic and apprehend its structure. Thereupon, we may develop a general description of it, define it, take note of its fundamental forms, offer some illustrations of it, and finally discuss briefly some of the problems related to its direction and to its evaluation.

§42. THE GENERIC SENSE OF DIALECTIC

Once dialectic referred to a well-regulated conversation in which the participants, by the exchange of information and ideas, brought each other into a state of agreement, or at least into mutual understanding. As many philosophers have believed, though, the pattern of an interchange of this kind is involved in many contexts other than the conversational. Some of these contexts are simpler than the conversational. We shall begin with the simpler contexts and work our way into the more complex, and in so doing be able to abstract more than one form of the pattern of dialectic. Also, the scope and limitations of dialectic will need to be indicated.

An acceptable and general first account of this term may be found, I believe, if it be specified as a sort of causal relation holding between entities of a certain kind, and directed toward an end. The suggestion that dialectic may be defined as a kind of causal relation may sound like an explanation *ignotum per ignotius*. Nevertheless, there exists some consensus that causality can be separated from anthropomorphic accretions and rendered both precise and widely applicable if it be translated into terms referring to sufficient conditions. Thus it is not the case that the cause occurs and the effect fails to occur; that is, only if the effect occurs does the cause occur. This is as much to say that the cause is the sufficient condition of the effect. Or again, utilizing a mathematical metaphor, we may say that the effect is dependent upon the cause in a functionally determined way.

Unfortunately, this definition logically entails that on the occasions when the effect fails to occur that the cause fails also. This possibility is often not intended by the usage of "cause." For example, if my reading an article is the cause of my understanding its subject matter, it does not seem to follow, in fact, that the contrapositive is true, that my failure to understand it causes my omitting to read it. Or again, if rain causes the crops to grow, it does not follow that a crop failure causes a drought. Thus, although the translation of causal language into logical language does not perfectly translate general usage and common meanings, still, logical entailment is analogous to causality, and the analogy is useful and sufficiently accurate for present purposes.

The causal relation is exemplified on many different kinds of occasions, for example, in efficient causation where contact with one particle is the sufficient condition for the change in momentum and velocity of another, and where the causing particle undergoes an alteration as a result of the impact. The momentum might be passed along an indefinitely long series of particles in this manner. Likewise, this causal relation is exemplified in organic systems and in psychological changes. In addition, premises are said to be the sufficient condition or cause of the conclusion, and certain theories of induction attempt to set up conditions under which the data might be said to cause the theory based upon them. Causality is a very general, even ambiguous, notion.

Some restriction is placed upon the generality of the definition of the causal relation by noting that the kind of entities it can relate must be at least partly homogeneous. The momentum of a billiard ball does not somehow cause a thought to appear in another billiard ball; the effect must be analogous to the cause. The causal event can communicate only such characteristics as it already possesses. This transmitted element may be thought of as a structure. The moving billiard ball is a mass-force structure. It alters the mass-force structure of the ball upon which it impinges so that the two are more nearly similar in structure; i.e., the former gives up some of its momentum to the latter.

This kind of correspondence between cause and effect was phrased by the

Medievals as an axiom: like causes like. Bertrand Russell has given this axiom a modern turn in his generalization: "It appears generally that if A and B are two complex structures and A can cause B, then there must be some degree of identity of structure between A and B."[1] For present purposes, this expression of the partial structural identity between cause and effect is introduced to define the kind of entity which can enter into a causal relation. It limits the causal relation to holding among partially homogeneous entities. An occasion of causation is an occasion where some identity in structure is transmitted from one event to another.

It will be useful to distinguish linear causal relations, as in the example of the billiard balls, from cyclical ones. To make this transition, an intermediate notion is needful: reciprocal causality. Suppose A and B are events in a relatively isolated system (B might be a ship's heading; A might be the rudder angle), then if A causes an effect in B, A will be changed as a consequence; such events are said to be related by reciprocal causality. But this statement is scarcely other than a generalized statement of Newton's third law. If, though, the relation between A and B is continuously reciprocal, the situation is altered. The change effected in B will react back on A, changing A to A′. The A′ will then react in a somewhat different way back upon the changed B, yielding B′, and so on. Thus a system of continuously and mutually changing events or entities is set up; this system may be called a cyclical system. When the relation of cyclical (or continuous reciprocal) causality holds among events, then they may be said to be related dialectically (using the term in its generic sense), or to interact dialectically.

Consider a linear causal series, in which A causes B and B causes C, etc. One can scarcely refer to an end of the series in any sense other than as a final temporal member of the series. In the cyclical or dialectical system, however, again the situation is different, for this kind of system moves in a direction; it moves in one specifiable manner rather than in another. The notion of end is a convenient way of defining this direction. The notion of end, however, is moot; it will be discussed in the next section. Here it is sufficient to note that a dialectical system of mutually changing elements, A and B, changes in the direction of the accommodation of A to B, an accommodation or similarity expressed by reference to their sharing a common structure or pattern. The end of the movement is the complete accommodation of A to B. Such a dialectical movement is often characterized as an evolution. It is illustrated by species of living beings which have, through the process usually described as mutation and natural selection, adapted themselves with increasing efficiency to the peculiarities of an environment.

Such a dialectical system will be continuously in the process of altering its characteristics while, in virtue of the principle of similarity of cause and effect, preserving some identity of structure. Dialectic is the changer changing in a continuous process. Here we need to consider some illustrations of this continuous reciprocal causality. I choose simple mechanical illustrations to indicate some further detail of this causal linkage.

One illustration is offered by a room whose heating unit is thermostatically controlled. A better illustration is a ship kept on course by an automatic pilot. Let us consider this last. The ship is, say, on a northerly course. Its heading changes to port (to the west), perhaps as the result of waves beating on its starboard bow. Now, an angle-measuring device in the automatic pilot responds to this variation from the desired heading, measures the angle of deviation, and sends electrical impulses proportional to this deviation to a machine (the output control), which alters the rudder angle by turning the rudder to the right so as to compensate for the error in the ship's heading. Thus the ship is gradually brought back on course. When the angle between the ship's heading and the desired course is zero, the rudder is amidships. Here the causal relation is made continuously reciprocal by (a) the "sensing device" which measures the angle of error,[2] and (b) by the "output control" which uses the latter measurement to control the ship's rudder. The end (telos, metaphorically understood), or state of mutual accommodation is reached when the ship's heading is identical with the desired course (MT §§28-30).

In old fashioned machines, the sensing device was a man, a pilot, whose eye and mind served to measure when and how far the ship was off course. Then his hands (the output control) moved the tiller appropriately to compensate for this error and so to bring the ship back on course. But these functions are all parts of one and the same person, the pilot, and thus are not noticed separately. The mechanical device has the advantage of separating these functions, and hence of letting us see just how the effect, the ship's wandering off course, is communicated back to a cause, the steering engine, by way of (a) the device for sensing error, and (b) the device for output control. If, generally speaking, dialectic is the product controlling the production, then the dialectical relation always requires some such sensing or measuring device which evaluates the product at a given stage of the process and, functioning as an interpretative principle, communicates this evaluation to an output control which determines the next step in the production (MT p. 231).

A dialectical system, then, is exemplified on any occasion when distinguishable yet partly homogeneous events are related by some means for producing a continuously reciprocal causal arrangement which moves toward a state of mutual information. Here the changer (the output control) changes by reason of the information sent it from the device which senses the difference between the present actual product and the desired product. Thus the means for producing a continuously reciprocal causal arrangement must fulfill at least two functions: it must sense (measure) the deviation of the system from some ideal, set, or desired state; it must be capable of using this measurement to control the system and bring it closer to this set, or desired state.

If, now, dialectic is formally a relation of continuous, reciprocal causality which moves toward mutual accommodation or information, it should be possible to distinguish, at least roughly, among dialectical systems by reference to the kinds of content entering into this dynamic relation. Perhaps there may be a mechanical dialectic where the mutually changing elements are material bodies, or a biological dialectic in which the elements are organisms or families of organisms in dynamic relationship with each other and with the environment. And surely there are various sorts of dialectical situations in which human beings participate. There is a question in the minds of many philosophers, though, whether "dialectic" retains the same specific sense when referred to mechanical and biological systems as it possesses when referred to human involvements. Let us consider these differences.

§43. THE GENERIC AND SPECIFIC SENSES

The generic sense of dialectic developed in the preceding section should be quite clearly distinguished from the specific and, as it seems to me, more proper sense restricted in its reference to human contexts. The question devolves, of course, upon the interpretation of the meaning of the end toward which dialectic moves. True, efforts have been made within behavioristic and naturalistic contexts to naturalize such notions as "purpose" and "movement toward an end." For example, in an important paper "Behavior, Purpose, and Teleology," by Arturo Rosenblueth, Norbert Wiener, and Julian Bigelow,[3] the authors attempted to effect just such a naturalization. This attempt was a failure, and it is important to see just why it was so.

In accordance with their naturalistic categories, the authors of this paper define as "purposeful" any act which may be interpreted as behaving so as to reach "a definite correlation in time or in space with respect to another object or event" (p. 23). They offer as examples human voluntary activity and the behavior of some (not all) machines, specifically those regulated by negative feedback so that they move toward a predesigned goal (i.e., are "teleological"). The reader will recognize in these machines allusion to the servo-mechanisms or self-regulating (cybernetic) machines with which Professor Norbert Wiener's name has long been associated. A ship's automatic pilot offers a good illustration. The suggested implication is that human voluntary effort differs only in degree of complexity from the behavior of servo-mechanisms.

Despite the extraordinary success of these self-regulating machines and the degree to which they seem to imitate human intelligent activity, the appropriateness of using such terms as "purposeful" and "teleological" to describe their behavior is certainly questionable. Indeed, the question has been put by Professor Richard Taylor in a paper entitled "Comments on a Mechanistic Conception of Purposefulness."[4] Professor Taylor points out that to speak of a machine as intending a goal or directing itself toward an end is to speak metaphorically. And if, for the sake of argument, these expressions are taken as literally descriptive of machines, then the most absurd consequences follow. For example, a machine is described as aiming at a goal if it is geared toward reaching a given coordination in time and space of its parts with certain objects. At every moment, however, such a coordination of its parts with innumerable other objects exists. By definition, each such coordination is a goal. Thus any machine is aiming constantly at innumerable goals. And there is no conceivable way of knowing at which goal, or at which correlation in time and space of machine parts and objects the machine especially "aimed."

In fact, all that can properly be said is that the machine parts are correlated at any moment with many objects, and such correlations may, therefore, be taken as just that toward which the machine's behavior was directed. Thus a wheel at any point of its rotation is in spatio-temporal correlation with something, and can, therefore, be considered to have been teleologically directed toward this something. At every moment, then, the wheel is achieving its goal, or, in other words, the "purpose" of the wheel, indeed of any object, is to be just where it is at any given moment. This conclusion, however convincing, is a tautology possessing absolutely no theoretical or explanatory value.

The error of the philosophers who ascribe purpose and teleology to machines lies in their concealing from themselves that they have picked out some one particular coordination of the machine parts with natural objects, just as the ship's captain picks out one particular course as the "correct" one. Consider that whatever way the ship heads defines a possible course. But all except the selected course are sensed by the automatic pilot as errors and used to bring the output control into play. Since the piloting machine was designed to produce just this one selected coordination of heading and course, achieving this "end" is hardly extraordinary, hardly a mechanical purpose.

The absurdity of supposing that the machine selects its own goal is avoided by confining expressions related to purpose and pursuit of ends to the meanings they have in common human experience, and to derivative uses. Human purposes and values are not to be found in machines or objects considered abstractly or in themselves; they are to be found in machines and objects only when considered concretely and in relation to human or human-derived projects, interests, values. That is, machines or objects have purposes or ends only if they are interpreted as acquiring this function from a source external to themselves. Thus when we interpret a mechanical system as having a dialectical character in that it moves toward an end, either we speak metaphorically (giving the genus the name of the species, as Aristotle expressed it), or we refer awkardly to a man's use of the mechanical system.

The difficulty into which the authors of "Behavior, Purpose, and Teleology" have plunged themselves is the consequence of failing to attend to the radical distinction between instrument and user, between natural processes and the ends or meanings discovered in, or attributed to, these processes by man. When the development of a geographical area is described as moving toward a mutually sustaining relation of rainfall to vegetation, the teleology seemingly attributable to this relation is the result of that particular ratio of rainfall to vegetation which men regard as desirable. Nature is, then, surreptitiously taken as a human artist subtly adjusting means to ends. Apart, however, from the context of human preferences and values, any relation whatsoever of rainfall to vegetation can be mutually sustaining. To speak of any one such adjustment as more desirable than another is to speak metaphorically. When a torpedo is said to direct itself by the sound of the target ship's propellors, or when a cybernetic device is said to keep a ship on its course, we must recall that the apparent teleology involved makes literal sense only within the context of the efficient design and correct use of these machines (MT §36; PC §21, pp. 258ff.).

"Mechanical dialectic," like natural dialectic, is a metaphorical notion; it refers to work automatically controlled by the difference between the present configuration of the machine and what the operator or his superior regards as the desirable outcome. Among the things a human worker may produce is a device which works automatically (by negative feedback) towards the end selected by another human worker. Unfortunately, the human user of many of the more complex instruments is often hidden; then the user is easily ignored. For instance, a computer adjusted to use part of its energy searching for a more efficient way of resolving the problem presented it is still an instrument of the worker who presents the original problem. It may improve, or simplify, as judged by the worker, both the statement of the problem and the original means of solving it; then it seems to be independent of the operator. But this appearance is deceptive. My point is that stories of harps that play music by themselves belong to Irish folklore.

Human work, on the other hand, may be described as labor controlled directly by its outcome. "Directly" is the fitting term here, for both the sensing device and the output control are parts of man's human nature; they are functions rendered possible by his sensitive field. More specifically, work is labor (output) controlled by the recognized or measured difference between its currently achieved stage and an ideal (or end) envisaged by the worker. This thoughtful envisagement of the ideal gives the dialectic a direction and a value altogether absent in the mechanical process (even when a direction or control is built into a mechanical process). Without this extrinsic evaluation and redirection, the next stage would remain merely a state on a par with any other. In addition, the worker himself is affected by this process. In the course of the work, his envisagement of the goal may change. Likewise, his technique, his manipulation of means to the end, may improve. Thus it could be said that the causality involved in the worker's relation to his work is continuous and mutual, and therefore his relation to his work is dialectical. Still, this dialectic is so different from the mechanical causality discussed earlier that only confusion could result from using the same term for both. Dialectic, in its proper and literal sense, refers exclusively to human involvements. However, the mechanical analogies serve a purpose in that they exhibit in a simplified form the articulation of the process of continuous reciprocal causality.

§44. THE LITERAL SENSE OF DIALECTIC

In addition to the generic and metaphorical senses of dialectic exemplified in nature and in machines, and to the more familiar and proper sense of dialectic instanced in human work, there are several other species.[5] The distinctions among them may be made by reference to the interpretative contexts within which this dynamic relation is operative. Let us consider three such contexts: A, interpretation of nature; B, interpretation of self; and C, interpretation of others.

A) The history of the development of any branch of our knowledge of nature is an objective dialectic in which interpretative theory and observation (ideally) tend toward more perfect correspondence. The scientific investigator responds to the difference between predictions inferred from his hypothesis and his actual observations; thus he measures the adequacy of his hypothesis. Then, where necessary, he introduces changes into his hypothesis (his output) in order to improve its correspondence with the observed facts. Some theory, even an incorrect theory, provided it is not too far wrong, can guide the student in the collection of data which may suggest a better use of the objective categories and concepts in the construction of an interpretative theory; in turn, this less imperfect theory functions as the guide to the collection of still more exact or more relevant interpretations of experience, and so on. A celebrated example was offered by Tycho Brahe, whose observations made within the context of Copernican-Ptolemaic theory were taken over by Kepler, thus helping him toward the discovery of the three laws of planetary motion which contributed to the establishing of Copernican theory. This more adequate theory rendered more accurate calculations and predictions possible and eventuated in still more precise observations.

The objective dialectic is, of course, more complex than the simple interchange between theory and data. The language of theory (e.g., mathematics), the instruments used in observation and experimentation, and various analogies likewise enter into these relations. For example, a dialectic movement is easy to observe in the development of many scientific instruments. Consider the thermometer. Measuring hot and cold by feel was rendered more exact with the invention of the mercury thermometer. By use of this instrument, the coefficient of expansion of various substances (e.g., glass) when heated could be determined. Knowledge of the coefficient of expansion of glass enabled the experimenter to correct the reading of his thermometer, and so to measure temperature to a far greater degree of accuracy, thus contributing to other improvements in theory and in instruments. Knowledge breeds knowledge, as theory and observation correct each other and lead to the development of new and better instruments in a seemingly limitless progress.

B) Another dialectic utilizing the existential categories in the interest of self-understanding and of character formation is less easy to characterize. Perhaps Plato's dialogues should be recalled as illustrations; however, I have in mind a dialectic rather less intellectualistic than Plato's is usually taken to be. What is given and is to be interpreted, and so united to the self-aware self, is probably to be identified as the flow of feeling and imagery, especially feeling, in which one's identity seems especially to be involved. It is also that illusive reflex of one's self to be sensed in all one's works and acts. What effects the interpretation is the store of existential categories and derivative interpretative principles (images, representations, concepts, and myths in which the self figures and which each of us has acquired from his culture and developed out of his own past experiences). The primary interpretative principle is that by which one interprets oneself as a possible protagonist. This principle is embodied in the conviction that some greater degree of freedom is always attainable and that even minimal natural freedom is sufficient to enable the individual who possesses it to make basic decisions and thus to enter in on the subjective dialectic, thereby eventually becoming a self-responsible person (MT §§21f.).

Natural freedom is the determining gift to the species *homo sapiens*; in this possession, the difference between man and other animals is to be found. By natural freedom, I mean liberation from the instincts which care for and guide the other animals at every critical turn of their lives. This freedom from instinctual determination is nothing less than the human possibility itself, man's sensitive field. Instincts are inherited patterns of action; we witness them in the southward flight of geese, in the squirrel's silage, and in the geometry of the spider. Instinct is the internal father of these animals, maintaining them still in their original paradise without responsibility or need of forethought. Evidently, instincts were Epimetheus' chief gift to the animals, for without instincts, other defensive or offensive equipment would be useless. And evidently, too, these instincts were virtually exhausted when he came to endow man. For this reason, Prometheus was led to replace them with the fire of intelligence, substituting calculation and prevision for automatisms.

Adam, so the story has it, was the first to yield to the Satanic temptation to reject natural routines and to relinquish the instinctive grasp of his own good. And, strangely, his lasting good lay in his yielding to this temptation, in his consequent exile from the pre-Adamic paradise, and in the evils and challenges which followed. Thenceforward, nourishing, sheltering, and protecting themselves presented problems men had to solve by conscious deliberation rather than by relying upon instinctive routines. Their new freedom, moreover, entailed the responsibility for taking a hand in working out their own survival and movement to maturity. Especially in this latter enterprise, they moved toward becoming more authentically themselves. Essential to anyone's envisaging himself as the protagonist of his own drama is the conviction that this natural freedom is a human possibility. Having this freedom, one can move toward becoming oneself through decision, struggle, and insight. Another reference to this dramatic pattern, translating it into terms used in this chapter, will be useful at this juncture (cf. §§16), and will recall the discussion of the existential categories in section 38.

The first fruit of intelligence, as the Greek dramatists conceived it (and as we recall from section 16 above), was a decision on the part of the chief actor, the protagonist, concerning his identity. The middle of a drama was formed by this actor's efforts to live out the identity he had chosen. But these efforts, being made in ignorance of his partial and quite human blindness, seem unexpectedly but constantly about to fail, until the catastrophic moment when the inadequacy of the decision becomes clear for all to see. The protagonist himself achieves some insight into the inappropriateness of his initial decision and his failure of self-knowledge. The end of the action is reached in this insight. Here, the insight, following upon the catastrophic failure of the struggle to embody the initiating decision, is something like a measure of the decision and exhibits its inadequacy. This insight and evaluation function as an interpretative principle. Thereupon the table is cleared, so to speak, and readied for formulating a new decision, a new and possibly more adequate output issuing from the protagonist's freedom. Here, the protagonist's insight into the divergence between his decision and his real nature, function, and impact upon the world takes the place of the mechanical "sensing device," and his reformulation of his decision corresponds to the "output control."

According to a humanistic view of man's condition, all of us possess the freedom enabling us to enter in on this dialectical pattern of decision, struggle, catastrophe, and insight. Indeed, it seems that all of us are involved in this dramatic dialectic, whether we will or not.

This human dialectic is unique. The making of the decision, the evaluation of it in the dramatic insight, the reformulation of it in the initial decision of the next drama, all are mediated through human language. Many philosophers have seen man's liberation from earlier biological conditions mirrored most clearly in his deliberate making and use of symbols, as contrasted with the animal's instinctive response to signals. The use of human symbols and language, however, has been attended with almost as much confusion as clarity, and this to such a degree that the human race has sometimes seemed to regret its decision and to wish for a return back to the primal paradise of unconscious art and unthinking self-care, where natural necessities smoothly and efficiently replace confused decisions, halting practice, and failing insight. This atavistic ideal is still very much alive among us, and philosophers from Hobbes through August Comte to B. F. Skinner have sought to lure men with the image of the mechanically organized and orderly society, where the average man plays only his preassigned role and where the major decisions are already made for him. Here every inclination to deviation, every unauthorized expression of individualism, is treated with operant conditioning, drugs, or force. Here the peace and order of the machine, the regularity of routine, bring the subjective dialectic to a halt, though the movement of the objective dialectic doubtless continues. So far, happily, history has always brought forth a savage, a hero, who could see through the promise of this frozen and mechanical paradise and could bring others to reject its destructive lure.

Although human talents can develop only in a human society, we have noted that a society will rarely permit the exercise of freedom beyong a certain point. Groups commonly develop a culture which discourages change and inhibits many kinds of work and human relation. Athens could not tolerate her own finest citizen, and the lives of repressed Galileos, exiled Spinozas, and martyred saints everywhere remind us that Athens is not unique in her antipathies. Nevertheless, all men do not endure these repressions and exiles with equanimity. The revolutionary, the champion of the negative, is always pitted against the status quo and the dead weight of traditional injustice. Every society is a battleground in which the forces of hallowed custom struggle against the harbingers of the new order. The chief contestant for the new order feels initially assured of protection since he feels that the movement of events lies in his own power and is subject to his freedom. Confidence in his own power and freedom is precisely what makes of a man a "chief contestant," or protagonist, and a potential hero, one who is willing to make the crucial decision and to take responsibility for it.

A protagonist, a person accepting the conviction of freedom and the duty and risk which go with that conviction, can then utilize the other existential categories in making decisions and in attempting to live with their consequences. Often, indeed usually, his final insight reveals that his initial decision, made in the blinding and deceptive light of hybris was, when measured by reality, catastrophically wrong.[6] Thus despite himself, he exemplifies the patterned movement toward self-revelation and self-determination. But other heroes, e.g., Socrates, make decisions whose appropriateness is verified in their final insight. Perhaps these heroes are correctly called martyrs. In any event, the hero's interpretative principles often strike more and more effective compromises between nature and freedom, culture and person, society and individual, everyday and mythological, as they interact with the events and circumstances surrounding the crises of human life.

The subjective dialectic ideally moves between the beginning category of the protagonist and the final category of authenticity. Then the three categories defining the tragic movement function as the means for moving from this beginning to the end. Nothing in human life, however, is quite so neat. And in this instance, we must admit to having no very clear grasp of the specific powers and state of freedom of any protagonist, nor do we know with precision just what his end, his authentic and true being, may be. We are, therefore, thrown back upon the tragic movement itself, which on any given occasion finds the *archē* in a hybritic vision of the protagonist's identity and develops thence through effort and suffering to a negative apprehension of the protagonist's *telos*, his true being. Cultures generally, however, have enshrined their most genial understanding of man in beliefs which can communicate some apprehension of his destiny and hence offer a clue for selecting his place of beginning (*archē*). Beginning and ending thus are interdependent and meet in the three categoreal principles of the tragic dialectic. Or to express the matter in a different way, our vision of our beginning and ending is generated out of reflection upon the tragic crises we have undergone. Thus through crisis and reflection, interpretative principles and the human life to be interpreted approach a harmony.

Not only dramas of great magnitude, but also successful psychiatric sessions or trivial occasions of self-inquiry and self-criticism exhibit a mutually clarifying and determining relation between interpretative principle and the matter of human life. Such an interpretation is not merely a means by which feelings and sensations are given meaning and determinateness, but the interpreting categories, images, concepts, and myths are clarified at the same time and so become more efficacious in their relation to feeling and sense. The clarification is mutual and developing.

Much of human growth may be conceived of as an effort toward rendering feelings, motives, and beliefs more determinate, more definite, with the purpose of coming finally into the unimpeded possession of all one's powers. When, for instance, on a lonely night near a remote and abandoned house, a person senses fear, he may pause and ask just what he is afraid of. Nothing overtly dangerous can be lying in ambush. Perhaps after a modicum of reflection, he concludes that he is merely afraid of being lonely. The fear has thereby become more determinate, less vaguely engulfing, and the person has matured in self-understanding, even though slightly in this instance, and has become more authentically himself. For now he has found a *logos*, an interpretative principle, which has given a unity and a meaning to confused fears. And now further, he can proceed to ask himself why he should be anxious about loneliness. In what sense is the absence of the other a threat? Thus this minor crisis has thrown the person in question back upon an unexpressed conviction, with the consequence that the conviction is expressed, criticized, and reformulated. The experience has been in its modest way maturing; it has revealed a principle.

No doubt an ideal of the mature and authentic self may be at least remotely envisaged in which the possibilities of experience have been rendered determinate by this subjective dialectic, leaving no unacknowledged and obscure part of the self remaining where self-deception and self-doubt may linger, blocking the use of one's powers; this is an ideal of human being, though, hardly to be actualized. In many of the more skillfully constructed dramas, a movement toward this being may be discerned; one thinks immediately of *Oedipus Rex*, *Antigone*, *Macbeth*, or *Murder in the Cathedral*. The property rendering these dramas effective lies in the revelatory return of their endings upon their beginnings. When the effect of the action upon the protagonist is sufficiently profound, it tends to force him back upon his basic views and convictions about himself and his world. Thus catastrophic action can lead to a revelation (a measurement) of one's deepest persuasions and perhaps to a revision of them. We recall Oedipus' recognition of his overweening self-confidence, Creon's realization of his foolish insistence upon kingly prerogative, Macbeth's insight into his short-sighted and egotistic hunger for power. And we can hardly doubt that any person could be caught up in a dialectic which could return him to his primary beliefs and principles and reveal to him how they are incorporated in a determining fashion, and in often self-destructive (yet sometimes redeeming) action.

This act of being thrown back upon one's basic principles I have called "archaic experience" (PC §§2f., 51; MT §11). It can be exemplified in the life history of movements, of peoples, and of cultures as well as in individuals. The Cartesian philosophy records such a return, consequent upon the development of the new sciences of the seventeenth century. In our own time, I suggest, the enormous growth of technology, now threatening to absorb the whole of human life, may invite a catastrophe and a return to basic beliefs and to a reassessment, perhaps a reformulation, of them. Doubtless we must always strive for such a consummation (PC pp. 28f.; MT pp. 215f.).

C) In the course of daily life, one engages in various kinds of dialectical relations with other persons. This "dialectic of the other" is different from the two kinds of dialectic just discussed in that the other person is both a body, an object located over against one in space and time, yet also a subjectivity. The other is not known directly as one knows oneself, but through empathy and through spontaneous interpretation of posture, movement, and behavior. No doubt there is an analogy between communication within the self between conscious and unconscious, and communication between the self and others. Communication with the other is specifically noticeable when the other is somehow disdained and so is easily made into a symbol of unworthy and rejected impulses, distinguished from the self and relegated to the unconscious. But even if the other is acknowledged to be a self, a person, perhaps a friend or another self, as Aristotle said, still undeniably the other is something in space and time, a kind of object with which one has to reckon in practical contexts as well as in biological and similar contexts. Hence dealings with him are in part objective. The curious status of the other, partly objective, partly subjective, suggests that dialectical relations with him are a mixture of the objective and subjective dialectics (PC pp. 195f.).

This mixture of the two dialectics is already evident in relation to objects where the primitive (and poetic) mind is operative. Only relatively late in one's own history, as in the history of man, does a person come to understand objects objectively. Similarly, the movement to interpreting another person as another self is not immediate but, as in the instance of the experience of objects, develops out of an original stage of identity. In sum, a modest degree of maturity must be developed before a person can withhold the inclination to personify objects and to think of them mythically as possessed of some animating and half-human or super-human power. Precisely the characteristic of certain mental illnesses lies in the inability of the patient to restrain the inclination to invest objects with human qualities. J.-P. Sartre writes of the feeling which came over him, during an apparent lapse of mental health, that buildings along the streets of Paris loomed over him threateningly and appeared to intend to engulf him. Similarly interpretation of another as an other person or another self is the product of maturity in dealing with the tension between individual and group. That is, the recognition of another as an other independent self is a development out of a more inchoate interpretation of others as something like an extension of or part of oneself. The sense of unity with the other or dependence on him precedes recognition of distinction from him. The growth is from unity with the other toward an analogical relation to him. The infant, for example, is usually thought unable to distinguish between himself and his mother, and even in later life the child may not succeed in outgrowing this initial identification. Unity and identification with another, thus, seem to precede recognition of the self as a self-responsible agent. Perhaps the infant's recognition of his difference from the mother comes about by taking rough note of the fact that some bodily movements (e.g., those of his "own" limbs) are more or less subject to his "own" desire, whereas those of another (the mother's) are not. At least some parts of the mother-infant are more tractable to his wishes than are other parts. Thus the mother comes to be set over against the infant as other, yet not totally other. Hence, dialectical relations with her can be initiated.

Development of the dialectic from some such beginning is a complex and often uneven process. Even persons of mature age can be observed to be anxiously concerned about pleasing or displeasing the image of a parent still an integral and obscurely determining part of their own neurotic and inauthentic personalities. They tend to see certain other persons not as they are, but rather as they announce or stand for others (e.g., for an important parent), and consequently they are unable to establish mature relations with these others. Opposed to this quirk of growth, on the other hand, the relation to other selves may develop unhealthily away from the capacity to identify with another, for there are persons who are quite incapable of grasping another as an other self. They are inclined to objectify persons and to think of them as instruments subservient to or resistant to their wishes. They may be very clever about concealing their disability; nevertheless, they fail to apprehend or to sense the human quality of another and no doubt of themselves as well. Persons of this schizophrenic sort, the true solipsists, can kill without compunction, even for trivial provocation, and figure frequently in crime reports.

These variations from the desirable norm of recognition of another self as a self possessing his own body (as I possess mine) suggest that a particularly important study should concern the means by which apprehension of the selfhood (or common humanity) of another independent self is communicated and developed. My suggestion, only to be sketched here, is that the selfhood of another self is displayed and understood, at least in an important part, through producing and reading "small signs," signs which we are, for the most part, unaware of making or interpreting (cf. §24). I refer to automatic movements such as the flushing of a face, the intonation of the voice, a movement of the hand, and the like. It is important to recognize that we respond to such spontaneous interpretative gestures mimetically. We respond, for example, to the small gestures of anger which the angry person produces unconsciously, by reproducing, perhaps to lesser extent, similar gestures and consequently we come to feel the anger ourselves. The spontaneous interpretation of these small signs by a mimetic response suggests a return toward the original state of identity or fusion with the other. Clearly, such a return is desirable, even necessary, for it insures some fellow feeling, some sameness and unanimity with the other. Also, this mimetic response is not only a communication in its own right (it says what it is like to be this person now), but it constitutes an important factor in the foundation upon which more complex communications may be constructed. No doubt it is an element in that complex state of mind called love. This fellow feeling, however, may also move beyond reasonable bounds; witness the sense of strong anger passing like wildfire from person to person in a mob, when the anger in each exacerbates that of the other. Here individualities are lost, fused together in an irrational and infantile group-unity which many a charismatic leader has known only too well how to manipulate.

This infantile group-unity may, however, be arrested by a reflection upon the sense of anger in relation to its occasioning circumstances. Is the anger felt appropriately or exaggeratedly? The anger thus measured may be purged and rendered more determinate whereupon the reflecting person begins to feel differently and hence to exhibit different communicative gestures. These latter affect his neighbors, and by this combination of the objective and subjective dialectics, the character of a group develops and may move toward some more complex and differentiated state. The spontaneous and unconscious interpretations of small signs is thus a significant element in identifying oneself with, or in distinguishing oneself from, the other.

This last example, and preceding ones as well, call to mind the fact that dialectic may follow alternative routes, and not all routes are equally desirable. A desideratum, then, is a standard for measuring and directing a dialectical movement.

§45. EVALUATION BY AN INTRINSIC STANDARD

Dialectic is a process, hence is normally judged by its outcome. There are two ways of looking at its outcome: it may be considered intrinsically, as that which internal factors direct; or it may be considered extrinsically, as leading to an outcome possessing a value beyond itself. Here our interest will center largely, though not wholly, upon the intrinsic end. If we use the term "end" in a metaphorical sense, as we did when discussing mechanical dialectic (§43), we may identify the intrinsic end of some dialectical processes as their most complex identifiable state. Consider some of the illustrations already utilized.

In the cybernetic illustration (§42), the effect of A's causal relation to B was "fed back" to A, thereby altering A so that its subsequent causal relation to B, thus changed, would more probably give rise to the B desired by the operator of the machine. Therefore, the outcome of the dialectical process at one state directs its movement to the subsequent stage. That is to say, the accomplishment of dialectic at an earlier stage (matter) can function as an interpretative principle (form) leading to a later state. What is fed by B back to A is technically called "information." Information relating several physical processes may be regarded as those elements the processes possess in common. The language of this description evidently assumes the partial homogeneity (or the accomodation) of the entities A and B, and recalls the prescription of the structural likeness required by Russell (see above §42). Thus the quantity of oxygen in my blood is "measured" and communicated to the mechanism controlling my rate of breathing. The more oxygen, the slower the breathing rate. This "end" is intrinsic; it is not imposed from outside the system.

The causal interrelations mediated by "information" move A and B toward the state identified as a goal or end, evidently a state in which A and B exhibit a more elaborately developed common structure. Here, as before, the information exchange was mediated through the sensing device and was fed into the output control. As an animal lives on, its efforts to survive change its environment, and the animal becomes changed by this activity, with the result that animal and environment approach a state of mutual adaptation or mutual information. Data and theory, knower and known, actor and acted-upon can likewise become mutually informed. The data of a theory, for example, become more and more amply available and increasingly precisely observed as improved theory enables the construction of more selective and accurate instruments of observation and measure. The final and ideal result would be the detailed and complete theory precisely reflecting the whole of the data.

And finally, the human being, the knower, entertains a dialectical movement between the imaginative and unconscious parts of his psyche and his conscious and rational mind. Probably most physicians would agree that the desirable development requires that both of these parts be closely related; then information, in the healthy mind, will move back and forth between imaginative and unconscious levels of the psyche and the conscious portion of the mind in the form of dreams, reverie, appreciation, and in motor, verbal and rational activity, with the final consequence that the several parts of the mind become harmoniously related, i.e., "integrated." The conscious and rational mind accepts the imaginative and the unconscious mind, and each reflects the other, one constantly translating the enlarging contents of the others into its own economy. (The reverse of this movement is illustrated in *Macbeth*. This reversal becomes evident when the Thane of Cawdor says "Macbeth hath murdered sleep," for here sleep refers to his sleeping self, the unconscious self yet to be, a self which a happier mate than Lady Macbeth might have helped. As it was, Macbeth yielded to the inclination to identify that self, his birthright, with the powers and possessions of his everyday world. Thus he lost touch with himself; consequently in the end, he saw that his life signified nothing.)

In each of these instances, the movement which the dialectical relation appears naturally to engender is toward a mutual reflection or conformity between the objects and events entering into this relation. This direction of movement may be described by saying that the events within such a context tend toward similarity of structure. With respect to this goal, dialectic may be regarded as mutual translation. Indeed, this way of expressing the matter can be seen in the definitions with which we began, but it is significant that it should be found so widely illustrated. This goal, the achievement of identity or similarity of structure, can be accepted as an intrinsic standard and used as a means for passing a rough judgement upon the efficiency of any dialectical system.

Dialectic moves toward harmonizing the structures of the events or objects participating in it, but the harmony actually achieved may not always be desired by someone using a dialectical process. For this reason, in part at least, dialectic has acquired a bad name among some philosophers. The only standard intrinsic to dialectic, however, seems to be the standard relative to the movement toward similarity in form or identity of structure among the events which participate in it. A dialectical process is intrinsically good if and only if the events involved in it do, in fact, move through mutual interaction toward increasing similarity in form. Whether the form is desired by someone making use of the process for his own ends can be decided only by reference to criteria extrinsic to the dialectic itself.

Are, though, such extrinsic measures trustworthy indicators that the dialectical process has reached a good and desirable issue? No doubt, the outcome of some dialectical development will, beginning with the indefinite notions of good and evil, formulate axiological categories and will proceed thence to the definition of such value concepts and interpretative principles as "the desirable," "the mature," "the complete," within the relevant contexts. And these principles, perhaps embodied in world symbols or myths, will have to function as the best criteria available at the time.

The case of the subjective dialectic is more complex. The course of events which swept an Oedipus or a Macbeth on to his end can scarcely be imagined to have been explicitly proposed by him. Rather, both were moved inexorably on to the intrinsic end of a vaguely grasped dialectic. In the larger sense, however, the sense in which any man may be thought to desire to be himself, these heroes may be said to have willed their unhappy histories, for thus they came further to know and to be themselves. A more determined and perhaps a more sophisticated hero might have designed, or at least have acquiesced in, such a series of events had there been a reasonable assurance of his moving through it into self-knowledge. He would thus have willed his own fate, and he would have judged the dialectical process by an external standard: its effectiveness in leading him to self-knowledge. Such a protagonist is possessed of *amor fati* and is by way of becoming an authentic person (PC pp. 151ff.).

Quite different, we must suspect, is the experience of one caught up in the mutually causal relations obtaining at present between man and modern machines, a technological dialectic, for the intrinsic end of this dialectic is the complete accommodation or similarity of man and machine. Such a person must, therefore, expect the growing homogeneity between men and machines to gain momentum in his own personal development, with the consequence that mechanical routines, not his own individual style of existing, become the end product (MT §37). For *amor fati* he must substitute an *amor machinae*. That machines should communicate their properties, their routines, to men seems an unhappy issue from this relationship, for if men are indeed radically different from machines, then their efforts to become mechanical, something they are not, cannot but be followed by frustration and unhappiness.[7] Important to consider, then, is the possibility that the technological dialectic of man and machine should be made to conform to some extrinsic standard more favorable to human kind and its growth. Just such an extrinsic standard was proposed in chapter 7 of my *Man and Technolgy*.

§46. EVALUATION BY AN EXTRINSIC STANDARD

The captain of a vessel, after consulting his charts, sets the automatic pilot upon a definite course. Thereupon the chosen course acts as an externally imposed standard which judges, so to speak, the correctness of the ship's actual heading at any moment of its movement. There seems to be no problem in understanding the operation of this standard; the measure of deviation and the output control provide a sufficient account. The matter is radically changed, however, where human beings and not machines enter into the dialectic. A man commonly is in possession of nothing more than a vague grasp of the desired or desirable relation to himself, others, nature, and the world, which he needs in order to steer his behavior aright. A further difficulty arises from the fact that his grasp upon these relations is, along with the rest of his activity, involved in the complex and concrete nexus of his whole life and, thus, is itself in process of change. Now, when the star by which the helmsman steers is not only difficult to see but is itself in movement, then the helmsman is — and should know himself to be — in a quandary.

This quandary is inevitable; it is intrinsic to the very conditions giving rise to and empowering the dialectic in the concrete and temporal world. For a loss of clarity is encountered whenever a concept is applied under actual conditions. Suppose a concept has been clarified and defined by the most approved logical and analytical techniques. It becomes a figure standing out sharply against its ground. Its relationships are, within its system (its ground), clearly known; its connections to other similar concepts have been precisely specified. Consider the way Euclid's 47th proposition as figure stands out against the remainder of his *Elements* as ground. This clarity and precision became one of the models which inspired Western thought, technological activity, and even much of its metaphysics. Unfortunately, as soon as such a concept is given an interpretation in the everyday temporal world, all is changed.

This change may be envisaged as a shift in context or ground, where the figure is still basically the same concept. But this new concrete context or ground is the reverse of clear. Its indefeasible complexity guarantees there will always be unsuspected relations which can place the concept in question in a completely new and unpredicted perspective. A simple illustration is provided by the Allies who early in World War I released chlorine gas when the wind was favorable, as a poison against their current enemies. But then the wind changed and the poison was carried back to the Allied troops. Exhaust gases from automobiles and factories, slowly but surely poisoning our atmosphere, offer a more poignant illustration. The annals of day-to-day life in our technological age are replete with such illustrations. Engineering is not a predictive science over the long range; it is a technique for gaining control over nature for purposes of present use.

In any event, a faultlessly predictive science is an impossibility in the temporal world, for a clear apprehension of *all* the effects of applying any given concept are in principle beyond grasp. The number of such effects, and effects of effects, is indefinitely large. And we and our machines are not Leibnizian gods who can entertain an infinite number of perspectives upon an indefinitely large number of individual substances or events. Somewhere a catastrophic surprise will always lie in wait; the finitude entailed by our ontological fault, our single perspective upon the multifarious world, insures that outcome. For such a reason, A. N. Whitehead was accustomed to recommend the search after clarity, together with a distrust of it.

The matter merits brief elaboration. I doubt that the opaqueness and irrationality of the concrete world are completely accounted for by complexity. Complexity, though, surely provides a partial reason for this opacity and for the unpredictability of experience. Consider that any object is the nodal point of indefinitely many relationships, only some of which can be mastered by any one person or group. For one thing, a culture is agent of the *aletheia* process which reveals objects and events in a characteristic guise. And there are indefinitely many possible cultures. Thus the object with which I am writing appears in one way to an unlettered Kurdish herdsman, in quite another way to a member of a literate culture. Again, this object may appear in many cognitive roles (to a member of a Western culture, it may be taken as an object of chemistry, of physics, of economics, and the like), or in many value relations (as having an aesthetic, an ethical, an ecological, or a religious function, and so forth). And each of these ways of appearing can be manifold. The all but unmanageable complexity of the object is intimated by mention of these few ways in which it may appear. Perhaps it may seem extraordinary that we should come to possess any truth about any object. Still, a certain temporary and practical clarity about concrete objects or events is achieved by ignoring (i.e., abstracting from) the greater part of the real contexts in which they may appear. But the ignored aspects and relations may retain a hidden importance and so may return, like the ancient fate, to take revenge upon the one who ignored them.

The point is essential to any reflection upon how ideas enter into history, and it calls for a re-evaluation of clear concepts when they are applied in the temporal world. A clear concept once introduced effectively into a concrete dialectical context is placed in a process apt to elicit obscure relationships, unexpected and conflicting interpretations. Such is the basis for the claim that concepts are both clarifying and obscuring, both specifying and distorting. Such, in addition, is one origin of the motive power of dialectic in its movement toward the resolution of conflicts. In the actual world, anything apparently offering satisfaction to our erotic urge toward harmony with ourselves, others, or nature cannot be far removed from renewed stress and conflict; in human experience one resolution commonly leads to another conflict. Thus the ideal of control over nature seemed, during the Renaissance, to define nicely a program which was to relieve men of economic insufficiency and of the hardships of labor. Only later was this idea seen to entail, at least to render inevitable, another: the control of man by man, an ideal which is being realized along with its sinister implications in one form by the consumer society and in an even more threatening form by totalitarian societies. Thus do the most constructive intentions turn out, upon insertion into the process of history, to be destructive.

And thus the end which men pursue appears differently as its context varies, for the end is an element within a dialectic of its own, whereby it, too, undergoes change. Once, the end of technology, the external standard by which it was guided, was the production of security and the means for living. Now, with this end achieved in principle, the new end has become the further development of technology as an end in itself (MT §35).[8] In general, the end by which Western man today evaluates the course his life has taken may not be what he is led to judge it by tomorrow, though both, within their respective contexts, may have been truly judged.

Is there, then, upon the human horizon, no recognizable and determinate end by which our own dialectical involvements may be judged? Once again, a cultural relativity seems to lie in wait (cf. §29). But according to an old tradition in Western philosophy, that which is properly called being provides this dependable evaluative element. And in fact, the changing beliefs concerning human being have offered, in the course of the dialectic of human growth, a flickering guidance over nearly three thousand years of history. Let us ask again what philosophy can say about this being or about the more basic being at its origin. What is this being? How is it to be designated? With these ontological questions in mind, we turn to the last chapter, with the intention of giving this philosophy its final characterization.

Notes

1. Bertrand Russell, *Human Knowledge, Its Scope and Limits* (N. Y.: Simon & Schuster, 1948), p. 468.
2. Perhaps the comparison of the angle of deviation from the desired course to the desired course itself should be recognized as a separate step in the process. But for present purposes, this additional complexity may be omitted.
3. This paper appeared in *Philosophy of Science*, vol. 10 (1943), pp. 18-24.
4. *Philosophy of Science*, vol. 17 (1950), pp. 310-17.
5. A quite different division of dialectic is offered by Professor A. Bahn in "Some Neglected Aspects of Dialectic," *The New Scholasticism*, vol. 43, no. 2 (1969), pp. 276-81.
6. On hybris, see §16 above, p. 100f. Also MT §5, pp. 230ff.
7. See my "On Dialectic: Mechanical and Human," in *Communication, Philosophy and the Technological Age*, ed. Michael J. Hyde (University of Alabama Press, 1982), pp. 15-47.

8. William Leiss, *The Domination of Nature*, chap. 8 (Boston: The Beacon Press, 1974). The author argues that today thinkers can properly doubt that the ideal of dominating and controlling nature, as this ideal was seemingly so reasonably expressed by Descartes, Bacon, and others up to and including B. F. Skinner, is now a fruitful or appropriate ideal by which to guide our history.

IX

The Beginning and End of Interpretation

§47. ON THE BEGINNING OF PHILOSOPHY

Plato said that philosophy begins in wonder. Which of the many senses of wonder did he mean? Surely not trivial wonder ("I wonder what time it is?"), and hardly practical wonder either ("How can I survive on my salary?"). He probably did not even have in mind a more curious and intellectual wonder ("What is the chemistry of the cell?"). Aristotle's categories are related to this latter kind of wonder, but direct it more broadly and more humanistically than does modern science. ("What was Socrates in his substance? What relations did he bear to others? What qualities did he exhibit? To what whole are these bits of knowledge related?") All these latter kinds of wonder are important. The progress of the sciences and of philosophy depends upon them. They are the provocations to extending our knowledge and to deepening our grasp upon ourselves, our society, and our environment. Still, they do not exhaust the possibilities of wonder, for there is another which goes beyond and behind them all and extends to another plane. How is it that I can raise any questions at all? Why do I, the questioner, exist? Why am I not, rather, nothing? Questions of this kind provoke a unique wonder and point to the beginning of philosophy.

To question is both a strange and an estranging act. And man who questions all things, even questions questioning itself, is strangest of all. To question, even trivially, throws what is interrogated, to some extent, into the region of wonder, for what is it to question? To question is to seek the meaning of what is questioned while admitting that that meaning is not present. It is to bring what is questioned into the open where its interpretation is as yet unset in a routine mold. To seek absent meanings seems to be the peculiar function and destiny of man himself. To question that questioning is to move man's nature and destiny beyond the bounds of confident belief and traditional certainties. To question the questioner is to abandon one's foothold in the familiar world; it is to take leave of the established and already interpreted world and to inquire into its possibility and into its source (its *archai*) or being. The great questions in philosophy possess this unsettling power.

Wonder at something, then, can invite us back to consider its original emergence into our consciousness and into our sensitive field. And consciousness itself, Husserl has said is "the wonder of wonders," for it is that to which itself and other things appear or come to be present. To be struck, thus, with wonder at man as the place of appearance, the agent of interpretation, is to be led back to his unique being and to catch a glimpse of the function he and perhaps no other being can exercise.

What is this presence, this appearance, to which man has the peculiar power of bringing other beings as well as himself? To tag it as consciousness seems to be an unnecessarily psychological mode of expression, unless consciousness be understood in a somewhat unusual sense as the power of transformation, the power of transforming, for example, the flow of feeling and presentations into experience. Heidegger is well known for his view that presence is the primary sense which the West has, since the Greeks, given to being.[1] Plato is said to have held that being in the fullest sense is that which is eternally present. Other things may approach and participate in eternal being, but can share only to a lesser extent in its timelessness. They can come to be present for a time, but not eternally. And Plato set the trend which still dominates the Western world.

Now, to see being primarily as timeless presence is to see that aspect of it which is susceptible to interpretation as timeless structures. Such structures are those the language and operations of mathematics are designed to exhibit. This mathematical view of being has proved itself to be enormously fruitful in many respects, and yet Heidegger is surely right: to confine our understanding of being to this one view is in the end destructive, for a consequence of this narrow view of being was that men tended to find their own being in what was most evidently related to eternal and timeless being. Now, the intellect apprehends timeless being and seems to have most in common with it; hence, men came to regard themselves as primarily rational and to devaluate their lesser rational and their non-rational qualities and powers. The result was that other parts of themselves were minimized or overlooked. Platonic intellectualist man thus tended to search for, and hence to find, both in himself and in the world around him, primarily unchanging traits, those most nearly resembling mathematical structures. He was, therefore, led by this mathematicism to overlook in nature and in himself much which is no less there than its mathematical structure, but which cannot be apprehended by mathematical or physical methods.

Intellectualist toward himself, mathematicist toward nature, typically modern man's limited interpretative principles have severely impoverished the world to which he has access. Whether or not Heidegger justly attributes this limiting Platonism to Plato himself is not the issue. The point is that limiting what can come to presence in man's experience to what is most like a mathematical structure clearly truncates experience. An important function the interrogative discourse of ontology can perform is to lead us to recognize the abstract character of doctrines of nature and man such as this one, and to do so by inducing in us an insight into concrete being. An indispensible step in inducing this insight is asking the kind of question which opens up a wider horizon and points to a genuinely philosophic beginning. And if this beginning may, with the tradition, be said to lie in something called "being," then a necessary result of the questioning of this being is a recognition of its temporal character, for observe that the indefeasibly temporal character of experience is a much more evident trait than its unchanging mathematical structure, so much more evident and even indispensable than its mathematical structure that one would suppose it to be the more reliable guide to the nature and being of experience. After all, concepts of timeless structures presuppose temporal beings in which they were earlier embodied. Thus, being, as far as it enters our experience and so becomes questionable, is undeniably temporal, and indeed, at some point obviously present.

Let us, therefore, follow tradition so far as to accept presence as a clue to the nature of being without assuming that it must be eternal presence. We must immediately recognize, though, that presence is complex, and one way of doing this is to glance at the etymology of the word. "Presence" derives from the Latin *praeesse*, or *praesēns*, to be in front of or near; it is the opposite of *abesse*, to be away from or distant; pre-sense suggests literally being positioned before one, geometrically opposite to one, occupying the same time and almost, though not quite, the same place. Likewise, the "before" in "before one" may also be taken, not altogether arbitrarily, as referring to time. The thing present must have existed before, so it must have a past; at least it must already have had a sense for one. To make sense now, it must have had a prior sense. Likewise, having a past time and a now moment as well, it is directed on toward a future. It is in three-dimensional time. Presence is not a static condition, it is a temporal movement, a presence now, away from, and toward.

I am saying that the word "presence" connotes not merely a now-dimension, but also the other two dimensions of time as well. Aristotle expressed something like this by noting that a present moment is always between a past and a future moment. Chapter 3 above endeavored to exemplify a similar point in its discernment and description of the periodic structure of time, although it envisaged a somewhat different relation between future and past. As that chapter and section 52 present the matter, a present moment of concrete time must come out of the future, through the past, then into the present, where it can become effective. The present, therefore, is the place of effectiveness, but as such it presupposes future and past. A present moment abstracted from its future and past dimensions is without direction, without meaning, hence not the sort of thing of which experience is made. It is not in lived time. Now, the eternal present is such an abstraction. Concrete, not abstract, time, however, is the presupposition of experience. Being, then, is scarcely eternal presence; it is more properly to be associated with concrete time. That there should be any recognized or recognizable thing to wonder at, that there should be we who wonder, we who question, is a consequence of being present in concrete and lived time.

Beyond recognizing that the time of questioning, of wonder, is concrete and dramatic time, we may ask what this more completely concrete context is wherein we are present and which makes possible one's life-world. We may term this more concrete context the ground, or being, or the power of world-making, or that which gives possibilities, but such terms merely designate the object of wonder, while saying little or nothing about it. If they could say something about it, we might then have an ontology, or the beginning of one.

I am inclined to believe that an ontology in a traditional sense, that which lays out a logical and complete doctrine of the structure of being, its definition, properties, functions, and relations to other studies, is often no more than a prejudice and an exercise in hybris. Being is not so much a thing or a class of things which has, or has been given, a meaning, as that which gives meaning in the first place. If so, then, ontology is not like a science of objects; it is more like a discipline which, if assiduously practiced, may yield insights into being, the possibility and source of meaning, the gift of world-making, the power of interpreting presentations into a world. Such insights may occasionally touch upon the world itself and issue in world symbols. I further suggest that this discipline is a process of awakening a sensitivity to, and skill in using, a kind of pointing. If so, then the kinds of questions expressed in the first paragraph of this section probably point in the right direction. We shall not, though, unless possessed of an unusual hybris, expect text-book answers to these questions.

Nevertheless, to have the directions indicated wherein an answer could be discovered is no inconsiderable achievement. In order to appreciate this achievement, the nature of pointing needs to be understood. Moreover, if being is not a thing, or not a kind which may be examined, manipulated, or studied in the ordinary way we study an object of everyday life, and not an object of one of the sciences either, then we shall have to employ some unusual means for pointing to it. I suggest a peculiar kind of pointing can be used to designate the preeminent object of wonder. To this peculiar gesturing we now turn.

§48. POINTING AND MEANING-GIVING

Pointing is a very simple kind of meaning-giving, a simplified act of naming. It may be illustrated by a temperature gauge. The pointer picks out one particular temperature from the range on the scale. It says that a specific temperature is there now, i.e., exists. What do *we* do when we point? For there to be any pointing at all, from the simplest to the most elaborate, there ordinarily is someone who points, as well as a pointing instrument, an object pointed to, something pointed away from, and finally, someone to whom the pointing is to some degree intelligible. One points, that is, with something, at something, away from something, and in order to indicate something to someone. The pointer's intention is to discriminate what he desires to talk about from irrelevancies.

Consider a gesture pointing toward an object. No natural (e.g., causal) tie between the object and the gesture is to be discovered. The same gesture might equally well point elsewhere, or toward another object. Or quite another gesture might have been used. Also, the place indicated by the gesture might be occupied by an object different from the one intended. What the gesture does do when pointing out an object in space is answer the question concerning the location of an object by separating out the place where the object is or is thought to be at that time. We know that some other object is not indicated since the gesture could always be repeated to designate a smaller area from which the other possible but unintended object is excluded. That is, the pointing can be brought under finer control so that it separates out a smaller region contained in the first one. Pointing limits and individualizes space. Finally, a conveniently small place is indicated by the gesture as the place intended. Then, we say, the communication is successful.

How does one know that a still smaller area need not be indicated? Just because the respondent indicates that he understands. But how does the respondent know that his own responsive pointing is successful? We must recall that this whole pointing action begins with a flow of feeling and an intention within an already developed culture, within contexts, and within an atmosphere of custom and convention. In this pervasive atmosphere of beliefs and things already known and familiar to all, where so many questions are already settled, the object becomes accessible. Here spontaneous identifications are the rule. When the demand of this custom is fulfilled, then the indicating is presumed to be successful. The familiarity of the atmosphere of culture and tradition lends this act its air of obviousness. Custom enters in both the initiation and the completion of the act and supplements it at every turn. Indeed, so efficiently do we use the gestural and linguistic customs of our culture that a brief movement or sound is quite sufficient to point out most objects of daily concern. For the more precise needs of the sciences, the conventions determining the limits of, say, experimental error, limits which bring pointing to a stop, are determined with more self-critical awareness. Or when the object to be designated is quite off familiar horizons, we must resort to poetic or mythic pointing.

In any case, without such generally accepted conventions, no one could tell that the index finger points rather than is pointed out, nor would one otherwise know that the index finger rather than other fingers (for example, the thumb) point, i.e., give direction rather than, say, indicate number; nor could one judge when this action is successful. Pointing is a statement drawn from the language of gesture; the grammar and vocabulary of this language are no less conventional than that of other languages. Consider the comparative complexity of the act. The one pointing out an X by hand assumes his respondent believes, in effect, that an imaginary line drawn from the pointer's wrist through his index finger and continued beyond will fall somewhere in the near vicinity of the X. Clearly, this language is in its own way as complex and as dependent upon convention as spoken language is. Clearly also, elements other than custom are involved. By the cooperation of these several elements, a *that*, an X, is brought into the open (the "area" activated by one's sensitive field) where it can be interpreted.

§49. ACTS OF POINTING

The method of pointing I have outlined was put to use in a more modern way by A. N. Whitehead in order to indicate geometrical elements by means of a set of regions having constantly decreasing dimensions. A point to be defined, for example, could be designated as the common member of an infinite series of concentric circles having constantly decreasing radii. In the point itself, the ratio of the radius to the circumference of the circle becomes not so much indefinitely small as irrelevant. In other words, the point itself is not another one of the circular regions which served to indicate it. It is not a member of the series of pointing regions, but rather is the limit upon which they converge. An equally familiar example is such a series as $^1/_2, ^1/_4, ^1/_8, ^1/_{16}, \ldots\ ^1/_{2^n}$, which converges upon a limit not a member of the series (here, zero), and thus points it out. The converging of such a series is its pointing.

The matter is not radically changed when we come to speak of applied mathematics.[2] Consider, for an illustration, the period closing this sentence. It is a circle which possesses, for the purpose of this illustration, a negligible radius. We may consider that the period is converged upon by a set of physically located concentric circles having continuously diminishing radii. Although the period itself, considered as an area, always possesses a small but finite radius, this radius is ignored — even if it were very large — when the area is the object pointed out. We ignore this radius and treat the period just as if it were a mathematical point. For many purposes, the point and the period possess the same being.

Thus, as one might express it, mathematical elements become applicable to, or substitutable for, other objects just because the being which is considered irrelevant can, in fact, be neglected within the given context. Hence the printed dot is the common member of the physical regions converging upon it, but it itself is not a region; rather, it is the limit of the converging regions. The movement of the finger pointing toward an object, as it moves through an arc and comes to rest on the line toward the object, is analogous to this convergence of the regions upon the dot. It is important to recall that the neglected radius is only an ignored being; it is not non-existent but only unintended or set aside, and may need to be drawn at some later time and for some different purpose out of the limbo to which the present intention consigned it.

These two illustrations have exemplified the act of pointing to mathematical or physical objects because the physical and the mathematical situations possessed some common elements, namely analogous regions, regions whose dimensions and areas could be sufficiently specified and controlled so that the common factor could be retained and so that convergence upon an element present in each — but identical with none — could be indicated. A region, a kind of context, is definable as any limited area or class in which an intended being is present. The structure is not quite that of figure-ground or point-horizon, for it is more complex. Given a region, another smaller region that contains the same being may always be defined within the first region. The diminishing regions converge upon the intended being. This converging is the pointing. The operations producing the smaller region are, in both instances, a kind of negation. In the physical situation this negating was illustrated by our neglect of the outer regions containing the object whose location we wished to indicate. Thus we pointed to a being by means of pointing away from another being. In both instances, this neglect was not just a chance omission; it was a regular neglect, a definite pointing-away-from. This negative aspect of pointing will be considered later. An additional matter of interest is the close parallel between the object of the physical or commonsensical and the object of the conceptual (mathematical) pointing. In fact, only a shift of intention is needed to convert the physical pointing to the mathematical one, or vice versa.

I do not know that this spatial pointing is privileged or in any way more basic than other kinds of demonstrative acts. But if it is privileged, as some philosophers believe, still there are other modes of pointing which in different contexts are similar to it. Thus a series of objects analogous to each other in some orderly and relevant respect can perform this indicating function admirably. A Platonic illustration might note that the ruler is to the citizens as the physician is to his patients (cf. *Statesman*, 276-E). Other analogues could be added to this series —for the physician is to his patients as the trainer is to the athletes under his care and, a little more remotely, as the shepherd is to his flock — but in this illustration these additional analogues are scarcely needed. The first two converge rather persuasively upon the point at issue: As the physician carefully and constantly trains himself in his art for the sake of the bodily health of his patients, so might the ruler make himself master of the political art for the sake of the common good of the citizens.

A not dissimilar pointing was suggested in chapter 5 where an effort was made to approach pure presentations. It is imaginable that strata of interpretations could be successively removed from an object and that the series of increasingly abstract objects could be conceived of as pointing to the uninterpreted presentations. Still another kind of pointing may be associated with fine art, for one may regard the activity of making as designating a product through successive regions which its material once occupied. The artist who knows how to carve stone directs his chisel, and defines, in ways hidden in the secrets of his knowing muscles, the stone which is to remain, while removing the stone which belongs to outlying and negated regions. He removes in successive approximations the stone which is not to be the statue. This removal is not the subtle neglect of applied mathematics but a forceful separation and rejection. But in the end it converges upon the object of the art. I say it converges upon the work of art, but not without leaving the work of organization and recognition to the viewer, for who can say what the work of art is? What angle of vision presents the genuine sculpture? Or should one view it from exactly eighteen different angles, left to right? Or perhaps the object, the sculpture, points through an aesthetic "space" to an aspect of an unique human activity, and the repeated effort to recreate this activity or its intention within oneself is convergence upon the experience of the object of art.

In addition, there are very interesting kinds of pointing which stretch through regions of time. These are exemplified in historical work which identifies themes, traits, and movements through several lengths of time, and focuses them in upon an event or period of special interest, endowing the event or period with a rationale and a sense it would not otherwise have had. Thus the past is interpreted and reinterpreted.

Such a convergence can also be engineered by the objective dialectic. Here a hypothesis may be established for a while, then destroyed by a crucial experiment, and often replaced by a more adequate hypothesis. The history of the concept of heat offers a familiar example. An even better one can be seen in the development of the concept of the solar system from Ptolemy through Newton. This latter development once seemed to promise an eventual convergence upon an ideally complete, coherent, and accurate rationale of all the solar and stellar phenomena available to us.

Illuminating in a quite different way is the dramatic pointing in dramatic time, developed by means of the pattern of decision, struggle, catastrophe, and insight (the subjective dialectic). This pattern of action has already been discussed in part and will be developed further in §51 below.

We have so far described or suggested several kinds of converging or pointing regions: a set of Euclidean areas converging upon their common member, which is a certain limiting line element; physical-spatial regions converging upon a physical point; regions of an artist's work-space and material converging upon a product; possibly regions of human activity and spatiality converging upon awareness of human being and relationships; and finally, periods of dramatic time converging upon the being, the determinate or determinable powers, of the protagonist. In each of these illustrations a being of a different type was pointed out. All of these instances of pointing, however different in most respects, share an essential property. All occur in the world and are what they are by reason of this location. Also all of these instances merely assumed the availability of this prior and omnipresent location. We now need, therefore, to designate this all-important and determining region.

§50. ON POINTING TO THE WORLD

All instances of pointing are instances of typical human activity. I do not refer, of course, to signals usually described as elements in some sort of causal sequence, but to pointers which are given meaning; such pointers do not exist in non-human nature. A sign along a woodland trail is scarcely differentiated from the earth where it is planted until the wanderer passes by and sees through it, so to speak, the direction he desires to go. It becomes a sign only in virtue of its use as a sign. All pointers contain this reference to their users, for without this use and rules of use, there would be no pointing. Differently said, any sign is by itself an incomplete instrument; a pointer, a sextant, a microscope, a violin, any instrument, is none of these things apart from the user's intention and meaning. Each is completed only in this meaning and use. Thus the being of a sign is dependent upon its maker and user. All kinds of pointing, all types of signs, are in the region of human use. This admission leads directly to an ancient problem.

Recognition of the dependence of all pointing upon the pointer brings to the fore a question concerning the origin of pointing. An object can be referred to only by virtue of being in a region. Given a region, that is, one may proceed to a more exact pointing by way of negating irrelevant portions of the region. The question concerns one's possession of an initial region, for an area is a region only in virtue of the presence in it of the object to be designated. But how is the object recognized as being there initially? Was there some prior pointing which led to the initial acquaintance? Is there, then, always pointing prior to any given instance of pointing?

This question about origins seems to place us in an infinite regress, perhaps indicating a false start on the problem. Some empiricists have sought to manage the difficulty by saying that the initial regions for pointing are learned from someone else. But here again the infinite regress recurs. How, we must ask, did the informant acquire his knowledge? From still someone else? Moreover, in order to recognize that one's informant is an informant and is pointing at something, one must already know the language of pointing and be in possession of the initial regions, customs, and contexts communication assumes. Thus this empiricist's answer merely presents the question in another form.

This problem has an air of the "odd," which has so often called forth essays on language. How, let us inquire, can one teach a Martian one's language? By beginning with gesture and counting on word-gesture association? But, it will be said, the Martian is ignorant precisely of one's language of gesture. Hence a word-gesture correlation cannot be initiated. How, then, can the Martian begin acquiring our gesture language? Because he already possesses some more basic and common language? Because he possesses some strange *a priori* connection of sign and signified? Both are improbable. Now, if by such rejoinders all points of communicative contact are progressively removed, then the difficulty at once becomes clear. The question concerned the means of communication, when in fact all means of communication are removed by the series of difficulties. That is, the question posited a frustrating or contradictory situation from the start and thus was unanswerable in the way it seemed it should be answered; nevertheless, in this kind of science fiction example, it seems to be assumed that Martians can learn languages, although an earth language might be very difficult for them. They are, in other words, the same sort of beings as men. They could live in the same world and hence could communicate with men. It is not fair, then, to be continually interposing difficulties to their learning. If they are like men, they do learn. Thus the problem seems to be eliminated when the linguistic and conceptual muddle is exposed. There is, therefore, a temptation to be satisfied with this exposure and to pass on, tackling other muddles without further concern about the sort of being a human language-user (or a Martian one) is.

The classic tradition in philosophy, on the other hand, attempts to make peace with the problem by pressing the question of being. What must be true, it asks, of one's kind of being in order that one should be able to raise questions of any sort, whether odd or conventional? It has concluded that we first recognize a being because, in a sense, we already cognize it. Thus pointing or any ostensive act of communication is circular in structure, presupposing a context or global region which includes (or probably includes) the object to be designated. For clearly, we must already know at least vaguely what we desire to point out before we can set about pointing it out more exactly; otherwise we can not recognize the object or even know if we fail to recognize it. We are already in possession, then, of something in virtue of which beings can appear to us. And indeed, we do possess our sensitive field, the possibility of receiving presentations, which contains among its originative powers the possibility of pointing to something contained in a region. Thus, though the sensitive field is not a region itself (for instance, it is not a spatial field since it is not in space), nevertheless it renders regions accessible to us and renders possible the utilization of an initial region or context (the world) which all further referring requires (cf. §28). The possession of such initial regions is exhibited in our intention of pointing at something or of meaning something. Intentionality, the power of intending something — the power, for example, of intending this black tubular thing in my hand as a pen, an object in the region of instruments — is presupposed by any meaning whatsoever and indeed is an essential power of consciousness. This power (and its activity) I call world in its noetic sense.

I could also have held the same object up against a physical and mathematical context. Then my intention would have been understood to refer to the object as a cylinder having a small radius compared with its height. Here again, two elements are presupposed in the one receiving my communication: the power to receive and to separate out the relevant presentations of the object, and the pre-possession of the context or region within which such reception and recognition become possible. To be conscious is to be conscious of something (e.g., of presentations). To be conscious of something is precisely to give meaning to that something of which one is conscious, and meanings fall within larger contexts of meaning, finally within a largest region structured by basic categories. This giving of meaning is otherwise called intentionality. Intending, in this broad sense, is the human way of being. Without it, no problem could be raised. Thus, instead of "solving" the problem about origins broached above, or dismissing it as odd, we are led to recognize a presupposition involved in any kind of meaning, involved in any pointing, one without which a problem, whether genuine or spurious, could not have been raised. (I do not mean to suggest that the presupposition of intentionality, the intending of meanings within larger regions of meaning, is a final and basic presupposition. Later, in fact, the dependence of intentionality upon lived time will be pointed out.)

Something like this intention of meaning is expressed in the Platonic doctrine of anamnesis (cf. *Phaedo* 76A-78E). The doctrine may be generally stated in this manner: Given a region, presumably containing the something intended, and a rule of negation, we can narrow the region down to designate the object intended, or else show that the object is not in the region. The thing recollected is present in an initial region, of which, say, the similar, the almost equal, or the apparently equal, are subsumed members or a participants. It should be added that mankind has shown itself possessed of a most remarkable talent for selecting appropriate initial regions out of the infinity of imaginable ones. Recognition of this talent lends weight to the hypotheses of anamnesis, and lends weight also to the conviction that by inhabiting a particular world, one is already predisposed to discover what is valued in such a world (MT pp. 104ff.).

Neither our method of pointing nor any other can be worked unless we know what we desire it to do. There must be a prior grasp of the method and the end to be reached by its means. If, now, we do not wish to maintain the doctrine of anamnesis, the supposition that this prior grasp is the consequence of our living in an atmosphere of human culture, custom, and society may suffice. There, one can practice one's art and recognize one's friends. Such an atmosphere is thought somehow to give the first bent to our intentions. But custom and culture are human products and are unintelligible apart from definite intentions. Indeed, custom and culture themselves are very general intentions, e.g., the intentions of being the kind of man one's culture accepts. In what do these very general intentions originate?

In chapter 5 (§§ 28-9) I tried to relate culture and custom to the more fundamental notion of world; here world is the form common to all our sensitive fields and imparts an initial direction to all our intentions. It is the all-inclusive project embodied in the culture that formed us. Being mythically invested, no further justification of it is felt to be necessary. We are accustomed to say we are born into our world and that being human is, in fact, being in such a world. Perhaps this sometimes vague yet always omnipresent world where we live may be accepted as a kind of myth of the primary region that enables pointing to be begun and continued. World is the initial region. Being in a world, one is aware of a spontaneous inclination to utilize spatial structures, for example, in directing attention toward an intended object in space, toward, say, the Saarinean Arch (PC §42 and pp. 242f.).

World, then, is not exactly something to which we may point in an easy and direct manner. It is, rather, more like a universal first region all must inhabit in order that any demonstrating be engaged. Perhaps it may be pointed toward by a series of kindred cultures. Even better, it is indicated in the living and effective world symbols of a culture. World is something like the prior and given intention of characteristic kinds of pointing; of this primary intention, anyone, whether man or Martian, must be possessed before any kind of pointing becomes a real possibility. Pointing is a rational act, perhaps the simplest one, not wholly learned but possessed by any living being having a world as a possibility prior to learning. Without world, there are no regions, hence no pointing. Thus, that there is any pointing at all, points to world.

§51. ON IDENTIFYING THE SELF

That there should be any pointing at all points not only to world, but also indicates the self who points. Every act of pointing, even acts of reflecting upon the self, point away from the one who points. To understand fully such an act, then, requires some grasp of the self who originates acts of pointing.

In our day, nothing is more obvious than that one can designate one's body and its parts by use of the objective categories, the objective dialectic, and techniques taken from anatomy, physiology, and genetics. But a body so designated is but a human shell; it is not yet interwoven in its world or possessed of its bodily schema, and no account is yet rendered of its selfhood. To take this last step, the existential categories must be brought into play. To bring them into play, consider a characteristic of Greek dramas.

The suggestion has already been made in passing that a series of dramas or a series of steps in the subjective dialectic may converge upon the self of the protagonist. Recall the habit Greek playwrights had of writing dramas in connected series where the decision of a preceding drama, seen in the insight to be defective, prepares the ground for a new decision in the succeeding drama. The Oedipus plays and the Orestia are examples. The related plays may be conceived of as moving through a dialectic and so to point with growing definiteness toward the protagonist himself: he is revealed with increasing clarity, both to himself and to others, as his excesses and self-ignorance are purged away through successive cycles of the tragic action. This purging effect of the dramatic insight has for a consequence a simplification (an effect not unlike the technique of epochē, as suggested above), which reveals the protagonist as he is, shorn of the pomp and circumstance, of the illusions and evasions used as concealment. This temporal pointing is a subjective dialectic which can be used to designate the actual bodily person himself, not man in general nor even man the role player, but something closer to the concrete individual person. It could be said to render his being evident if, by his being, we mean the protagonist's power of giving his own unique sense and value to the events of his life, however catastrophic they may sometimes be. This power is made manifest by the simple expedient of exhibiting it in operation upon the stage or in the world. A series of tragic actions in dramatic time, then, can point to the being of the protagonist (MT § 16).

It is pertinent here to inquire whether any general direction can be perceived in the drift of many individual dramas, whether literary or living. Do — or should — the many dramas which presumably converge upon the being of the protagonist point in some common direction? The question is equivalent to asking whether there is any common human nature. From the *coign* of vantage of this essay, a position may reasonably be taken. Anyone setting out to describe human being cannot but hew scrupulously to the phenomena of human changes. We are not unaccustomed to saying, and hardly without paradox, that a person characteristically is not who or what he is. His being is being in becoming. And in becoming, a person is transcending what he is toward some other being. We cannot, however, rest content with this indefinite notion of transcendence: We need to have some grasp of the being toward which he transcends. The present method of pointing can play a part in designating the limit of human transcendence.

Now, an important point develops from the observation that any series of dramatic insights are commonly negative; they agree in establishing that the protagonist is not the person he believed himself to be, not the person he had resolved to be in the decision initiating the dramatic movement. Upon making such a discovery, the protagonist can always settle upon some other role or function with which he may identify himself. But he may at last conclude not merely that he has made unfortunate interpretations of himself in the past, but that any such positive identification embodied in a decision will inevitably be made in hybris and will surely lead to catastrophe; he may even apprehend his ontological fault.[3] Consequently, he may perceive the essential negativity of the self. In the language of this study, he would then have achieved a grasp of the essential character of himself or of his sensitive field. He would have discovered that the sensitive field, his *sine qua non*, is never a being. It is the "place" where beings appear, but it is not any one of these beings which appear (cf. §21 and §36 above). The sensitive field, in comparison with things, is a nothing. Any identification attributing to it the specific and limited character of an object, a role, a function, even membership in a group, cannot but be in error, and such an error proves destructive under trial by circumstances. The protagonist, then, who has received that universal communication tragedy finally has to offer, has learned that he is himself a kind of permanent question, that the positive identifications at his disposal are all illusory, temporary at best, and always clearly false when prolonged beyond a relatively brief interval. At least all definite interpretations prove false in death. The protagonist who perceives this final truth about himself, that he is that strange being, a non-thing, a non-being, has moved a step beyond the usual subjective dialectic; he has approached what we may call "The Tower beyond Tragedy."

Recognition of the non-objective status of the self is and should be startling. For if the self is always different from any being, any object whatsoever, then the intending self emerges as non-being. It loses content. It is not anything specifiable. At best, the self is only the possibility of something specifiable. It is no object, no thing, a mere nothing. At this point, metaphor, poetry, and myth are often invoked. The invocation of these modes of description serves at least to emphasize the non-objective character of the intending self; his direction of movement, of development, is toward non-being.

This outcome is predictable. If the analogy of pointing to a series holds, a series which converges upon a limit not itself a member of the series, then the limit will not be a definite identification such as protagonists are wont to make: I am the avenger of my father's death; I am the Thane of Cawdor, destined to become King; I, King Lear, am the beloved father of my two daughters. Inevitably, such definite identifications prove to be tragic errors. But if the series of dramatic insights converges upon nothing definite, then upon what will it converge? The present suggestion is that it converges upon the *sine qua non* of man, his sensitive field. But again, this sensitive field is no thing. It is a limited power-to, a readiness for human acts and thought, but nothing with the definiteness of a specific being or act. Any philosophy identifying the self as some object-like being — such as a substance, a subject, an ego, a functionary, or any other reified something — will have to pay the price for illusion.

We may at this point risk an identification of the *archē* of human experience. This *archē*, the beginning of being human, is surely no initial event, however notable, nor is it a presupposition or anything like a logical beginning point. One must already be a person of some maturity in order to experience or recognize such beginnings as these. Rather, this *archē* is precisely the power to engage in the dramatic movement by which the self is discovered to itself and comes into explicit possession of itself. It is the power of initiating decisions and of moving through their consequences with insight. This power is always with one, even at the end. Without it, one may be some other being, though not a human one. But again, this power, this readiness, is no ordinary being; at most, it is that which is necessary for becoming such a one. Let us say it is the being of a man.

This nothing which the self is, the sensitive field, is, however, not a mere empty nothing, not a *nihil negativum*. It is better described as a rich and structured nothing, a field of possibilities. It is the fruit of perhaps a lifetime of exercise in the arts, of many friendships, of reflection upon life and its paradoxes, of practice in the perception of the strangeness of the human self and its career. But it itself is nothing more than an open receptiveness toward the world, its contents, others, and itself, all of which it appropriates through acts of interpretation in word and deed.

Traditionally, this full and rich nothingness, the developed self, has been described as having established a characteristic relation with being, its source, and the limit of its transcendence. Not a few religions, following something like this line of reflection, have also perceived the self as basically nothing. Buddhism, so I am given to understand, arrived as a view somewhat like the present one and proceeds further to conclude that the nothing which is a human self is somehow the Buddha spirit itself. Christianity, too, holds that the self must move through suffering to the discovery of its nothingness; it must lose itself in order to win itself. This self, this Christian nothingness is, no less than the Buddhist self, the reverse of a mere vacancy. As the *imago* doctrine teaches, it possesses a structure, indeed something like a family structure, and participates somehow in divinity. I cite these religious parallels in order that my conclusion regarding the nothingness of the self may not appear captious or strained.

If the view of the self as a nothing were to become convincing and if this conviction were to penetrate to and inform emotional life, then an ethical change would surely ensue. A new objectivity, tolerance, and acceptance could be envisaged, for then the person involved would recognize that he has no vulnerable ego to expose and to save. More exactly, he would see that the ego he was accustomed to protect and nourish is nothing essential, only a product of conviction and culture, a mortal growth perhaps better left behind, better transcended. Such a belief, though, will scarcely be so much as caviar to the general.

If, therefore, this doctrine of the nothingness of the self and its Tower beyond Tragedy, seems too mystical or too pessimistic to be plausible, another way out of the tragic cycle may be attractive and may throw further light upon the self. This is the comic way. A comedy may be viewed as a connected series of minor actions, each having its beginning, middle, and end, where again the end reaches some new insight into the beginning decision.[4] The actions are minor, as is the insight achieved, but the insight is sufficient to anticipate and so to avert or moderate the minor catastrophe and to invite a new decision. Socrates may be viewed as a comic hero. From time to time he bills himself as a powerful or wise man, then looks ahead Prometheus-like and humorously withdraws or recants (e.g., *Euthydemus* 23A-B; 41E).

The term "comedy" suggests something about the Socratic comic spirit. "Comedy" derives from *kōmos* and refers to a village festival, as Aristotle notes (*Poetics*, 1). Characteristic of the village and its festivals, as contrasted with the populous city, is the small number of its inhabitants and its consequent simplicity. In the city, a person feels himself safe by reason of the number of persons like himself, but he finds himself tempted to reach for power, wealth, and influence, just as others do. He is also constrained by the many laws and customs necessary to civil life. The occasions for hybris, for stepping beyond boundaries, are therefore many. One can, however, escape the complexity of city living and its invitations to hybris by the expedient of moving beyond its walls, as Socrates once did, sensing the move as a "divine release from the yoke of custom and convention" (*Phaedr*. 265B). Such is the release which can be reached by situating oneself in the rustic *kōmos*. Though Socrates only once voluntarily left Athens, still he was always beyond its political intrigue, its economic competition, and its social perplexities. In this sense, he was always beyond the Athenian walls.

Moreover, he constantly recommends a kind of straightforward simplicity in living and thinking. He continually talks about such common things as carpenters, shoemakers, pilots, and physicians, and always says "the same about the same." He is not as other men are; he is the simple and unambitious comic hero, convinced that all men ultimately are nothing (*Apology* 41E). Yet until that ultimate moment, he will continue to play out his role of questioning the comforting routines of Athenian social life.

The rapid and repeated movement of comedy through beginning, middle, and end is more within the bounds of human endurance than tragedy is, and, additionally seems to offer a continuous approach to the self, which constitutes the limit of this movement. Thus the comic protagonist is not tempted to take refuge in a doctrine of the nothingness of the self, though the comic movement certainly is not incompatible with that doctrine. Still, comedy continually avoids so radical and dark a decision; rather, it is content merely to depict the self in continuous movement through the human and social complexities of living.

Comedy may also be imagined a natural sequel to tragedy, for upon reaching the final tragic insight into the nothingness of the self, the tragic protagonist may have to ask himself, "What next?" The next move may quite reasonably be a series of social (or other) roles he can accept while seeing ironically and in advance that they must collapse; yet these roles may appear to be not without value in spite of their mortal character. Again Socrates offers the best illustration, for though he sees that he himself is as nothing, he nevertheless examines the oracle about himself in such a way as to become the gadfly of Athens. Now surely, revealing to the Athenian people of his day their lack of virtue and trying to awaken in them a hunger after justice is a ridiculous undertaking, one befitting a veritable Don Quixote. In dialogue after dialogue, Socrates tilts with stupidity, confusion, sophistry, hostility, and tyranny, but he picks himself up after each fall, and seeing no reason for changing his role, moves on to the next encounter. His professed ignorance of final things, together with his willingness to risk success-in-failure, designates him a sort of model comic hero, knowing but not knowing himself. In the end, he is interrupted by his condemnation, which offers to the Athenian people the occasion for a genuine tragic insight and radical change, but because these people are incapable of profiting, their seeming triumph is only the failure of self-recognition.

The comic hero, then, postpones indefinitely a full recognition of the nothingness of self by continuing ironically to play the social game. He is the eternal self-questioner who anticipates his failure to be an enduring self.

§52. ON HUMAN BEING AND MEANING

This moment is as good as any to attempt a succinct summary of all I have said about human nature. Man is both a directed and a directing power, and this opposition is the source of many other conflicts. He is an embodied, meaning-giving, non-object who feels, knows, and acts within a culture, who tends to hybris, but who can achieve an understanding of his non-being. The reader will see, I trust, that this brief remark refers more or less directly to all the topics discussed in this essay — to the essential items, to power to . . . or not to . . . to the sensitive field, and to interpretation, categories, dialectic, self-manifestation, and world (in its two senses).

The modest success achieved thus far in designating the self suggests that the present method may be utilized in an even more difficult task. Can we, then, use this method of pointing in an effort to indicate what we vaguely apprehend as the common origin of ourselves and our world? This origin the tradition has, since the Greeks, called being (*ousia*). The name is easy; it appears in almost every sentence. But its meaning is another matter. Our task is to express this meaning so far as it refers us to the origin in question. The task is important not merely because its achievement would satisfy a theoretical demand, but even more because the establishment of an appropriate relation with this origin is the end and goal of human being.

We approach this task through that which is essential to human being as well as to any pointing. A man lays claim to humanity in virtue of possessing, or being, a sensitive field through which he himself and other beings can appear as phenomena of some particular kind. Or we may say that a being, a *that*, emerges into the human world by means of his sensitive field and by means of the interpretative principles developed from this field, whence it acquires at least a minimal *what*. Earlier, this point was made by use of Plato's metaphor of the marriage between the stream of reflected light from the object and the interpretative stream from the eye (§30). The sunlight reflected from the object contributes, so to speak, the *that*; the light from or in the human eye elicits the *what*, the interpretation. The outcome of this marriage is a *that* united with a *what*, a something having a meaning, a particular, though even a mere "something" is already some meaning, a vague particular which later reflection can specify and ramify.

Now, the protagonist (or anyone) is to be identified, at least in respect to his being, with his sensitive field. As his experience accumulates and develops, his sensitive field may become structured in an altogether individual way, so that his way of perceiving, of expressing himself, and of acting is pervaded by his own unique character. That is, certain possibilities constituting his sensitive field, through repeated embodiment in acts and in interpretative principles, become distinctive of his personal being. They bespeak his style, whereas other possibilities remain dormant. He is consistently who he is because of being exactly this sensitive field, structured in consequence of his own repeated interpretations, decisions, and acts. In spite of this distinctiveness, the common means for communicating with others through language remains — at least in the saner instances — possible, for language can refer not only to objects, their properties, and relations, but it can also be made to communicate some of the subtler organization of the speaker's sensitive field and its pervasive properties (moods, attitudes, habitual feelings, and the like), which is the *way* the speaker experiences and communicates himself. This sensitive field *is* the protagonist. These ways of responding and interpreting, of developing individually and commonly, indicate the being of the protagonist. This is the being (the nothing) to which, as we have seen, the protagonist points as he moves through the crises of his life.

There is, however, a still more inclusive sense of the term "being." Here we come again to a question which the tradition has dubbed the chief speculative question, one difficult to phrase. A first expression of it might be this: what is the common meaning of, and unity among, these several sensitive fields? What is the unity of a man's being, of men's being? But the questions expressed thus are susceptible of a superficial answer. The unity of these sensitive fields, so the easy response goes, follows upon their living in a common culture and society and is the product of training in a common language, common ways of feeling, thinking, evaluating, and producing. The metaphysician who maintains that his culture provides the unquestionably true basic principles has baptized this superficial response.

My question, though, bears not upon these elements of the common life but upon their origin and possibility. The question is transcendentally directed. But how shall we secure access to the transcendental? Can the many sensitive fields (persons) be made to point to or to converge upon a being in which they all originate, a being which, therefore, must in some significant sense be effectively present in all their acts? Just as my sensitive field is related to perceived beings (by originating their sense), so may there not be a being which originates in some fashion the many sensitive fields and which perhaps also originates the *thats*, the objects, to which these sensitive fields respond? Is individual subjectivity related to a man's being, somewhat as intersubjectivity is related to a still more primary being? Such being may be thought to lie at the origin of a world and its cultures. Our question about the originative function of such being can best be answered by the attempt to execute a pointing toward it.

Perhaps someone will think, judging from the last of the above questions, that I am going to suggest placing persons in some sort of order so that they will point somehow, somewhere. But in what order? The plethora of orders would be matched only by the diversity of preconceived ideas of being. A more promising way of proceeding will be through an analysis of the most characteristic of human acts, namely, interpretation or the giving of meaning, understood in its most concrete sense, the sense in which it is actually lived in time. We shall, accordingly, select one essential and invariably present characteristic of all concrete beings and investigate its relation to the most characteristic acts and effects of human beings, the giving of meanings, of "whats." Now, existing in time, a primary qualification for being a concrete something, a *that*, is essential to the giving of meaning. More specifically, the possibility of living in human (dramatic) time is surely the *sine qua non* of maturing human being. Only by way of a progress through dramatic time does the humanoid animal move from barbarism and savagery to humanity, for living in this kind of time is precisely the process of giving meaning to one's acts in their relationship to the formative decisions of one's life. Time, then, which all things have in common and through which all things communicate, may be just the needed clue to human being. We proceed, therefore, to analyze the process of meaning-giving in its relation to temporality. Predictably, we find the first appearance of temporal structure in intentionality.

Intention is not purpose, for purpose is an explicit, conscious, even articulated directedness toward an end. Intention is a far more subtle and inarticulate directedness. One may entertain the purpose of writing a book. An outline of the book and, perhaps, offers of support from a foundation are evidence that the purpose is seriously entertained. Such a purpose is one kind of meaning; it is formed, whole, and communicated or explicitly ready for communication. Intention, on the other hand, is an element present at every point in the formation of such a purpose. It is the first felt impulse toward such an act and continues through each moment until the act is complete. As one proceeds with such an act, e.g., enunciating a purpose, words come to mind and are put in place by the skilled speaker with unhesitating spontaneity. The intention is the "knowledge ahead" which initiates, guides, and orders the selection and positioning of words. Any statement or act, any experience, thus gives evidence of the presence of intentionality. It is that which leads us to saying — to use A. N. Whitehead's illustration — "United Fruit Company" (when that is intended) rather than "United States" (to which a mechanical association would have led).

Intention, thus, is related to the immediate future. It may come to awareness in the felt confidence that one can give a meaning of a certain kind to an act, a statement, a gesture. Thus, it comes to one, as it were, out of the future. It is the birth of meaning, a readiness for seeing and communicating, a sense (direction) entering the present from the future. This function of intentionality, the bringing to mind of the meaning one is about to see or to express, is difficult to describe, for ordinarily one is aware of it only in the process of giving it expression. Nevertheless, there are occasions when actual expression is inhibited and when the power or intention to express or to give meaning can come to the fore. Elsewhere I have cited John Cage's "Silent Concerto" as effective in this respect (MT pp. 132-4). Certain other works of art seem to call forth a similar grasp upon unfulfilled intention, the intending itself; Michelangelo's "Awakening Slave" belongs in this class. The sudden death of a promising young person may do the same, as does a love affair prematurely arrested yet still pregnant with a future. Such cases yield a transcendental experience, an awareness of one's power to be or of the limitations upon this power. They give sense to my phrase, "power-to . . ."

Such a sense, a readiness-for . . . , may be clothed with words as other kinds of acts are clothed with or expressed in conventional forms and familiar movements, shapes, or sounds. These words, conventions, movements, principles, are prior possessions. They have already been acquired through practice and past experience and are now disposable means, memorial objects, awaiting the call of intention. They are accumulated and lie dismembered in one's memory awaiting the need for them. These images, principles, thoughts, being already acquired, belong to the past, the partly forgotten yet still available past. The past, I want to say, is the fertile region from which the meaning of an intended object may be collected, the region whose content is already distinct enough to allow of the recognition of its kinship with the object presently to be designated (cf. §16).

An intention, for instance, some specific but yet unphrased meaning about to be spoken, elicits, as it were, the relevant elements from the available past. This combining of (future) intention with past acquisition is the present speaking, the actual action. My intention to point out an X with my finger, as part of some on-going project, was shown in section 48 to have been executed only through a learned and rather complexly elaborated custom which I recalled as an imaginary line drawn through the wrist and the index finger toward the X. Without the initiating intention calling upon some such convention available in memory, my intention to point to X could not now be rendered evident, even to myself. When our intentions, emerging from our concrete future, are clothed with meanings acquired in and remembered from the past, there the present is constituted. A statement, an action, a perception is the present offspring of future and past, of future originated and oriented intention and prior retentions. The intention guides memory or restructures past possessions in the present expression. Thus, *the structure of an act of meaning is a temporal structure*, and like time itself its parts are qualitative parts, distinguishable in thought but in existence always unified.[5] Whether time is appropriately described as living meaning, the act of giving meaning, or whether meaning is more properly said to be essentially temporal, is difficult to say. The structures are the same whichever the descriptive phrase.

I offer here a small-scale but paradigmatic example, the "I-am-me" experience, a not infrequently recorded and often dramatic recognition that one is an independent human person, like others. In *Man and Technology* (pp. 133-5) I interpreted this experience as a kind of birth into self-responsible human status, an initiatory experience. Here I add that this birth is a giving of new meaning to one's self precisely as a self-manifesting being. It is (or can be) an acknowledgment that one is and will always be in some way responsible for one's self and world, that one is (in my terms) the uncoverer of one's self or that one intends one's self as discoverer. The exact sense of this intention is drawn from already discovered senses of self, acquired probably from literature, history, or experience. The present uncovering is the uniting of this intention with those acquired meanings. Thus, "I-am-me" means the present discovering self ("I"), finds its being ("am") in intending always to be the "me" gathered in part from my past. That is, self as discoverer is now discovering (interpreting) the self as discovered. Here future, present, and past senses of self are joined. The three moments are inseparable, but the first, intending the self as discoverer, is the *conditio sine qua non*, for it calls the other moments into being. I do not so much want to say that there are three functionally differing selves indissoluably united as that there is one self having three functionally differing moments of its meaning, and these moments constitute a beginning of self-knowledge.

Intention, selection and restructuring the already acquired, become actual and effective in the present. Thus the present meaning is the product of a marriage, the union of the fecundating future and the fallow past. The present book, uniting two former books, offers another and moderately large-scale example of such a marriage. *Man and Technology* expressed an attempt to understand and evaluate a present and possibly dangerous development in cultural change (a change toward a totally technological society). This possible change was seen as an outgrowth of past possibilities assembled and lying available in our history, combined with alternatives; this "inherited conglomerate" was described in *Philosophy at the Crossroads*. Then these two books were united in the present study in a manner designed to elicit the principles of such a change, not only regarding the process of interpretation but also regarding the goal, so that present action and change might be understood as expressing that which called them into being.

The act of meaning as thus analyzed is plainly related to the categories, for the categories have been identified as the basic principles or primary intentions of meaning. The formal categories are prior, always relevant, and contentless apprehensions whose only content is to be derived from past experience and presentations. The issue of this union is particular phenomena and classes of phenomena (beings) which inhabit the present.

§53. ON POINTING TO BEING

Let us now utilize our analysis of the concrete act of interpretation or meaning-giving in an attempt to point to being. We begin with the series of categories developed in chapters 6 and 7. These categories contain the formal elements of our primary intentions. The formal categories represent the abstract possibilities of the modes of meaning and organization attributable to presentations and experience, as these meanings and intentions come to us, as it were, wordlessly out of the future. Categories having content are selections from the formal ones appropriate to that content. The formal and non-formal elements become fitted and unified by the dialectical process described in chapter 8 and in accord with the interests, conventions, and ideals of some particular culture.

Several modes of categories have been distinguished: the abstract but precise and partitioned categories of mathematics; the less abstract but still rather exact categories belonging to a science like physics; the more subtly interrelated categories of common experience; the existential categories of human living and maturing; and finally, the mythological categories used to set in order the rare and ultimate experiences symbolized by world symbols. This gamut of categories runs by degrees from the precise and abstract to the less exact but more concrete. Our usual thought, moving with what is generally conceded today as the general direction appropriate to the civilized world, would conclude that this series of kinds of categories (or of categoreal matrices) points away from the concrete, let alone from the mythological. Clearly, it points toward science (and of course, toward the applications of science in technology); in so doing, it indicates the currently desirable direction of development, the kind of objects we expect to find, and the direction of future as well as past civilization. Such, at least, is the judgment of philosophers like August Comte and of the generations of scientific humanists. They point to an inclination of the categories on the right hand side of the sketch below to be accommodated to, and to be judged in reference to, the categories on the left side. The gamut of categories looks something like this:

Categories of mathematics	categories of physics	categories of everyday life	categories of existence	categories of myth
abstract				concrete

As I have drawn the picture, the pointer seems to be indicating the direction of increasing exactness, the direction of precise and practically effective thought. Earlier, though, we observed that any pointing toward is also a pointing away. Now, this pointing away also indicates a direction, no less than a pointing toward. Let us consider this new direction, for just this inverse pointing away from the exact and applied sciences, away from the values, the achieved successes, and the hopes which have so fascinated our technological era in history, may be the direction pointing to being. Ontology, then, must consider the possibility that the subject of its study lies in a direction the reverse of that customarily traveled. Indeed, ontology looks not to the constructions, images, concepts, and interpretative principles which much usage has made familiar, but rather to the sensitive fields by which these familiar objects come to be, and looks further toward some being which, like these sensitive fields, is neither a particular thing nor a universal thing, but a something which has the power to originate these sensitive fields where particulars and universals may come to present awareness. The categories, then, placed as above, and if read inversely and in the order of increasing concreteness, may be thought to converge toward being itself, as upon a limit.

This ordering of the categories in the direction of the more concrete becomes explicit and effective in relation to the existential. For the existential categories are just the ones used to strip away from the protagonist the rags and tatters of power and glory he has used to blind himself to his fate. They are the efficient means used to discover to the protagonist his hybris, his self-deception, and finally his ultimate nothingness. The character and traits of the protagonist not purged away by the succession of catastrophies and insights must be seen to converge upon his being. So, it seems that the categories of myth may function with respect to being. Have we, then, succeeded in pointing to being? If so, only paradoxically. We only see *that*, though not *what*, this being may be.

Being, we have suggested, is what all sensitive fields have in common, and is what, therefore, they may be conceived to point toward. Likewise, various myths hint of it. This being, common to all sensitive fields, is the temporally structured power of giving meaning. It may also be called presence (or presencing) if this presence be understood not as eternal presence but as the unifying of the temporal dimensions of dramatic time (cf. §16), which is also the process of giving meaning. Utilizing the mythological categories, we may say that being is the movement or process whereby Ouranos and Gaea give birth to the cosmos of phenomenal beings, rendering them manifest.

Significant among these phenomenal beings is man himself to whom beings appear, for his nature offers the most pregnant suggestions regarding being itself. As we have identified a man ontologically with his sensitive field (his power or freedom to give meaning to presentations which thereby become the things of his experience), so we suggest the identity of being *simpliciter* with that which gives possibilities. But being so understood is not in space and time, is not a *that* in the sense this pen is a *that*, even though the pen also gives possibilities. (It allows me the possibility of writing.) Rather, being gives me the possibility of being myself, a structured sensitive field, and so gives me the possibility of writing, of using my pen in the work of communication (for which the pen was designed), and marks me as having been given the directing power of extending my ways of perceiving and acting by means of tools, even so far as using these powers as a tool (a directed power) for pointing to the same being which gives these possibilities. They point, that is, to being as a power of self-manifestation.

Again, this pen is a *that* having its peculiar *what*, e.g., its meaning as an instrument for writing. Being *simpliciter*, though, not only is not such a *that*, but it can be assigned no such definite *what* or meaning. It seems, rather, to be involved in all such meanings in so far as they *are* what they are, as if being were what unifies the separable elements of meaning; for instance, it unifies in the present a future-oriented intention and past acquisitions. And man in his presence, where his future and past are united, is a man manifesting the being which brings together these dimensions of time. Being, then, is the unifying power of giving a *that*, revealed as a *what*, to a person in the process of discovery, a process which has come to be known as *aletheia*.

The point needs emphasis that being — neither a *that* nor a *what* in the usual sense of these terms — cannot be any one of the phenomenal things to which a meaning has been imparted. If it is not a *that*, or a particular being of some sort, how then can it be singled out and indicated? How can it have meaning? We must constantly remind ourselves that the world symbols which point to being as it is thought to be known do not mean what they initially appear to mean. Evidently the recent philosophers are correct who see being as no thing at all. Have, then, all our efforts to point to being eventuated in pointing to a vacancy? But let us again try to interpret this nothing as a pointer in its own right, for evidently this effort to point to being in its positive sense requires completion in a negative pointing.

§54. THE NEGATION OF BEING

The tangle in which the last section seemed to terminate is susceptible of yet further complication. If being is no recognizable thing, then it is present in no defining region; hence, it is present in nothing. Therefore, it would appear not to be present. But that which is not and cannot be present is again just nothing. What, then, have we pointed to? Nothing? This paradox may be elucidated if attention be turned upon another aspect of pointing.

Any oriented set of regions, converging upon an object intended, points away from something else. In order to refer to a being, a demonstration refers also in a reverse sense to what the object is not. "Is not" in this last statement may be understood in more than one way. This notion of negation or limitation has already been singled out as a constitutive relation involved in organizing any simple set of demonstrating regions. Each region converging upon a being to be demonstrated is not the preceding region in some definite respect. A rule of negation requires placing aside or negating some aspects or part of the preceding region irrelevant to, and discriminated from, the object intended. This regular and specific negation is the means by which a converging set of regions is constructed. The convergence points to an object by pointing away from what the object is not. This is constructive or restricted negation. Thus, for example, part of the definition of 6 is that it is not 5; a concept of man as a human being is constructed by showing that it excludes aspects of the concept of animal being (e.g., rule by instinct, or communication exclusively by signals).

Pointing away is surely also a kind of pointing and may be so read in a number of different senses by the sophisticated reader. To begin with, notice that the negative element in the pointing act is exactly that factor in the act without which it is not complete. Were there no such pointing away it would not be possible to distinguish between a region and the object contained within it. Even the indication of a very general region is achieved only by discriminating it from something else by means of this constructive negation. Thus the property of space, as that which makes distinctions possible, is utilized. The negated regions are pointed away from. All pointing toward something entails pointing away from something else.

In a slightly different sense, a given set of demonstrating regions may refer to other sets of regions which in some definite manner it is not. Thus one shepherd dog is not another one in a sense different from that in which a shepherd dog is not a sheep. Again, animals such as these are different in yet another way from minerals. No doubt, demonstrating regions may be regularly organized by inclusion, exclusion, and overlapping in complex patterns as determined, finally, by a set of categories. These categories determine the relations we can envisage among the things pointed out, and dominate our speech and thought about them. They express the general structure of our familiar environment. But this whole environment is exactly that away from which we turned when we undertook to point to being.

This same being, however, not being *a* being at all, seemed curiously to point away from even itself. This negation of being seems to refer us to non-being or to nothing. Can this reference be used somehow to help constitute a clearer apprehension of being? Let us look again at the act of pointing.

We have noted that pointing is a typically human act and that pointers do not exist in non-human nature. This fact is often ignored. There are several reasons why this essential element in any pointing tends to be ignored. Familiarity and cultural blindness have a hand in the matter. But there are more interesting reasons why the pointer is so often passed over, more interesting to us because those reasons throw some light upon the paradoxical relation of being to nothing.

Consider a person who is attempting to point out to a stranger the way to the next town. He ordinarily makes directions distinct by pointing away from his own location. The negative of his own position is a constitutive element in his interpreting location and in his communicating the direction intended. This act and this kind of pointing is suggestive of the sophisticated pointing which may be termed objective; indeed, objective pointing has become the most carefully considered kind of pointing in the modern world (MT p.214).

Clearly and necessarily, a great deal of human communication includes a specific reference to the speaker himself. This sort of communication is or can be practical, dramatic, or mythological. In contrast to this, a vast deal of pointing requires a "distance" from the pointer or an impersonality which sets it apart from the former types. It seeks to point out not "the being as it is or might be for me" but rather "the being as being" (MT p.214). That is, it seeks to disconnect impulses to appropriate or to reject an object, and to allow its theoretical entertainment and its impersonal consideration from some definite point of view. (Of course, theoretical and objective thought is supposed to spring from and serve practical needs in the present industrial and technological epoch. Perhaps this supposition is correct. But here I am confining attention strictly to the theoretical moment of thought, its objective aspect.) This aspect, this objective pointing requires, thus, a general and intentional pointing away from the person who points. Its development represents an effort to de-anthropomorphize the world, and it ends by positing a world-without-man, seeking that end by denying the attributes of human subjectivity to all the objects in the world. Human subjectivity, thus, is nothing in this object universe; it is a non-object which, however, constitutes object meanings (PC §13).

Objective pointing was systematically cultivated during and after the Renaissance and initiated a new epoch of intellectual history. With this Cartesian or objective pointing began the vision of a natural world from which human characteristics were specifically extruded as secondary or tertiary qualities. All scientific pointing, presumably, is of this type. I cite it here, not for its intrinsic interest, but rather to illustrate the crucial importance of the "away from" aspect of pointing. The character of the modern objective universe is a function of what it is not. It is pointed out by distinguishing it from the subject who knows, experiences, and values it. The giving of objective meanings is achieved in an important part by explicitly excluding non-objective meanings.

Just this extrusion of subjectivity from the objective world might be used, conversely, in helping point to and define human being, the being possessing a sensitive field. However difficult it may be to point to this subjectivity, at least a start toward specifying it may be got by observing that it is not in the region of the objective. We have observed already that the total context must include this subjectivity whose pointing systematically determines the region of objects pointed out and the human region of objects-as-related-to-pointing-subjects. The former is abstract as compared to the latter. Now, I suggest that as the objective region is related to the human one, so the everyday human one is related to being. Or inversely, just as the objective region is defined by excluding the human being who points it out, so the whole everyday human universe is defined by excluding being. No doubt in virtue of this exclusion of being, the source of its meaning, the universe is as we daily experience it. Now, upon recognizing this circumstance, we are pointing toward being in an inverse sense. Thus the average and common human context does point to being indirectly, that is, by pointing away from it. Being is what the human universe or any particular or general being, for that matter, primarily is not; a being's first movement toward manifesting itself occurs in its ontological distinction from being. Any region, whether human, objective, or any other with which we commonly have to do, diverges first from its origin, and points explicitly toward the various beings and kinds which must be distinguished from this origin. Perhaps we have here hit upon another sense of Aristotle's remark (already cited, §40), to the effect that being falls into the categories. Its falling into the categories of objects is a falling away from its origin.[6]

To observe, as we did in the beginning, that being is nothing, is not merely to express its transcendence in relation to the region of things, but is also to indicate, at least by suggestion, the usual direction of human transcendence, for human transcendence normally moves away from any apprehension of being it may have and toward some specific being. Conversely, the ontological orientation is back toward being, just the opposite of the everyday human movement toward beings or objects. Thus there are two possible directions of human transcendence: into the world of objects, and back to the origin of the world, for man is a being who can look in these two directions. He is the being in passage, a Janus, the being continually at the crossroads, continually in the gateway.

At the crossroads where these two directions of transcendence divide, individuals and whole eras often choose the direction recommended by local convention and unreflective opinion. They are given to try this direction to the exclusion of any alternative way, only to find that this neglect of an essential part of their human possibilities is distorting and produces unhappiness. In our own time of technological culture, and in response to our prevailing materialist and economic myths, transcendence into the world of objects is all but the exclusive choice, and personal observations as well as multitudes of sociological tests demonstrate the pervasive and conscious unhappiness of the population.[7] Well-known, too, is the fact that the incidence of alcoholism, murder, and suicide is highest in the technologically advanced nations of the West. And yet, if practice of the non-objective dialectic in the transcendence toward being is the answer to unbalanced development and consequent unhappiness, one must wonder whether we can ever seriously expect any healthful change, for practice of the non-objective dialectic would take time and attention away from meeting the imperious demands of the technological machine upon which we now depend for the satisfaction of our material needs.

The excuse that we do not have the time to pursue our own balanced development is a bit thin, however, even though this pursuit does require that we think upon our own nothingness. The only virtue discoverable in this excuse is that it may have the effect of again raising the question concerning our own paradoxical non-being.

Let us, therefore, resume our discourse upon non-being.

The being of the universe of beings is the non-being of the origin of that universe. Non-being is that pregnant nothing whose neglect or negation is the first step toward the recognition of specific beings and objects; thus it indicates, perhaps, an answer to the question which first pointed us toward being: Why are there beings and not nothing?

To say that being is present in nothing or is not present as a thing in any sense, may be taken as an oblique way of saying that being may be pointed out only in a unique manner. It is not a being in our world of beings. It is not in any region whatsoever. Thus, in sum, being is pointed out only by recollecting that it is not designated by the familiar use of pointing; its meaning begins subtly to become evident only when we observe that we move away from it toward beings.

Perhaps being may be thought of as what remains after all things are pointed out. Yet it is not just a residue. We might say that it is a nothing which is a silence, the silence from which language and pointers draw their meaning. We become aware of it only when we take the direction of ontological transcendence and travel back up the path toward this earlier silence, toward the non-being which renders meaning-giving possible.

Reflection upon the familiar use of pointing reveals this other perspective upon the operation — and from it — which is concealed by our naively looking always in just the direction pointed out. Our reflection has indicated that whether that which is now being questioned can properly be called being or nothing is a function of the way pointers are used.

Perhaps a combined practice of both kinds of dialectic will help to correct the blindness which could develop from the exclusive use of one or the other. Anyone who refuses the objective dialectic and rejects transcendence into the region of bodily objects condemns himself to starvation and to other creature discomforts. On the other hand, anyone who refuses the subjective dialectic and rejects relation to transcendental being — whether to his own being, his sensitive field, or to being which is the source of his own being — must fail to grasp himself in his full extent, and lives, therefore, only a partial, alienated, and abstract existence, for wholeness requires a tie to the source. Either kind of blindness is a type of hybris and probably a prelude to catastrophe.[8]

§55. CONCLUSION: TOWARD THE MEANING OF BEING

We were able to point to being positively as self-manifesting presence, as the temporality which originates meaning, or as a unifying presence which of itself does not have or present the meaning of any being. And we pointed to being negatively by pointing away from the world of beings. Then the attempt to give further content to the notion of being ended in nothing. Yet nothing is no reason for anything. We are led, therefore, to conclude that there is no particular reason why there should be being rather than nothing. Being is that nothing distinguishing beings from the absolute nothing which may be imagined as the indefinite and utter absence of the possibility of all those elements constitutive of meaning. Any more specific reason for there being something rather than nothing would make reference to one of those things already in being. Thus we may observe, somewhat cryptically, that nothing is the reason for being. I hope that the rather facile and sophistical tone of this "answer" will be sufficiently diminished if this answer itself continually returns us to the opening where the question can be re-experienced. For the question, "Why are there beings rather than nothing?", is itself a being, and one pre-eminently fitted to point away from itself and toward its origin, or *archē*.

Being, understood as the origin or ground of phenomenal beings (beings experienced as having particular and general senses), is first expressed as regionality and is apprehended as the idea of being and the intention of more specific recognitions. At the same time, being is a nothing in the world and is that away from which one turns for orientation in the conventional and familiar environment. It is the nothing away from which all directions point, and provides one with a starting point, a transcendental basis, to move away from and into the world of things. Whether, therefore, we speak of being or of nothing, of transcendence or of the transcendental, is a function of the way we attend to our pointing.

The pointing which was intended to indicate being as a whole and as transcending our familiar distinctions now seems to be indistinguishable from the present inverse pointing to transcendental being or to the nothing prior to distinctions and *a fortiori*, to the objective world. For as the familiar world recedes, being may come into view, being where end and origin are the same. Such is the being to which beings point, and such is its meaning as disclosed by our method.

"Being" then, is the name for that which originates our world and our own possibilities, our sensitive field. Chief among these possibilities is what follows upon the separation of human powers from their natural directedness, for after this separation, direction falls into our own hands, at least in part. We are freed from instinctual ties and become, to a limited extent, responsive to and responsible for more and more of our own possibilities. This taking over of our own possibilities is precisely manifesting them or giving them meaning in the world. The meaning-giving being must in the end give itself meaning.

And what is the appropriate meaning? We have seen that all beings are in time and communicate through it, and that the meaning (the *what*) of these beings is temporal in its structure. Furthermore, a sense has been indicated in which the unity or unifying operation of this temporal structure is being itself, the being which, as Aristotle said, is the same as unity. Being unifies the dimensions of (dramatic) time that are just the moments of the act of interpretation or meaning-giving. Man, then, who gives himself meaning in and beyond the "I-am-me" experience, still does so in accordance with the temporal structure of meaning-giving, which has its unity in his being. He needs, in consequence, to achieve some apprehension of being. Knowing himself requires that he establish a relation to that which is his source, which gathered him into a unity in the first instance. He needs to seek, so far as possible, to grasp the meaning of this being, for therein lies the key to being himself, to his freedom, and to his own meaning. In this apprehension, we may speculate, lies his end.

"In my beginning is my end," remarked a poet. Perhaps he meant that in human affairs, the place from which one sets out (with its orientation) determines the place one reaches. The *terminus ad quem* specifies the *terminus a quo*. Thus all depends upon making a good beginning. A difficulty lies in the fact that the beginning (*archē*) cannot be envisaged or fittingly determined until a person is completely himself or in his end (*telos*), since otherwise hybris and circumstance conspire to blind a man.

Perhaps a hesitating faith can be placed in the myths and world symbols which express the nature and value of the world and yield hints to men of their destiny. Reliance, too, needs to be placed upon the purifying effect of the authentic and dramatic time which men are capable of living, and upon those crucial interpretations, the decisions, struggles and insights which are constitutive of this time, and move men toward their destiny. These guiding myths and symbols, these decisions and insights are the noematic correlates, the expressed principles of that essential human power to return in the end toward one's beginning. The *archē* (noetically understood) is precisely the power which can direct the end illuminatingly into the beginning and collect, thus, a man into such completeness as he is able to achieve. The awareness of this power is, or approaches, archaic experience and opens the way to the discovery of the meaning of human being. Such an experience, a reduction to the *archē-telos*, is a good place to begin the direct doing of philosophy. It initiates the subjective dialectic which, thus guided toward an apprehension of being, takes on a significance far outweighing the objective.

It must, nevertheless, be remembered that man's end and goal is that of a concrete and embodied being, not of a merely intellectual or spiritual one. Thus the objective dialectic, a necessary means, is not to be lightly treated or forgotten, as contemplatives are sometimes thought to do, but integrated. An inspired vision of this embodied wholeness of being is the message of Dostoyevsky's *The Brothers Karamasov*, especially the chapter entitled "Cana of Galilee."[9] This ideal and goal may appear strange to many Westerners today. Some of us are said to have little notion of spiritual self-discipline or of a responsibility extending beyond our own time. Goethe and Kant effectively gave a sense of identity, wholeness, and direction to the German nation; Pascal and Bergson performed the same service for the French. It would be distressing were Americans to offer only superficial recognition to their great ones and to act as if history began with Henry Ford, reached maturity in the latest technology, and will end with our command of interstellar travel (and with the complete organization for technology such travel will surely demand). We would live, were such critics correct, only an impoverished present. We would have failed as guardians of that freedom and dignity for which Americans have avowedly stood.

As a medicine for this possible impoverishment, I offer a paradox, remembering that Plato intimated that the perception of paradox is the beginning of wisdom. The paradox is this: that being is quite the same as nothing. To discover ourselves, therefore, in the position of Wallace Steven's Listener will not be amiss,

> "Who listens in the snow
> And, nothing himself, beholds
> Nothing that is not there and the nothing that is."[10]

Or again we may broach the question whether meaning-giving, the act of the human *logos*, is nothing more than the power of pushing buttons to get a reward, a reward like that which satisfies pigeons or chimps, or whether meaning-giving is, rather, dissatisfied with any such reward. Does the human *logos* not lie, instead, in the power of raising questions about meaning-giving itself and in pushing such questions to their beginning, however mysterious, however near to nothing this beginning may appear? In such activity would seem to lie the end of human being. Let me summarize:

ἐν ἀρχῆ ἦν ὁ λόγος και ὁ τέλος

In the beginning was the power of meaning-giving and its end.[11]

Notes

1. Cf. Martin Heidegger, *Introduction to Metaphysics*, trans. Ralph Manheim (New Haven, Conn: Yale University Press, 1959), chaps. 1 and 2. On questions concerning the meaning of being, and on the role of questions in philosophy generally, see Hans-Georg Gadamer, *Truth and Method*, trans. G. Barden and J. Cumming (New York: The Seabury Press, 1975), pp. 325-33; also Charles P. Bigger, *Kant: Methodology and the Ontological Difference* (unpublished), chap. 10.
2. Others have made use of the generalized method of pointing. Cf. Charles Bigger, "Speculative Demonstration" *J. of Philos.*, 58, (1961), pp. 785ff.; William S. Weedon, "A Theory of Pointing" *Southern J. of Philos.* 1, (1963), pp. 20ff. Likewise cf. my use of this method in "Reason and Convention," *Tulane Studies in Philosophy*, 1, (1952), pp. 21ff; and in *Art and Analysis* (The Hague: Nijhoff, 1957), passim.
3. Cf. MT. §15 and p. 230f., also above chap. 3, pp. 100-106.
4. See my "Sense of the Comic" in *The Dictionary of the History of Ideas*, vol. 1, ed. Philip Wiener (New York: Chas. Scribner's Sons, 1973).
5. This analysis of time and meaning structure provides a rationale for the association of noesis and noema observed by Husserl (cf. *Ideas*, §§34ff). For time, or rather being in time, is a unifying of the future-oriented noesis synthesizing past acquisition in the present noema or meaning (cf. §54 below, also Heidegger, *Being and Time*, §§61-71).
6. For some extremely interesting comments on and developments of the theme that philosophy is the examination of archaic experience, see *Philosophy and Archaic Experience*, ed. John Sallis (Pittsburgh: Duquesne University Press, 1982); also *Tulane Studies in Philosophy* vol. 29, ed. Robert Whittemore (New Orleans, La.: Tulane University, 1980).
7. Nicholas Rescher, *Unpopular Essays on Technological Progress*, (Pittsburgh, University of Pittsburgh Press, 1980), pp. 3-23.

8. Cf. my "Man or Technology: Which Shall Rule?" in *Technology and Understanding of Human Destiny*, ed. Stephen Skousgaard (NY: University Press of America, 1982).
9. See also Nicholas Berdyaev's comments on this chapter in his *Dostoevski*, trans. Donald Attwater (NY.: New Amer. Library, 1974), pp. 206-12.
10. From the poem, "The Snow Man." For another approach to nothingness see the delightful article "Nothing," by P. L. Heath in *The Encyclopedia of Philosophy*, ed. Paul Edwards (1967); I am indebted to Professor Charles P. Bigger for these two references.
11. I have obviously changed the wording and secularized the meaning of St. John I,1.

A summary of the meanings associated with 'beginning' (*archē*) may be useful. *Archē* may refer to a beginning in time (e.g., a decision) or to a beginning in the sense of a principle (whether a logically first principle or a principle of an activity or operation). *Archē* may also be used in the noetic sense to refer to a basic operative principle, or in a noematic sense to refer to the result of the operation of a principle, i.e., to a concept or stated rule. The context of usage should make evident the sense intended.

Index